S0-ACY-054

Intermediate Japanese

Written by
Mamori Sugita Hughes and Kumiko Ikeda Tsuji

Edited by
Suzanne McQuade

LIVING LANGUAGE®

Copyright © 2012 by Living Language, an imprint of Random House, Inc.

Content in this program has been modified and enhanced from *Complete Japanese: The Basics*, published in 2008.

Living Language is a member of the Random House Information Group.

Living Language and colophon are registered trademarks of Random House, Inc.

All rights reserved.

Published in the United States by Living Language, an imprint of Random House, Inc.

www.livinglanguage.com

Editor: Suzanne McQuade
Production Editor: Ciara Robinson
Production Manager: Tom Marshall
Interior Design: Sophie Chin
Illustrations: Sophie Chin

First Edition

ISBN: 978-0-307-97190-6

This book is available at special discounts for bulk purchases for sales promotions or premiums. Special editions, including personalized covers, excerpts of existing books, and corporate imprints, can be created in large quantities for special needs. For more information, write to Special Markets/ Premium Sales, 1745 Broadway, MD 3-1, New York, New York 10019 or e-mail **specialmarkets@ randomhouse.com**.

PRINTED IN THE UNITED STATES OF AMERICA

10 9 8 7 6 5 4 3 2

Acknowledgments

Thanks to the Living Language team: Amanda D'Acierno, Christopher Warnasch, Suzanne McQuade, Laura Riggio, Erin Quirk, Heather Dalton, Amanda Munoz, Fabrizio LaRocca, Siobhan O'Hare, Sophie Chin, Pat Stango, Sue Daulton, Alison Skrabek, Ciara Robinson, Andrea McLin, and Tom Marshall.

Course Outline

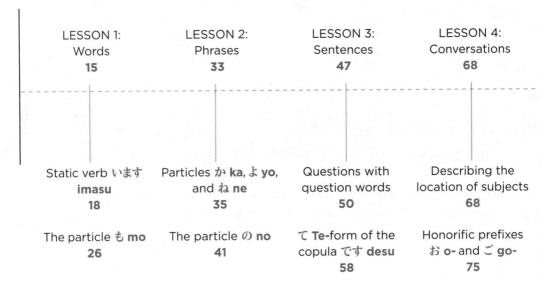

COURSE

OUTLINE

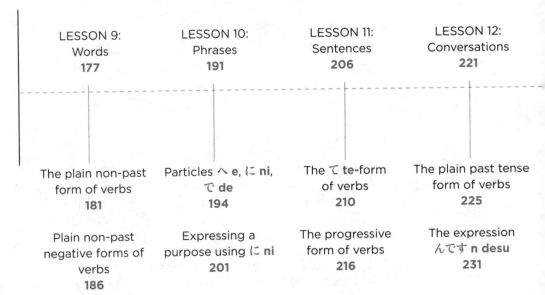
C O U R S E

OUTLINE

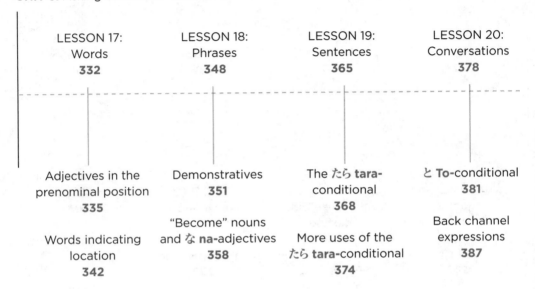

How to Use This Course

Konnichiwa ! Welcome to *Living Language Intermediate Japanese*! Ready to learn how to speak, read, and write Japanese?

Before we begin, let's go over what you'll see in this course. It's very easy to use, but this section will help you get started.

CONTENT

Intermediate Japanese is a continuation of *Essential Japanese*. It will review, expand on, and add to the foundation that you received in *Essential Japanese*. In other words, this course contains:

- an in-depth review of important vocabulary and grammar from *Essential Japanese*;

- an expanded and more advanced look at some key vocabulary and grammar from *Essential Japanese*;

- an introduction to idiomatic language and more challenging Japanese grammar.

UNITS

There are five units in this course. Each unit has four lessons arranged in a "building block" structure: the first lesson will present essential *words*, the second will introduce longer *phrases*, the third will teach *sentences*, and the fourth will show how everything works together in everyday *conversations*.

At the beginning of each unit is an introduction highlighting what you'll learn in that unit. At the end of each unit you'll find the Unit Essentials, which reviews the key information from that unit, and a self-graded Unit Quiz, which tests what you've learned.

LESSONS

There are four lessons per unit for a total of 20 lessons in the course. Each lesson has the following components:

- **Introduction** outlining what you will cover in the lesson.

- **Word Builder 1** (first lesson of the unit) presenting key words and phrases.

- **Phrase Builder 1** (second lesson of the unit) introducing longer phrases and expressions.

- **Sentence Builder 1** (third lesson of the unit) teaching sentences.

- **Conversation 1** (fourth lesson of the unit) for a natural dialogue that brings together important vocabulary and grammar from the unit.

- **Take It Further** providing extra information about the new vocabulary you just saw, expanding on certain grammar points, or introducing additional words and phrases.

- **Word/Phrase/Sentence/Conversation Practice 1** practicing what you learned in Word Builder 1, Phrase Builder 1, Sentence Builder 1, or Conversation 1.

- **Grammar Builder 1** guiding you through important Japanese grammar that you need to know.

- **Work Out 1** for a comprehensive practice of what you saw in Grammar Builder 1.

- **Word Builder 2/Phrase Builder 2/Sentence Builder 2/Conversation 2** for more key words, phrases, or sentences, or a second dialogue.

- **Take It Further** for expansion on what you've seen so far and additional vocabulary.

- **Word/Phrase/Sentence/Conversation Practice 2** practicing what you learned in Word Builder 2, Phrase Builder 2, Sentence Builder 2, or Conversation 2.

- **Grammar Builder 2** for more information on Japanese grammar.

- **Work Out 2** for a comprehensive practice of what you saw in Grammar Builder 2.

- **Drive It Home** ingraining an important point of Japanese grammar for the long term.

- **Tip** or **Culture Note** for a helpful language tip or useful cultural information related to the lesson or unit.

- **Word Recall** reviewing important vocabulary and grammar from any of the previous lessons in *Intermediate* or *Essential Japanese*.

- **How Did You Do?** outlining what you learned in the lesson.

UNIT ESSENTIALS

You will see the **Unit Essentials** at the end of every unit. This section summarizes and reviews the key information from the unit, but with missing vocabulary information for you to fill in. In other words, each Unit Essentials works as both a study guide and a blank "cheat sheet." Once you complete it, you'll have your very own reference for the most essential vocabulary and grammar from the unit.

UNIT QUIZ

After each Unit Essentials, you'll see a **Unit Quiz**. The quizzes are self-graded so it's easy for you to test your progress and see if you should go back and review.

PROGRESS BAR

You will see a **Progress Bar** on each page that has course material. It indicates your current position within the unit and lets you know how much progress you're making. Each line in the bar represents a Grammar Builder section.

AUDIO

Look for the symbol ⊙ to help guide you through the audio as you're reading the book. It will tell you which track to listen to for each section that has audio. When you see the symbol, select the indicated track and start listening! If you don't see the symbol, then there isn't any audio for that section. You'll also see ⦿, which will tell you where that track ends.

The audio can be used on its own—in other words, without the book—when you're on the go. Whether in your car or at the gym, you can listen to the audio on its own to brush up on your pronunciation or review what you've learned in the book.

GLOSSARY

At the back of this book you will find an extensive Japanese–English and English–Japanese glossary, including all of the essential words from all three levels of this Japanese course, as well as some additional vocabulary.

GUIDE TO READING AND WRITING JAPANESE

Three different types of characters are used to write Japanese: ひらがな **hiragana**, カタカナ **katakana**, and かんじ **kanji** characters. You will learn about each type gradually through this book and in the **Guide to Reading and Writing Japanese** included with this course. You'll also see the Japanese sounds transcribed into the Roman alphabet (also called **romaji**) throughout this course.

FREE ONLINE TOOLS

Go to **www.livinglanguage.com/languagelab** to access your free online tools. The tools are organized around the lessons in this course, with audiovisual flashcards, as well as interactive games and quizzes for each lesson, plus a grammar summary for all three levels. These tools will help you to review and practice the vocabulary and grammar that you've seen in the lessons, providing some extra words and phrases related to the lesson's topic as well.

Unit 1:
Talking About Family

In Unit 1, you will learn how to talk about your and other people's families and occupations. You'll expand some key Japanese grammar and your vocabulary, as well as building your conversation skills. By the end of the unit, you'll be able to:

☐ use key vocabulary related to family

☐ use key vocabulary related to occupation

☐ use the static verb います imasu

☐ use the particle も mo

☐ use the sentential particles か ka, よ yo, and ね ne

☐ use the particle の no

☐ ask questions with question words

☐ use the て te-form of the copula です desu

☐ describe the location of subjects using the particle に ni

☐ use the honorific prefixes お o- and ご go-

Lesson 1: Words

In this lesson you'll learn how to:

☐ use key vocabulary related to family

☐ use key vocabulary related to occupation

☐ use the static verb います imasu

☐ use the particle も mo

Word Builder 1

▶ 1A Word Builder 1 (CD 4, Track 1)

ちち 父	chichi	*father (one's own)*
とう お父さん	otoosan	*father (someone else's)*
はは 母	haha	*mother (one's own)*
かあ お母さん	okaasan	*mother (someone else's)*
あに 兄	ani	*older brother (one's own)*
にい お兄さん	oniisan	*older brother (someone else's)*
あね 姉	ane	*older sister (one's own)*
ねえ お姉さん	oneesan	*older sister (someone else's)*
いもうと 妹	imooto	*younger sister (one's own)*

妹<ruby>いもうと</ruby>さん	imootosan	*younger sister (someone else's)*
弟<ruby>おとうと</ruby>	otooto	*younger brother (one's own)*
弟<ruby>おとうと</ruby>さん	otootosan	*younger brother (someone else's)*
そふ	sofu	*grandfather (one's own)*
おじいさん	ojiisan	*grandfather (someone else's)*
そぼ	sobo	*grandmother (one's own)*
おばあさん	obaasan	*grandmother (someone else's)*
夫<ruby>おっと</ruby>、主人<ruby>しゅじん</ruby>	otto or shujin	*husband (one's own)*
ご主人<ruby>しゅじん</ruby>	goshujin	*husband (someone else's)*
つま、家内<ruby>かない</ruby>	tsuma or kanai	*wife (one's own)*
おくさん	okusan	*wife (someone else's)*
子<ruby>こ</ruby>ども	kodomo	*child*
お子<ruby>こ</ruby>さん、子<ruby>こ</ruby>どもさん	okosan or kodomosan	*child (someone else's)*
むす子<ruby>こ</ruby>	musuko	*son (one's own)*
むす子<ruby>こ</ruby>さん	musukosan	*son (someone else's)*
むすめ	musume	*daughter (one's own)*
むすめさん、おじょうさん	musumesan or ojoosan	*daughter (someone else's)*
いとこ	itoko	*cousin*

Take It Further

Throughout this course, you'll encounter some words written in 漢字 kanji, such
as 父 and 母 . In Unit 1, you'll see about a dozen kanji, just to get you warmed
up. From Unit 2 onward, kanji will be used wherever possible, just as in every
day reading materials targeted to adult Japanese audience. But don't worry; in
Complete Japanese, every single kanji has 振り仮名 furigana over it, which is
basically a reading guide written in small hiragana. You don't have to learn how to
write kanji at this point, but you may want to start seeing them. The goal here is
to get a lot of exposure. You don't have to try to memorize anything. For detailed
guidance on kanji characters and some reading rules, please refer to the *Japanese
Script Guide*. For now, here are two quick key hints for reading kanji to get you
started. First, everyday Japanese is written in a combination of kanji and hiragana
(or katakana for foreign loan words), which means that only some Japanese words
can be written in kanji. Second, a single kanji character usually has more than
one possible reading. The character 兄 , for example, can be read as あに ani (as
in 兄 ani [*one's own older brother*]), にい nii (as in お兄さん oniisan (*somebody
else's older brother*), or きょう kyoo (as in 兄弟 kyoodai [*siblings*]). The specific
reading of a character depends on in which word the character is used.

✎ Word Practice 1

Translate the new vocabulary you just learned in the list below. You may write
using either hiragana or the roman alphabet. Don't use kanji unless you know the
correct stroke order.

1. *grandfather (one's own)* _____

2. *grandfather (someone else's)* _____

3. *grandmother (one's own)* _____

4. *grandmother (someone else's)* _____

5. *husband (one's own)* _____

6. *husband (someone else's)* _____

7. *wife (one's own)* _____

8. *wife (someone else's)* _____

9. *child* _____

10. *child (someone else's)* _____

11. *cousin* _____

ANSWER KEY

1. そふ sofu; 2. おじいさん ojiisan; 3. そぼ sobo; 4. おばあさん obaasan; 5. 夫 otto or 主人 shujin; 6. ご主人 goshujin; 7. つま tsuma or 家内 kanai; 8. おくさん okusan; 9. 子ども kodomo; 10. お子さん okosan or 子どもさん kodomosan; 11. いとこ itoko

Grammar Builder 1
STATIC VERB います IMASU

▶ 1B Grammar Builder 1 (CD 4, Track 2)

Let's begin our grammar lessons by reviewing the verb います imasu (*to exist*), which you already started studying in *Essential Japanese*. います Imasu (*to exist*) is used to describe the existence of animate subjects, such as people and animals. It is used in the following construction with the particle が ga:

X がいます。

X ga imasu.

There is/are X.

It is very important to remember that the subject of います imasu has to be animate. In Lesson 6, we'll review another static verb, あります arimasu, which is used to describe the location of inanimate subjects. Note that the English *there is/are* construction requires a mention of a location, but in Japanese, the location does not have to be explicit. If a location is mentioned, the location noun is followed by the particle に ni (*at, in*), as in ニューヨークに nyuuyooku ni (*in New York*). The following sentences show how this structure is used.

父がニューヨークにいます。

Chichi ga nyuuyooku ni imasu.

My father is in New York.

やまださんがいます。

Yamada san ga imasu.

Mr./Ms. Yamada is there.

います Imasu can also be used to express possession with animate subjects. When used in the meaning of possession, the possessor noun can be expressed as a topic of a sentence followed by the topic particle は wa; the possessed is the subject of the verb います imasu.

わたしは家族がいます。

Watashi wa kazoku ga imasu.

I have a family. (lit., As for me, there is a family.)

やまださんは弟さんがいます。

Yamada san wa otootosan ga imasu.

Mr./Ms. Yamada has (a) younger brother(s). (lit., As for Mr./Ms. Yamada, there is/ are (a) younger brother(s).)

Note that since Japanese, unlike English, doesn't distinguish between the singular and plural forms of nouns, there are two possible translations for most of the sentences above. In actual use, the context decides which meaning is intended.

If you want to turn an います imasu sentence into a question, place the particle か ka at the end. In addition, yes/no questions in Japanese often employ the particle は wa in place of the particles が ga or を o. In the case of an います imasu sentence, you replace the particle が ga with は wa.

弟さんはいますか。

Otootosan wa imasu ka.

Is there a younger brother?/Do you have a younger brother?

It is not absolutely necessary to replace the particle. Sometimes you will hear a question without any particle replacement.

弟さんがいますか。

Otootosan ga imasu ka.

Is there a younger brother?/Do you have a younger brother?

The choice of particles in questions results in slight differences in nuance, and using the particle が ga can be more appropriate in certain contexts. Don't worry about this yet. For now, it is good practice to use the particle は wa in all yes/no questions. Please note that Japanese question words (なに nani *what*, どこ doko *where*, だれ dare *who*, etc.) should not be followed by は wa. You'll be reminded of this rule in Lesson 4 where you'll see actual examples.

The negative form of います imasu is いません imasen. Just as in the question, it is common to use the particle は wa instead of the particle が ga in a negative sentence.

<ruby>弟<rt>おとうと</rt></ruby>はいません。

Otooto wa imasen.

There isn't a younger brother./I don't have a younger brother.

Again, this is not an absolute rule, and using the particle が ga may be more appropriate in certain contexts. However, it is fine for now to keep using the particle は wa in all negative sentences until you're confident enough to make this distinction.

✎ Work Out 1

A. Translate the following sentences into English.

1. たなかさんがいます。 **Tanaka san ga imasu.**

_____

2. わたしは<ruby>姉<rt>あね</rt></ruby>がいます。 **Watashi wa ane ga imasu.**

_____

3. スミスさんはお<ruby>子<rt>こ</rt></ruby>さんはいますか。 **Sumisu san wa okosan wa imasu ka.**

_____

4. ご<ruby>兄弟<rt>きょうだい</rt></ruby>はいますか。 **Gokyoodai wa imasu ka.**

_____

5. <ruby>子<rt>こ</rt></ruby>どもはいません。 **Kodomo wa imasen.**

_____

B. Translate the following sentences into Japanese. You may write using either hiragana or the roman alphabet. Don't use kanji unless you know the correct stroke order.

1. *Mr. Smith is there.*

_____

2. *Children are there./I have children.*

_____

3. *Do you have a younger sister?*

_____

4. *I don't have an older brother.*

_____

5. *Mr. Tanaka is not there.*

_____

ANSWER KEY

A: 1. *Mr./Ms. Tanaka is there. 2. I have an older sister. 3. Does Mr./Ms. Smith have a child? 4. Do (you/they)/Does (he/she) have siblings? 5. I don't have a child./There isn't any child.*

B: 1. スミスさんがいます。 **Sumisu san ga imasu.**; 2. 子どもがいます。 **Kodomo ga imasu.**; 3. 妹さんはいますか。 **Imootosan wa imasu ka.**; 4. 兄はいません。 **Ani wa imasen.**; 5. たなかさんはいません。 **Tanaka san wa imasen.**

Word Builder 2

▶ 1C Word Builder 2 (CD 4, Track 3)

（ご）家族	(go)kazoku (polite with go)	family
（ご）両親	(go)ryooshin (polite with go)	parents
（ご）兄弟	(go)kyoodai (polite with go)	siblings
（ご）夫婦	(go)fuufu (polite with go)	married couple
（ご）親せき	(go)shinseki (polite with go)	relatives
うち	uchi	house, one's home, one's family
みなさん	minasan	everyone
ちゅうがっこう	chuugakkoo	junior high school
こうこう	kookoo	high school
だいがく	daigaku	university, college
せんせい、きょうし	sensee or kyooshi	teacher
すうがく	suugaku	mathematics
けいざい	keezai	economy
けいざいがく	keezaigaku	economics
主婦	shufu	housewife
しごと	shigoto	job, work

かいしゃ	kaisha	company
かいしゃいん	kaishain	company employee
ぎんこういん	ginkooin	bank clerk
ウェブデザイナー	webudezainaa	web designer
エンジニア、ぎし	enjinia or gishi	engineer
でんきぎし	denkigishi	electrical engineer
けいり	keeri	(business) administration, accounting
たんとう	tantoo	being in charge
(お) きゅうりょう	(o)kyuuryoo (polite with o)	salary
(ご) しゅっしん	(go)shusshin (polite with go)	place of origin, hometown
でも	demo	however, but (at the beginning of a sentence)
にほん人	nihonjin	Japanese (person)
アメリカ人	amerikajin	American (person)

Take It Further

In English, words like *Japanese* and *French* can refer to several things, including people, languages, and cuisines. In Japanese however, each of these descriptions requires a different word. If you want to talk about people, the rule is to attach 人 jin (*person*) to the name of the country. Thus, you get にほん人 nihonjin

(*Japanese*), アメリカ人 amerikajin (*American*), メキシコ人 mekishikojin
(*Mexican*), etc. The following chart lists further examples:

COUNTRY		NATIONALITY	
フランス furansu	France	フランス人 furansujin	French (person)
カナダ canada	Canada	カナダ人 kanadajin	Canadian (person)
スペイン supein	Spain	スペイン人 supeinjin	Spanish (person)
ちゅうごく chuugoku	China	ちゅうごく人 chuugokujin	Chinese (person)
ドイツ doitsu	Germany	ドイツ人 doitsujin	German (person)
イギリス igirisu	England	イギリス人 igirisujin	English (person)

✎ Word Practice 2
Translate the vocabulary below.

1. *family* _____

2. *parents* _____

3. *married couple* _____

4. *relatives* _____

5. *house, one's home, one's family* _____

6. *everyone* _____

7. *housewife* _____

8. *company* _____

9. *bank clerk* _____

10. *Japanese (person)* _____

ANSWER KEY

1. (ご) 家族 (go)kazoku; 2. (ご) 両親 (go)ryooshin; 3. (ご) 夫婦 (go)fuufu; 4. (ご) 親せき (go) shinseki; 5. うち uchi; 6. みなさん minasan; 7. 主婦 shufu; 8. かいしゃ kaisha; 9. ぎんこういん ginkooin; 10. にほん人 nihonjin

Grammar Builder 2
THE PARTICLE も MO

▶ 1D Grammar Builder 2 (CD 4, Track 4)

The particle も mo corresponds to the English *too, also,* or *both... and.* It is used in the constructions X も mo (*X too, also X*) and X も mo Y も mo (*both X and Y*). も Mo can follow a noun, a time adverb, a demonstrative, or a numeral, but it cannot follow a verb or an adjective. Take a look at some examples.

妹 はがくせいです。

Imooto wa gakusee desu.

My younger sister is a student.

弟 もがくせいです。

Otooto mo gakusee desu.

My younger brother is also a student. (lit., My younger brother too is a student.)

兄のしごとはウェブデザイナーです。

Ani no shigoto wa webudezainaa desu.

My older brother is a web designer. (lit., My older brother's job is [a] web designer.)

いとこのしごともウェブデザイナーです。

Itoko no shigoto mo webudezainaa desu.

My cousin is also a web designer. (lit., My cousin's job is also [a] web designer.)

むす子はやきゅうをします。

Musuko wa yakyuu o shimasu.

My son plays baseball.

むす子はフットボールもします。

Musuko wa futtobooru mo shimasu.

My son plays football, too.

これは DVD です。

Kore wa DVD desu.

This is a DVD.

それも DVD です。

Sore mo DVD desu.

That is a DVD, too.

こんしゅうはいそがしいです。

Konshuu wa isogashii desu.

This week is busy.

らいしゅうもいそがしいです。

Raishuu mo isogashii desu.

Next week will be busy, too.

Note that も mo can also follow a postposition.

アメリカからがくせいがきます。

Amerika kara gakusee ga kimasu.

Students will come from the U.S.A.

メキシコからもがくせいがきます。

Mekishiko kara mo gakusee ga kimasu.

Students will also come from Mexico.

Note that in the above examples, も mo replaces particles は wa, が ga, and を o, but occurs in sentences with other particles and postpositions, such as に ni (*to*), と to (*with*) and から kara (*from*) and others. Now let's look at a few examples where も mo is used in the structure X も mo Y も mo.

妹も 弟もがくせいです。

Imooto mo otooto mo gakusee desu.

Both my younger sister and younger brother are students.

兄のしごともいとこのしごともウェブデザイナーです。

Ani no shigoto mo itoko no shigoto mo webudezainaa desu.

Both my older brother and my cousin are web designers. (lit., Both my older brother's job and my cousin's job are web designers.)

むす子はやきゅうもフットボールもします。

Musuko wa yakyuu mo futtobooru mo shimasu.

My son plays both baseball and football.

✎ Work Out 2

Combine the two sentences you're given using the construction X も mo Y も mo by filling in the blanks with the appropriate words and placing the appropriate particles in parentheses. You have the option of using either the roman alphabet or Japanese characters.

1. すずきさんはにほん人です。もりさんもにほん人です。 Suzuki san wa nihonjin desu. Mori san mo nihonjin desu.

   _____ (_____) _____ (_____) にほん人です。_____ (_____) _____ (_____) nihonjin desu.

2. わたなべさんはかいしゃいんです。もりさんもかいしゃいんです。 Watanabe san wa kaishain desu. Mori san mo kaishain desu.

   _____ (_____) _____ (_____) かいしゃいんです。_____ (_____) _____ (_____) kaishain desu.

3. さとうさんのお母さんは主婦です。 ほんださんのお母さんも主婦です。 Satoo san no okaasan wa shufu desu. Honda san no okaasan mo shufu desu.

   さとうさん (_____) _____ (_____) ほんださん (_____)

The particle も mo   The particle の no

_____ (_____) 主婦です。 Satoo san (_____) _____

_____ (_____) Honda san (_____) _____

_____ (_____) shufu desu.

4. はやしさんはこうこうのせんせいです。かわむらさんもこうこうのせんせい
です。 Hayashi san wa kookoo no sensee desu. Kawamura san mo kookoo no
sensee desu.

_____ (_____) _____ (_____)

こうこうのせんせいです。 _____ (_____)

_____ (_____) kookoo no sensee desu.

5. たかはしさんはジャズを聞きます。たかはしさんはロックも聞きます。

Takahashi san wa jazu o kikimasu. Takahashi san wa rokku mo kikimasu.

たかはしさんは_____ (_____) _____ (_____)

ききます。 Takahashi san wa _____ (_____) _____

(_____) kikimasu.

ANSWER KEY

1. すずきさんももりさんも Suzuki san mo Mori san mo; 2. わたなべさんももりさんも Watanabe
san mo Mori san mo; 3. のお母さんも no okaasan mo, のお母さんも no okaasan mo; 4. はやしさん
もかわむらさんも Hayashi san mo Kawamura san mo; 5. ジャズもロックも jazu mo rokku mo

✎ Drive It Home

By now, you're familiar with Drive It Home exercises, which may seem easy,
but are meant to make grammatical structures more intuitive by helping you
establish grammatical patterns through practice and repetition. We'll mostly use
these exercises for practicing particles, which are an essential part of Japanese
grammar, so don't skip over these exercises! They'll help you in the long run.

A. Complete the following phrases and sentences by inserting appropriate particles.

1. はやしさん _____むすめさん _____います。

   Hayashi san _____ **musumesan** _____ **imasu.**

   Mr./Ms. Hayashi has a daughter.

2. たなかさん _____お兄さん _____います。

   Tanaka san _____ **oniisan** _____ **imasu.**

   Mr./Ms. Tanaka has an older brother.

3. やまださん _____妹 さん _____います。

   Yamada san _____ **imootosan** _____ **imasu.**

   Mr./Ms. Yamada has a younger sister.

4. きむらさん _____ ぎしです。

   Kimura san _____ **gishi desu.**

   Mr./Ms. Kimura is also an engineer.

5. 兄_____ 弟 _____やきゅうをします。

   Ani _____ **otooto** _____ **yakyuu o shimasu.**

   Both my older brother and younger brother play baseball.

B. Complete the sentences by inserting appropriate words.

1. いとこが五人 _____。

   Itoko ga gonin _____.

   I have five cousins.

2. 兄弟が五人 _____。
   きょうだい ごにん

   Kyoodai ga gonin _____.

   I have five_____ siblings.

3. 家族が五人 _____。
   かぞく ごにん

   Kazoku ga gonin _____.

   There are five people in my family.

ANSWER KEY
A: 1. は wa, が ga; 2. は wa, が ga; 3. は wa, が ga; 4. も mo; 5. も mo, も mo
B. 1. います imasu; 2. います imasu; 3. います imasu

⊕ Culture Note

There are different ways of addressing one's own parents in Japanese. The most common way is to address your father as お父さん otoosan and your mother as お母さん okaasan. In the western part of Japan, such as Kyoto and Osaka, one's father is often addressed as お父ちゃん otoochan and one's mother as お母ちゃん okaachan, especially by children and teenagers. Children often address their father as パパ papa and their mother as ママ mama, but some people continue to use these words even after they have grown up. It is just a matter of preference. To some people, it sounds awkward if people in their thirties or forties use パパ papa and ママ mama when addressing their own parents, but to others, the use of these loanwords is fine and even fashionable.

How Did You Do?

Let's see how you did! By now, you should be able to:

☐ use key vocabulary related to family (Still unsure? Jump back to page 15)

☐ use います imasu (Still unsure? Jump back to page 18)

☐ use key vocabulary related to work and school (Still unsure? Jump back to page 24)

☐ use the particle も mo (Still unsure? Jump back to page 26)

✎ Word Recall

1. そふ sofu	a. *relatives*
2. つま tsuma	b. *grandfather (someone else's)*
3. 親せき shinseki	c. *wife (someone else's)*
4. おくさん okusan	d. *grandmother (someone else's)*
5. そぼ sobo	e. *grandfather (one's own)*
6. かいしゃ kaisha	f. *wife (one's own)*
7. おばあさん obaasan	g. *child (someone else's)*
8. 夫 otto	h. *company*
9. おじいさん ojiisan	i. *grandmother (one's own)*
10. お子さん okosan	j. *husband (one's own)*

ANSWER KEY

1. e; 2. f; 3. a; 4. c; 5. i; 6. h; 7. d; 8. j; 9. b; 10. g

Lesson 2: Phrases

By the end of this lesson, you should be able to:

☐ use the particles か ka, よ yo, and ね ne

☐ use the particle の no

Phrase Builder 1

▶ 2A Phrase Builder 1 (CD 4, Track 5)

ごにんかぞく 五人家族	gonin kazoku	*five people in a family*
さんにんきょうだい 三人兄弟	sannin kyoodai	*three children in a family*
ひとり　こ 一人っ子	hitorikko	*only child*
りょうしん 両親といっしょに	ryooshin to issho ni	*together with parents*
それから	sorekara	*and then*
それじゃまた。	Sore ja mata.	*See you then.*
そうですか。	Soo desu ka.	*Is that so?*
そうですか。	Soo desu ka.	*I see.*
そうですね。	Soo desu ne.	*Yes, it is./Let me see.*

Take It Further

Note that the particle と to above is used in the meaning of *with*. Remember that we encountered it used with the meaning of *and* earlier.

The じゃ ja in それじゃまた sore ja mata is a contracted form of では de wa in それではまた sorede wa mata. The expression それじゃまた sore ja mata is informal while それではまた sorede wa mata is formal.

✎ Phrase Practice 1

Translate the expressions you just learned below.

1. *five people in a family* _____

2. *three children in a family* _____

3. *only child* _____

4. *together with parents* _____

5. *and then* _____

6. *See you then.* _____

7. *Is that so?* _____

8. *I see.* _____

9. *Yes, it is./Let me see.* _____

ANSWER KEY
1. 五人家族 gonin kazoku; 2. 三人兄弟 sannin kyoodai; 3. 一人っ子 hitorikko; 4. 両親といっしょに ryooshin to issho ni; 5. それから sorekara; 6. それじゃまた。 Sore ja mata. 7. そうですか。 Soo desu ka. 8. そうですか。 Soo desu ka. 9. そうですね。 Soo desu ne.

Grammar Builder 1
PARTICLES か KA, よ YO, AND ね NE

▶ 2B Grammar Builder 1 (CD 4, Track 6)

The particle か ka is used when making questions, but it can also be used to express surprise. In this case, か ka is often pronounced as かあ kaa.

こばやしさんはだいがくのせんせいですよ。
Kobayashi san wa daigaku no sensee desu yo.
Mr./Ms. Kobayashi is a college professor.

だいがくのせんせいですかあ。
Daigaku no sensee desu kaa.
College professor, right?

だいがくのせんせいですか。

Dagaku no sensee desu ka.

College professor? Really?

だいがくのせんせいですかあ Daigaku no sensee desu kaa, with a falling intonation, expresses a speaker's mild surprise. だいがくのせんせいですか Dagaku no sensee desu ka. with a rising intonation can either be used as an echo-question, confirming what a speaker heard, or as an expression of the speaker's surprise. The difference between か ka with a falling intonation and か ka with a rising intonation is also demonstrated in the following examples.

こばやしさんはだいがくのせんせいですよ。

Kobayashi san wa daigaku no sensee desu yo.

Mr./Ms. Kobayashi is a college professor.

そうですか。

Soo desu ka.

I see ... /Really ...

そうですか。

Soo desu ka.

Is that so?/Really?

When used with a falling intonation, そうですか soo desu ka indicates that a speaker is accepting the information he or she received with mild surprise. When そうですか soo desu ka is pronounced with a rising intonation, it indicates that a speaker does not fully accept the information he or she received.

In addition to か ka, the particles ね ne and よ yo are often added to sentences in daily conversations. ね Ne is used when seeking or expressing agreement.

おいしいですね。

Oishii desu ne.

It's delicious, isn't it?

そうですね。

Soo desu ne.

Yes, it is.

ね **Ne** is also used when confirming a piece of information.

それからフットボールもしますね。

Sorekara futtobooru mo shimasu ne.

And you also play football, right.

そうですね。

Soo desu ne.

Right?

Note that, depending on the intonation, そうですね **soo desu ne** can be used to express (falling intonation) as well as seek (rising intonation) agreement. そうですね **Soo desu ne** can also mean *Let me see*, but in this case, ね **ne** is often lengthened to ねえ **nee**.

なにをのみますか。

Nani o nomimasu ka.

What are you going to drink?

そうですねえ・・・。コーヒーをのみます。

Soo desu nee ... koohii o nomimasu.

Let me see ... I'll have a coffee.

The particle よ yo is used when making assertions.

わたしは五人家族ですよ。
<ruby>五人家族<rt>ごにんかぞく</rt></ruby>

Watashi wa gonin kazoku desu yo.

There are five people in my family. (I assure you.)

こばやしさんのしゅっしんはながのですよ。

Kobayashi san no shusshin wa nagano desu yo.

Mr./Ms. Kobayashi is from Nagano. (lit. Mr./Ms. Kobayashi's hometown is Nagano.)
(I assure you.)

Note that よ yo is usually not translated directly into English. The particles ね ne
and よ yo are frequently used in everyday conversation, but they are not used in
formal writing.

✎ Work Out 1

Fill in the blank with the correct particle: か ka, ね ne, or よ yo. (Take your clue
from the given answer or the hints in parentheses.)

1. *A:* ご兄弟はいます ＿＿＿＿＿＿＿。

    Gokyoodai wa imasu ＿＿＿＿＿＿.

    B: はい、兄がいます。

    Hai, ani ga imasu.

2. *A:* いいバッグです _____。 *(seeking agreement)*

   Ii baggu desu _____.

   B: いいえ、やすいバッグです _____。

   Iie, yasui baggu desu _____.

3. *A:* ブラウンさんはアメリカ人です。

   Buraun san wa amerikajin desu.

   B: へえ、そうです _____。

   Hee, soo desu _____.

4. たかはしさんはぎんこういんです _____。 *(assertion)*

   Takahashi san wa ginkooin desu _____.

5. たなかさんのしゅっしんはとうきょうです _____。 *(confirming the information)*

   Tanaka san no shusshin wa tookyoo desu _____.

   ANSWER KEY
   1. か ka; 2. ね ne, よ yo; 3. か ka; 4. よ yo; 5. ね ne

Phrase Builder 2
▶ 2C Phrase Builder 2 (CD 4, Track 7)

父も母も	chichi mo haha mo	*both my father and mother*
こうこうのすうがくの せんせい	kookoo no suugaku no sensee	*high school mathematics teacher*
ちゅうがくのえいごの せんせい	chuugaku no eego no sensee	*junior high school English teacher*

だいがくのけいざいの せんせい	daigaku no keezai no sensee	university economics teacher
けいりのたんとう	keeri no tantoo	being in charge of accounting
スミスさんのおきゅう りょうのたんとう	Sumisu san no okyuuryoo no tantoo	being in charge of Mr./ Ms. Smith's salary
どんなしごと	donna shigoto	what kind of work
アメリカにいます	amerika ni imasu	to be in the U.S.A.
そして	soshite	and, and then
しごとのあとで	shigoto no ato de	after work

✎ Phrase Practice 2

Complete the following by inserting appropriate particles.

1. 父 _____ 母 _____
   ちち   はは

   chichi _____ haha _____

   both my father and mother

2. こうこう _____ すうがく _____ せんせい

   kookoo _____ suugaku _____ sensee

   high school mathematics teacher

3. けいり _____ たんとう

   keeri _____ tantoo

   being in charge of accounting

4. スミスさん _____ おきゅうりょう _____ たんとう

   Sumisu san _____ okyuuryoo _____ tantoo

   being in charge of Mr./Ms. Smith's salary

5. アメリカ _____ います

   amerika _____ imasu

   to be in the U.S.A.

6. しごと _____ あとで

   shigoto _____ ato de

   after work

ANSWER KEY

1. も mo, も mo; 2. の no, の no; 3 の no; 4. の no, の no; 5. に ni; 6. の no

Grammar Builder 2
THE PARTICLE の NO

▶ 2D Grammar Builder 2 (CD 4, Track 8)

As you learned in Essential Japanese, the particle の no can be used to connect nouns, essentially allowing one noun to modify the other.

<ruby>父<rt>ちち</rt></ruby>のかいしゃ

chichi no kaisha

my father's company

アメリカのかいしゃ

amerika no kaisha

an American company

妹のちゅうがっこう

imooto no chuugakkoo

my younger sister's junior high school

こうこうのすうがくのせんせい

kookoo no suugaku no sensee

high school mathematics teacher

の No can also connect more than two nouns, as in the structure X の no Y の no Z.

やまださんのお父さんのかいしゃ

Yamada san no otoosan no kaisha

Mr./Ms. Yamada's father's company

たなかさんのだいがくのせんせい

Tanaka san no daigaku no sensee

a professor at Mr./Ms. Tanaka's university (lit., Mr./Ms. Tanaka's university's
professor)

スミスさんのおきゅうりょうのたんとう

Sumisu san no okyuuryoo no tantoo

being in charge of Mr./Ms. Smith's salary (lit., Mr./Ms. Smith's salary's being
in charge)

In these sentences, keep in mind that the main noun being described will appear
at the end. In the previous examples, かいしゃ kaisha is modified by やまださん
のお父さん Yamada san no otoosan, せんせい sensee is modified by たなかさん
のだいがくの Tanaka san no daigaku no, and たんとう tantoo is modified by
スミスさんのおきゅうりょう Sumisu san no okyuuryoo.

Just remember to be aware of the word order in these constructions to determine the main noun.

たなかさんのだいがくのせんせい

Tanaka san no daigaku no <u>sensee</u>

a professor at Mr./Ms. Tanaka's university

✎ Work Out 2

Choose the correct translation for the following noun phrases.

1. *Mr. Miller's mother's older sister*
   a. お母さんのミラーさんのお姉さん okaasan no Miraa san no oneesan
   b. ミラーさんのお母さんのお姉さん Miraa san no okaasan no oneesan
   c. お姉さんのお母さんのミラーさん oneesan no okaasan no Miraa san

2. *Ms. Suzuki's math teacher*
   a. すずきさんのすうがくのせんせい Suzuki san no suugaku no sensee
   b. すうがくのせんせいのすずきさん suugaku no sensee no Suzuki san
   c. せんせいのすずきさんのすうがく sensee no Suzuki san no suugaku

3. *a job at a Japanese company*
   a. かいしゃのしごとのにほん kaisha no shigoto no nihon
   b. にほんのかいしゃのしごと nihon no kaisha no shigoto
   c. かいしゃのにほんのしごと kaisha no nihon no shigoto

4. *an economics class at a university*
   a. だいがくのクラスのけいざいがく daigaku no kurasu no keezaigaku
   b. クラスのけいざいがくのだいがく kurasu no keezaigaku no daigaku
   c. だいがくのけいざいがくのクラス daigaku no keezaigaku no kurasu

5. *my English student Mr. Mori*

a. わたしのえいごのもりさんのがくせい

watashi no eego no Mori san no gakusee

b. わたしのえいごのがくせいのもりさん

watashi no eego no gakusee no Mori san

c. わたしのもりさんのえいごのがくせい

watashi no Mori san no eego no gakusee

ANSWER KEY

1. b; 2. a; 3. b; 4. c; 5. b

✎ Drive It Home

Complete the following phrases and sentences by inserting appropriate particles.

1. そうです＿＿＿＿＿。

Soo desu ＿＿＿＿＿.

I see...

2. そうです＿＿＿＿＿。

Soo desu ＿＿＿＿＿.

Really?

3. そうです ＿＿＿＿＿。 *(agreement)*

Soo desu ＿＿＿＿＿.

Yes, it is.

4. ぎんこういん＿＿＿＿＿ おきゅうりょう

ginkooin ＿＿＿＿＿ okyuuryoo

bank clerk's salary

5. むすめ ＿＿＿＿＿ だいがく ＿＿＿＿＿ せんせい

   musume ＿＿＿＿＿ daigaku ＿＿＿＿＿ sensee

   a professor at my daughter's university

6. わたしはでんきぎしです ＿＿＿＿＿。 *(assertion)*

   Watashi wa denkigishi desu ＿＿＿＿＿.

   I am an electrical engineer.

7. 子どもさんがいます ＿＿＿＿＿。

   Kodomosan ga imasu ＿＿＿＿＿.

   You have children, right?

ANSWER KEY
1. か ka; 2. か ka; 3. ね ne; 4. の no; 5. の no, の no; 6. よ yo; 7. ね ne

⊕ Culture Note

There are subtle differences in how everyday greetings are used in the United States and in Japan. For example, in the U.S., people may repeatedly say *hello* or *hi* to greet someone they have already seen on the same day. The Japanese こんにちは konnichi wa cannot be used for such repeated greetings. Instead, people usually just bow by moving their heads slightly downward to acknowledge the person; sometimes, the greeting どうも doomo may also be used. This type of bow is called えしゃく eshaku. Similarly, although the Japanese phrase おげんきですか ogenki desu ka can be translated as *How are you?* this phrase is actually not used in the same way as the English phrase. おげんきですか Ogenki desu ka (*How are you?*) is used only with someone whom you have not seen in a while, and unlike the English phrase, it is meant as a real question demanding an answer.

How Did You Do?

Let's see how you did! By now, you should be able to:

☐ use the sentential particles か ka, よ yo, and ね ne (Still unsure? Jump back to page 35)

☐ use the particle の no (Still unsure? Jump back to page 41)

✎ Word Recall

1. みなさん minasan	a. *place of origin, hometown*
2. 主人 shujin	b. *however, but*
3. でんきぎし denkigishi	c. *wife (one's own)*
4. 一人っ子 hitorikko	d. *husband (one's own)*
5. それから sorekara	e. *everyone*
6. にほん人 nihonjin	f. *only child*
7. 家内 kanai	g. *mathematics*
8. しゅっしん shusshin	h. *Japanese (person)*
9. すうがく suugaku	i. *electrical engineer*
10. でも demo	j. *and then*

ANSWER KEY

1. e; 2. d; 3. i; 4. f; 5. j; 6. h; 7. c; 8. a; 9. g; 10. b

Lesson 3: Sentences

By the end of this lesson, you should be able to:

☐ ask questions with question words

☐ use the て te-form of the copula です desu

Sentence Builder 1

▶ 3A Sentence Builder 1 (CD 4, Track 9)

<ruby>何人家族<rt>なんにんかぞく</rt></ruby>ですか。

Nannin kazoku desu ka.

How many people are there in your family?

<ruby>五人家族<rt>ごにんかぞく</rt></ruby>です。

Gonin kazoku desu.

There are five people in my family.

<ruby>何人兄弟<rt>なんにんきょうだい</rt></ruby>ですか。

Nannin kyoodai desu ka.

How many children do your parents have?

<ruby>三人兄弟<rt>さんにんきょうだい</rt></ruby>です。

Sannin kyoodai desu.

My parents have three children.

<ruby>兄弟<rt>きょうだい</rt></ruby>は<ruby>何人<rt>なんにん</rt></ruby>いますか。

Kyoodai wa nannin imasu ka.

How many siblings do you have?

兄弟が二人います。

Kyoodai ga futari imasu.

I have two siblings.

ご家族はみなさんアメリカにいますか。

Gokazoku wa minasan amerika ni imasu ka.

Is your family all in the U.S.A.?

姉と弟は両親といっしょにいまとうきょうにいます。

Ane to otooto wa ryooshin to issho ni ima tookyoo ni imasu.

My older sister and younger brother are now in Tokyo with my parents.

それじゃまたしごとのあとで。

Sore ja mata shigoto no ato de.

See you after work, then.

✎ Sentence Practice 1

Fill in the missing words in each of the following sentences.

1. _____ ですか。

   _____ desu ka.

   How many people are there in your family?

2. _____ です。

   _____ desu.

   There are five people in my family.

3. _____ ですか。

_____ desu ka.

How many children do your parents have?

4. _____ です。

_____ desu.

My parents have three children.

5. ご兄弟は_____ 。
   <ruby>兄弟<rt>きょうだい</rt></ruby>

Gokyoodai _____.

How many siblings do you have?

6. 兄弟が_____ 。
   <ruby>兄弟<rt>きょうだい</rt></ruby>

Kyoodai ga _____.

I have two siblings.

7. 姉と弟は_____ いまとうきょうにいます。
   <ruby>姉<rt>あね</rt></ruby> <ruby>弟<rt>おとうと</rt></ruby>

Ane to otooto wa _____

ima tookyoo ni imasu.

My older sister and younger brother are now in Tokyo with my parents.

8. それじゃまた _____。

Sore ja mata _____.

See you after work, then.

ANSWER KEY
1. 何人家族 Nannin kazoku; 2. 五人家族 Gonin kazoku; 3. 何人兄弟 Nannin kyoodai; 4. 三人兄弟
Sannin kyoodai; 5. 何人いますか nannin imasu ka.; 6. 二人います futari imasu; 7. 両親といっしょに
ryooshin to issho ni; 8. しごとのあとで shigoto no ato de

Grammar Builder 1
QUESTIONS WITH QUESTION WORDS

▶ 3B Grammar Builder 1 (CD 4, Track 10)

As you already know, the formation of simple yes-no questions and questions with question words is very easy in Japanese. You've already learned some question words in *Essential Japanese*. Let's review them as well as adding a few more to your vocabulary. First look at the following examples where questions with なに nan(i) (*what*) and its variants are listed.

なんですか。
Nan desu ka.
What is it/he/she?, What are they?

なん人ですか。
Nannin desu ka.
How many people?

なんさつですか。
Nansatsu desu ka.
How many books/magazines?

なに人ですか。
Nanijin desu ka.
What nationality are you?

Remember that only なん nan can appear before the copula です desu. Also, some measure words are combined with なん nan, like なん人 nannin and なんさつ nansatsu, but others take なに nani, such as なに人 nanijin. Now, let's look at questions with other question words.

どこですか。 / どちらですか。
Doko desu ka./Dochira desu ka. (*polite*)
Where is it?

いくつですか。 / おいくつですか。
Ikutsu desu ka./Oikutsu desu ka. (*polite*)
How many?/How old are you?

だれですか。 / どなたですか。
Dare desu ka./Donata desu ka. (*polite*)
Who is/are he/she/they/it?

いつですか。
Itsu desu ka.
When is it?

いくらですか / おいくらですか。
Ikura desu ka./Oikura desu ka. (*polite*)
How much is/are it/they?

どんなしごとですか。
Donna oshigoto desu ka.
What kind of job is it?

どうしてですか。 / なぜですか。 / なんでですか。
Dooshite desu ka./Naze desu ka./Nande desu ka.
Why is it?

Note that どちら **dochira** and どなた **donata** are polite forms of どこ **doko** and だれ **dare**, respectively.

Remember that the question word replaces the information you are asking for, so when answering, the answer will appear in the same sentence position as the question word. Look at the following examples; note the position of the question word and the answer.

Q: ごしゅっしんはどちらですか。
Goshusshin wa dochira desu ka.
Where are you from? (lit., Where is your place of origin?)

A: (しゅっしんは) おおさかです。
(Shusshin wa) Oosaka desu.
I'm from Osaka. (lit., (My hometown) is Osaka.)

Q: なん人
にん
いますか。
Nannin imasu ka.
How many people are there?

A: 三十人
さんじゅうにん
います。
Sanjuunin imasu.
There are thirty people.

Q: はい、どなたですか。
Hai, donata desu ka. *(A doorbell rings.)*
Yes, who is it?

A: こやまです。
Koyama desu.
It's Koyama.

Q: パーティーはいつですか。

Paatii wa itsu desu ka.

When is the party?

A: (パーティーは) あしたです。

(Paatii wa) ashita desu.

(The party) is tomorrow.

Q: おすしはいくらですか。

Osushi wa ikura desu ka.

How much is sushi?

A: (すしは) 三^{さん}ぜんえんです。

(Sushi wa) sanzen en (*three thousand yen*) **desu.**

(Sushi) is three thousand yen.

Q: たなかさんはどんな人^{ひと}ですか。

Tanaka san wa donna hito desu ka.

What kind of person is Mr./Ms. Tanaka?

A: たなかさんはいい人^{ひと}です。

(Tanaka san wa) ii hito desu.

(Mr./Ms. Tanaka) is a good person.

Q: どうして / なぜ / なんでですか。

Dooshite/Naze/Nande desu ka.

Why (is it)? (For example, if your friend says he/she cannot come to the party.)

A: いそがしいですから。

Isogashii desu kara. (*because*)

Because I'm busy.

✎ Work Out 1

Fill in the blanks with appropriate question words from the word bank.

だれ dare, いつ itsu, なん人 nannin, なに人 nanijin, どちら dochira

1. *A:* ごしゅっしんは _____ですか。

   Goshusshin wa _____ desu ka.

   B: さっぽろです。

   Sapporo desu.

2. *A:* ご家族は _____ ですか。

   Gokazoku wa _____ desu ka.

   B: 五人です。

   Gonin desu.

3. *A:* ミラーさんは _____ ですか。

   Miraa san wa _____ desu ka.

   B: アメリカ人です。

   Amerikajin desu.

4. *A:* パーティーは _____ ですか。

   Paatii wa _____ desu ka.

B: あしたです。

Ashita desu.

5. *A:* _____ ですか。 (*You are pointing to a woman in a photograph.*)

_____ desu ka.

B: ロバーツさんのお姉さんです。

Robaatsu san no oneesan desu.

ANSWER KEY

1. どちら dochira; 2. なん人 nannin; 3. なに人 nanijin; 4. いつ itsu; 5. だれ dare

Sentence Builder 2

▶ 3C Sentence Builder 2 (CD 4, Track 11)

弟さんはかいしゃいんですか。

Otootosan wa kaishain desu ka.

Is your younger brother a company employee?

父も母もきょうしです。

Chichi mo haha mo kyooshi desu.

Both my father and my mother are teachers.

父はこうこうのすうがくのせんせいで、母はちゅうがくのえいごのせんせいです。

Chichi wa kookoo no suugaku no sensee de, haha wa chuugaku no eego no sensee desu.

My father is a high school mathematics teacher, and my mother is a junior high school English teacher.

お姉さんもせんせいですか。

Oneesan mo sensee desu ka.

Is your older sister also a teacher?

スミスさんのご家族は？

Sumisu san no gokazoku wa?

What about your family, Mr./Ms. Smith?

うちは父はいしゃで、母は主婦です。

Uchi wa chichi wa isha de, haha wa shufu desu.

As for my family, my father is a doctor, and my mother is a housewife.

スミスさんのおしごとは？

Sumisu san no oshigoto wa?

What's your occupation, Mr./Ms. Smith?

わたしはでんきぎしです。

Watashi wa denkigishi desu.

I'm an electrical engineer.

おのさんはけいりのたんとうですね。

Ono san wa keeri no tantoo desu ne.

Mr. Ono, you are in charge of accounting, right?

しゃいんのおきゅうりょうのたんとうです。

Shain no okyuuryoo no tantoo desu.

I'm in charge of employees' salaries.

✎ Sentence Practice 2

Fill in the missing words in each of the following sentences.

1. 弟さんは ＿＿＿＿＿＿＿＿＿＿＿＿＿＿＿＿＿＿＿＿。
   <small>おとうと</small>

   Otootosan wa ＿＿＿＿＿＿＿＿＿＿＿＿＿＿＿＿＿＿.

   Is your younger brother a company employee?

2. 父も母も ＿＿＿＿＿＿＿＿＿＿＿＿＿＿＿。
   <small>ちち　はは</small>

   Chichi mo haha mo ＿＿＿＿＿＿＿＿＿＿＿＿＿＿＿＿.

   Both my father and my mother are teachers.

3. 父はこうこうの ＿＿＿＿＿＿＿＿＿＿＿＿＿＿＿＿＿ で、母はちゅうがくの
   <small>ちち</small>　　　　　　　　　　　　　　　　　　　　　　　　　　　　　<small>はは</small>

   ＿＿＿＿＿＿＿＿＿＿＿＿＿＿＿＿＿ です。

   Chichi wa kookoo no ＿＿＿＿＿＿＿＿＿＿＿＿＿＿＿＿＿＿＿ de,

   haha wa chuugaku no ＿＿＿＿＿＿＿＿＿＿＿＿＿＿＿＿＿＿＿＿desu.

   My father is a high school mathematics teacher, and my mother is a junior high school English teacher.

4. ＿＿＿＿＿＿＿＿＿＿＿ せんせいですか。

   ＿＿＿＿＿＿＿＿＿＿＿＿＿＿＿＿＿ sensee desu ka.

   Is your older sister also a teacher?

5. ＿＿＿＿＿＿＿＿＿＿父はいしゃで、母は主婦です。
   　　　　　　　　　　<small>ちち</small>　　　　　　<small>はは　しゅふ</small>

   ＿＿＿＿＿＿＿＿＿＿ chichi wa isha de, haha wa shufu desu.

   As for my family, my father is a doctor, and my mother is a housewife.

6. しゃいんのおきゅうりょうの _____ 。

Shain no okyuuryoo no _____.

I'm in charge of employees' salaries.

ANSWER KEY

1. かいしゃいんですか kaishain desu ka; 2. きょうしです kyooshi desu; 3. すうがくのせんせい suugaku no sensee, えいごのせんせい eego no sensee desu; 4. お姉さんも Oneesan mo; 5. うちは Uchi wa; 6. たんとうです tantoo desu

Grammar Builder 2
て TE-FORM OF THE COPULA です DESU

▶ 3D Grammar Builder 2 (CD 4, Track 12)

The particle と to (*and, with*) is used in Japanese to connect more than one noun to express a group.

せんせいとせいと

sensee to seeto

a teacher and a student

But the same word cannot be used to connect verbs, adjectives, and the copula. To connect two or more actions, events, or descriptions, you will need to use the て te-form of verbs, adjectives, and the copula です desu. The following English sentences show the contexts where て te-forms would need to be used in Japanese.

I got up at six, had breakfast, and left home at 7:00.

This apartment is clean, spacious, and inexpensive.

Mr. Yano is Japanese and a college student.

We will discuss the て te-form of verbs and adjectives in later lessons; for now, let's focus on で de, which is the て te-form of the copula です desu. Let's look at how two sentences are combined into one sentence using this formula.

スミスさんはアメリカ人です。
Sumisu san wa amerikajin desu.
Mr./Ms. Smith is American.

スミスさんはぎんこういんです。
Sumisu san wa ginkooin desu.
Mr./Ms. Smith is a bank clerk.

スミスさんはアメリカ人で、ぎんこういんです。
Sumisu san wa amerikajin de, ginkooin desu.
Mr./Ms. Smith is American and a bank clerk.

Here are some more examples.

わたなべさんはだいがくせいです。
Watanabe san wa daigakusee desu.
Mr./Ms. Watanabe is a college student.

わたなべさんの妹さんはこうこうせいです。
Watanabe san no imootosan wa kookoosee desu.
Mr./Ms. Watanabe's sister is a high school student.

わたなべさんはだいがくせいで、妹<small>いもうと</small>さんはこうこうせいです。

Watanabe san wa daigakusee de, imootosan wa kookoosee desu.

Mr./Ms. Watanabe is a college student, and his/her sister is a high school student.

父<small>ちち</small>はいしゃです。

Chichi wa isha desu.

My father is a doctor.

母<small>はは</small>は主婦<small>しゅふ</small>です。

Haha wa shufu desu.

My mother is a housewife.

父<small>ちち</small>はいしゃで、母<small>はは</small>は主婦<small>しゅふ</small>です。

Chichi wa isha de, haha wa shufu desu.

My father is a doctor, and my mother is a housewife.

The て te-form does not express tense; tense is expressed by the final copula, verb, or adjective in each sentence.

✎ Work Out 2

Connect sentences using て te-form of the copula です desu.

1. わたしはアメリカ人<small>じん</small>です。しゅっしんはニューヨークです。

   Watashi wa amerikajin desu. Shusshin wa nyuuyooku desu.

   _____

て Te-form of the copula です desu | Honorific prefixes お o- and ご go-

2. 兄はすうがくのきょうしです。姉はぎんこういんです。

   Ani wa suugaku no kyooshi desu. Ane wa ginkooin desu.

   _____

3. ロペスさんはメキシコ人です。ロペスさんはやきゅうとサッカーをします。

   Ropesu san wa mekishikojin desu. Ropesu san wa yakyuu to sakkaa o shimasu.

   _____

4. コリンズさんはだいがくせいです。コリンズさんの弟さんはこうこうせい
   です。

   Korinzu san wa daigakusee desu. Korinzu san no otootosan wa kookoosee desu.

   _____

5. 父も母もきょうしです。父も母もとうきょうにいます。

   Chichi mo haha mo kyooshi desu. Chichi mo haha mo tookyoo ni imasu.

   _____

ANSWER KEY
1. わたしはアメリカ人で、しゅっしんはニューヨークです。Watashi wa amerikajin de, shusshin wa nyuuyooku desu. 2. 兄はすうがくのきょうしで、姉はぎんこういんです。Ani wa suugaku no kyooshi de, ane wa ginkooin desu. 3. ロペスさんはメキシコ人で、やきゅうとサッカーをします。Ropesu san wa mekishikojin de, yakyuu to sakkaa o shimasu. 4. コリンズさんはだいがくせいで、弟さんはこうこうせいです。Korinzu san wa daigakusee de, otootosan wa kookoosee desu. 5. 父も母もきょうしで、とうきょうにいます。Chichi mo haha mo kyooshi de, tookyoo ni imasu.

✎ Drive It Home

A. Fill in the blanks by choosing appropriate words from the word bank.
だれ dare, なに人 nanijin, なん nan, どんな donna, なん人 nannin, どこ doko, いくつ ikutsu, いつ itsu

1. それは _____ ですか。

   Sore wa _____ desu ka.

   What's that?

2. _____ 家族ですか。

   _____ kazoku desu ka.

   How many people are in your family?

3. ロペスさんは _____ ですか。

   Ropesu san wa _____ desu ka.

   What nationality is Mr./Ms. Lopez?

4. ごしゅっしんは _____ ですか。

   Goshusshin wa _____ desu ka.

   Where are you from?

5. _____ ですか。

   _____ desu ka.

   How old are you?

6. あのおんなの人は _____ ですか。

   Ano onna no hito wa _____ desu ka.

   Who is that woman?

7. コンサートは _____ ですか。

   Konsaato wa _____ desu ka.

   When is the concert?

8. _____ がくせいですか。

_____ gakusee desu ka.

What kind of student is he/she?

B. Complete the sentences by inserting the て te-form of the copula です desu.

1. たかはしさんはにほん人（じん）_____ 、がくせいです。

Takahashi san wa nihonjin _____, gakusee desu.

Mr./Ms. Takahashi is Japanese and a student.

2. 父（ちち）はかいしゃいん _____ 、母（はは）はきょうしです。

Chichi wa kaishain _____, haha wa kyooshi desu.

My father is a company employee and my mother is a teacher.

ANSWER KEY
A: 1. なん nan; 2. なん人（にん） nannin; 3. なに人（じん） nanijin; 4. どこ doko; 5. いくつ ikutsu; 6. だれ dare; 7. いつ itsu; 8. どんな donna
B. 1. で de; 2. で de

⏻ Tip!

Describe your family using て te-form of the copula です desu as much as possible. You can talk about their place of origin, occupation, etc. Next describe someone else's family, for instance your friend's family, again using て te-form of the copula です desu. This will help you practice two different forms of family terms as well as connecting two or more sentences together.

How Did You Do?

Let's see how you did! By now, you should be able to:

☐ ask questions with question words (Still unsure? Jump back to page 50)

☐ use the て te-form of the copula です desu (Still unsure? Jump back to page 58)

✎ Word Recall

1. 家族 kazoku
2. かいしゃいん kaishain
3. ご主人 goshujin
4. 子ども kodomo
5. ちゅうがっこう chuugakkoo
6. 両親といっしょに ryooshin to issho ni
7. 五人家族 gonin kazoku
8. けいざい keezai
9. そして soshite
10. きょうし kyooshi

a. *husband (someone else's)*
b. *together with parents*
c. *and, and then*
d. *five people in a family*
e. *child*
f. *teacher*
g. *junior high school*
h. *economy*
i. *company employee*
j. *family*

ANSWER KEY
1. j; 2. i; 3. a; 4. e; 5. g; 6. b; 7. d; 8. h; 9. c; 10. f

て Te-form of the copula です desu   Honorific prefixes お o- and ご go-

Lesson 4: Conversations

By the end of this lesson, you should be able to:

☐ describe the location of subjects using the particle に ni

☐ use the honorific prefixes お o- and ご go-

ⓐ Conversation 1

▶ 4A Conversation 1 (Japanese: CD 4, Track 13; Japanese and English: CD 4, Track 14)

Mr. Smith and his Japanese colleague Mr. Ono are talking about their family on their way to their work.

おの/Ono: スミスさんはなん人家族ですか。
Sumisu san wa nannin kazoku desu ka.

スミス/Sumisu: 五人家族です。父と母と兄と妹とわたしです。
Gonin kazoku desu. Chichi to haha to ani to imooto to watashi desu.

おの/Ono: そうですか。ご家族はみなさんアメリカにいますか。
Soo desu ka. Gokazoku wa minasan amerika ni imasu ka.

スミス/Sumisu: 両親と妹はアメリカにいます。でも、兄はいまメキシコにいます。
Ryooshin to imooto wa amerika ni imasu. Demo, ani wa ima mekishiko ni imasu.

おの/Ono: へえ。メキシコですか。
Hee. Mekishiko desu ka.

スミス/Sumisu: おのさんはご兄弟はいますか。
Ono san wa gokyoodai wa imasu ka.

おの/Ono: ええ、三人^{さんにん}います。姉^{あね}と妹^{いもうと}と弟^{おとうと}です。

Ee, sannin imasu. Ane to imooto to otooto desu.

スミス/Sumisu: じゃあ、四人兄弟^{よにんきょうだい}ですね。おのさんのご家族^{かぞく}はみなさん とうきょうにいますか。

Jaa, yonin kyoodai desu ne. Ono san no gokazoku wa minasan tookyoo ni imasu ka.

おの/Ono: いいえ。姉^{あね}はいまおおさかにいます。それから妹^{いもうと}と 弟^{おとうと}は両親^{りょうしん}といっしょにながのにいます。

Iie. Ane wa ima oosaka ni imasu. Sorekara imooto to otooto wa ryooshin to issho ni nagano ni imasu.

スミス/Sumisu: そうですか。じゃあごしゅっしんはながのですか。

Soo desu ka. Jaa, goshusshin wa nagano desu ka.

おの/Ono: ええ、そうですよ。ああ、かいしゃですね。じゃあ、 またしごとのあとで。

Ee, soo desu yo. Aa, kaisha desu ne. Jaa, mata shigoto no ato de.

スミス/Sumisu: それじゃ、また。

Sore ja, mata.

Ono:	*Mr. Smith, how many people are in your family?*
Smith:	*There are five people in my family. My father, mother, older brother, younger sister, and I.*
Ono:	*I see. Are they all in the U.S.A.?*
Smith:	*My parents and younger sister are in the U.S.A. But, my older brother is currently in Mexico.*
Ono:	*Oh, Mexico.*
Smith:	*Do you have any siblings, Mr. Ono?*
Ono:	*Yes, I have three siblings. An older sister, a younger sister, and a younger brother.*
Smith:	*Then, there are four children in your family, right? Is your whole family in Tokyo, Mr. Ono?*

Ono: No. My older sister is now in Osaka. And, my younger sister and younger brother are in Nagano with my parents.

Smith: I see. Then, are you from Nagano?

Ono: Yes, that's right. Oh, we arrived at the company. So, see you again after work.

Smith: See you then.

Take It Further

Note that there is an important distinction between the sentences 兄弟が三人<ruby>兄弟<rt>きょうだい</rt></ruby><ruby>三人<rt>さんにん</rt></ruby>います Kyoodai ga sannin imasu and 三人兄弟<ruby>三人兄弟<rt>さんにんきょうだい</rt></ruby>です Sannin kyoodai desu. The first sentence means the subject has three siblings and the second sentence means there is a total of three children in a family.

(わたしは) <ruby>兄弟<rt>きょうだい</rt></ruby>が<ruby>三人<rt>さんにん</rt></ruby>います (Watashi wa) kyoodai ga sannin imasu is easier to understand because its English translation is *I have three siblings*, and it indicates that there are three siblings besides the speaker. However, (わたしは) s16 <ruby>三人兄弟<rt>さんにんきょうだい</rt></ruby>です (Watashi wa) sannin kyoodai desu may be a little confusing. In this case, <ruby>三人兄弟<rt>さんにんきょうだい</rt></ruby> sannin kyoodai is treated as a unit, and the direct translation of the sentence is *(As for me,) there are three siblings*, indicating that the speaker is counting him or herself in the group of three siblings.

✎ Conversation Practice 1

Fill in the blanks in the following sentences with the missing words. If you're unsure of the answer, listen to the conversation one more time.

1. スミスさんはお父さんとお母さんと＿＿＿＿＿と＿＿＿＿＿＿がいます。

Sumisu san wa otoosan to okaasan to ＿＿＿＿＿＿＿＿＿＿ to

＿＿＿＿＿＿＿＿ ga imasu.

2. スミスさんのお兄さんは＿＿＿＿＿＿＿＿＿にいます。

Sumisu san no oniisan wa ＿＿＿＿＿＿＿＿＿ ni imasu.

3. おのさんは＿＿＿＿＿＿兄弟です。

Ono san wa ＿＿＿＿＿＿ kyoodai desu.

4. おのさんの＿＿＿＿＿＿はおおさかにいます。

Ono san no ＿＿＿＿＿＿ wa oosaka ni imasu.

5. おのさんの＿＿＿＿＿＿＿はながのです。

Ono san no ＿＿＿＿＿＿＿ wa nagano desu.

ANSWER KEY
1. 妹さん imootosan, お兄さん oniisan; 2. メキシコ mekishiko; 3. 四人 yonin; 4. お姉さん oneesan;
5. しゅっしん shusshin

Grammar Builder 1
DESCRIBING THE LOCATION OF SUBJECTS

▶ 4B Grammar Builder 1 (CD 4, Track 15)

You learned how to describe the existence of animate subjects, such as people and animals in Lesson 1. Now let's learn how to express the location of such subjects. As mentioned in Lesson 1, the location is marked by the particle に ni in the following structure.

Y に X がいます。

Y ni X ga imasu.

There is/are X in Y.

おおさかにそふとそぼがいます。

Oosaka ni sofu to sobo ga imasu.

I have my grandfather and grandmother in Osaka.

ホンコンにいとこがいます。

Honkon ni itoko ga imasu.

I have a cousin in Hong Kong.

おきなわにしんせきがいます。

Okinawa ni shinseki ga imasu.

I have my relatives in Okinawa.

Note that these sentences generally describe who is at a certain location. So, the first sentence above can be the answer to the following question.

Q: **おおさかにだれがいますか。**

Oosaka ni dare ga imasu ka.

Who is in Osaka?

A: (**おおさかに**) **そふとそぼがいます。**

(Oosaka ni) sofu to sobo ga imasu.

My grandfather and grandmother (are in Osaka).

When answering the question, it is therefore not necessary to express おおさかに oosaka ni (*in Osaka*) because it is understood from the context.

Please note that the question word だれ dare (*who*) should not be followed by the particle は wa. This is true of all question words — なに nani (*what*), だれ dare (*who*), どこ doko (*where*), いつ itsu (*when*), なに人 nanijin (*what nationality*), いくら ikura (*how much*), etc. Therefore, in the case of います imasu, you should use the default particle が ga, just as you would use it in a declarative sentence.

To describe where someone is, the following structure is used.

X は Y にいます。
X wa Y ni imasu.
X is in/at Y. (lit., As for X, it/he/she is in Y.)

兄はフランスにいます。
Ani wa furansu ni imasu.
My older brother is in France.

姉はカナダにいます。
Ane wa kanada ni imasu.
My older sister is in Canada.

父と母はとうきょうにいます。
Chichi to haha wa tookyoo ni imasu.
The father and mother are in Tokyo.

Since these sentences are describing where the subject is, the first sentence above can answer the following question.

Q: お兄さんはどこにいますか。
Oniisan wa doko ni imasu ka.
Where is your older brother?

て Te-form of the copula です desu   Honorific prefixes お o- and ご go-

A: (兄は) フランスにいます。

(Ani wa) furansu ni imasu.

My older brother is in France. (lit., As for my older brother, he is in France.)

In this case, 兄は ani wa can be dropped in the answer because it is understood from the context.

✎ Work Out 1

A. Answer the following questions with sentences using the structure Y に X がいます Y ni X ga imasu. X is provided in parentheses.

1. とうきょうにだれがいますか。(むす子)

   Tookyoo ni dare ga imasu ka. (musuko)

   _____

2. オフィスにだれがいますか。(やまださん)

   Ofisu ni dare ga imasu ka. (Yamada san)

   _____

3. だいがくにだれがいますか。(むすめ)

   Daigaku ni dare ga imasu ka. (musume)

   _____

B. Answer the following questions with sentences using the structure X は Y にいます X wa Y ni imasu. The location is provided in parentheses.

1. ご両親はどこですか。(アメリカ)

   Goryooshin wa doko desu ka. (amerika)

   _____

2. 妹 さんはどこですか。(がっこう)

   Imootosan wa doko desu ka. (gakkoo)

   _____

3. お姉さんはどこですか。(うち)

   Oneesan wa doko desu ka. (uchi)

   _____

ANSWER KEY

A: 1. (とうきょうに) むす子がいます。(Tookyoo ni) musuko ga imasu. 2. (オフィスに) やまだ さんがいます。(Ofisu ni) Yamada san ga imasu. 3. (だいがくに) むすめがいます。(Daigaku ni) musume ga imasu.

B: 1. (両親は) アメリカにいます。(Ryooshin wa) amerika ni imasu. 2. (妹は) がっこうにいます。(Imooto wa) gakkoo ni imasu. 3. (姉は) うちにいます。(Ane wa) uchi ni imasu.

◖ Conversation 2

▶ 4C Conversation 2 (Japanese: CD 4, Track 16; Japanese and English: CD 4, Track 17)

Mr. Smith and Mr. Ono are walking to the station after work.

スミス/Sumisu:	おのさんのお父さんはかいしゃいんですか。
	Ono san no otoosan wa kaishain desu ka.
おの/Ono:	いいえ、父も母もきょうしです。父はこうこうのすうが くのせんせいで、母はちゅうがくのえいごのせんせいで す。
	Iie, chichi mo haha mo kyooshi desu. Chichi wa kookoo no suugaku no sensee de, haha wa chuugaku no eego no sensee desu.

スミス/Sumisu:	じゃあ、お姉さんと妹さんもせんせいですか。
	Jaa, oneesan to imootosan mo sensee desu ka.
おの/Ono:	姉はおんがくのせんせいです。でも、妹はウェブデザイナーです。スミスさんのご家族は？
	Ane wa ongaku no sensee desu. Demo, imooto wa webudezainaa desu. Sumisu san no gokazoku wa?
スミス/Sumisu:	うちは父はいしゃで、母は主婦です。兄はぎんこういんで、妹はかんごしです。
	Uchi wa chichi wa isha de, haha wa shufu desu. Ani wa ginkooin de, imooto wa kangoshi desu.
おの/Ono:	そうですか。そして、スミスさんはエンジニアですね。
	Soo desu ka. Soshite, Sumisu san wa enjinia desu ne.
スミス/Sumisu:	ええ、でんきぎしです。おのさんはけいりのたんとうですね。
	Ee, denkigishi desu. Ono san wa keeri no tantoo desu ne.
おの/Ono:	うん、スミスさんのおきゅうりょうのたんとうですよ。
	Un, Sumisu san no okyuuryoo no tantoo desu yo.
スミス/Sumisu:	そうですかあ。ははははは。
	Soo desu kaa. Hahahahaha. (laughing)

Smith:	*Mr. Ono, is your father a company employee?*
Ono:	*No. Both my father and mother are school teachers. My father is a high school math teacher, and my mother is a junior high school English teacher.*
Smith:	*Then, your older sister and younger sister are also teachers?*
Ono:	*My older sister is a music teacher, but my younger sister is a web designer. What about your family, Mr. Smith?*
Smith:	*As for my family, my father is a doctor, and my mother is a house wife. My older brother is a bank clerk, and my younger sister is a nurse.*

Ono:	I see. And, Mr. Smith, you are an engineer, right?
Smith:	Yes, I'm an electrical engineer. Mr. Ono, you are in charge of the accounting, right?
Ono:	Yes, I'm in charge of your salary, Mr. Smith.
Smith:	I see. (laughing)

✎ Conversation Practice 2

Fill in the blanks in the following sentences with the missing words. If you're unsure of the answer, listen to the conversation one more time.

1. おのさんのお父さんとお母さんは＿＿＿＿＿＿＿＿です。

   Ono san no otoosan to okaasan wa ＿＿＿＿＿＿＿＿ desu.

2. おのさんの＿＿＿＿＿はウェブデザイナーです。

   Ono san no ＿＿＿＿＿＿＿＿ wa webudezainaa desu.

3. スミスさんのお父さんは＿＿＿＿＿です。

   Sumisu san no otoosan wa ＿＿＿＿ desu.

4. スミスさんのお母さんは＿＿です。

   Sumisu san no okaasan wa ＿＿＿＿＿＿ desu.

5. おのさんはスミスさんの＿＿＿＿＿＿＿＿のたんとうです。

   Onosan wa sumisu san no ＿＿＿＿＿＿＿＿ no tantoo desu.

ANSWER KEY

1. きょうし kyooshi; 2. 妹さん imootosan; 3. いしゃ isha; 4. 主婦 shufu; 5. きゅうりょう kyuuryoo or おきゅうりょう okyuuryoo

Grammar Builder 2
HONORIFIC PREFIXES お O- AND ご GO-

▶ 4D Grammar Builder 2 (CD 4, Track 18)

Honorifics are words, prefixes, and suffixes that convey respect towards other people. Honorifics are similar to titles like *Mr., Ms., Sir,* or *Dr.* You already know the honorific suffixes さん **san** and せんせい **sensee**. The system of Japanese honorifics is complex. For instance, verbs can have honorifics attached to them, creating two different forms: the honorific form and the humble form.

In this lesson, we'll look at the honorific prefixes お **o-** and ご **go-** which are usually attached to nouns to make them sound more polite. Some nouns take お **o** and others take ご **go**, but not every noun can take お **o** or ご **go**. At this level, it is not necessary to worry about which nouns take お **o** or ご **go** and which nouns do not. As you are exposed to the language, you will learn it naturally. Here are some examples of words with their honorific prefixes.

家族 (かぞく)	**kazoku**	ご家族 (かぞく)	gokazoku	*family*
兄弟 (きょうだい)	**kyoodai**	ご兄弟 (きょうだい)	gokyoodai	*siblings*
なまえ	**namae**	おなまえ	onamae	*name*
でんわ	**denwa**	おでんわ	odenwa	*telephone*
しごと	**shigoto**	おしごと	oshigoto	*job, work*
両親 (りょうしん)	**ryooshin**	ご両親 (りょうしん)	goryooshin	*parents*
夫婦 (ふうふ)	**fuufu**	ご夫婦 (ふうふ)	gofuufu	*married couple*

親せき	shinseki	ご親せき	goshinseki	*relatives*
きゅうりょう	kyuuryoo	おきゅうりょう	okyuuryoo	*salary*

If you add an honorific prefix to words when talking to someone, you will sound more polite , showing respect towards the person you are addressing. For instance, when giving your own name, you will say なまえは X です Namae wa X desu (*My name is X*), whereas when asking someone else's name, it's more polite to say おなまえはなんですか Onamae wa nan desu ka (*What is your name?*).

It is important to remember that an honorific prefix cannot be added to words when talking about yourself. In some cases, however, you will be unable to avoid an honorific prefix, even when talking about yourself, because over time some of them became inseparable from the word. For instance, very common words おかね okane (*money*) and おちゃ ocha (*tea*) are usually used in their formal forms; かね kane and ちゃ cha are seldom used. Additionally, female speakers tend to add an honorific prefix more often when talking about others to be more polite or to sound more sophisticated.

✎ Work Out 2

Pick the right form of the word according to the context.

1. _____（兄弟 / ご兄弟）はなん人ですか。

   _____（Kyoodai / Gokyoodai) wa nannin desu ka.

2. わたしは ___（兄弟 / ご兄弟）が二人います。

   Watashi wa _____ (kyoodai / gokyoodai) ga futari imasu.

3. わたしの ___（両親 / ご両親）はいまとうきょうにいます。

   Watashi no _____ (ryooshin / goryooshin) wa ima

   tookyoo ni imasu.

4. _____（両親 / ご両親）はおげんきですか。

   _____ (Ryooshin / Goryooshin) wa ogenki desu ka.

5. _____ （でんわ / おでんわ）ですよ。

   _____ (Denwa / Odenwa) desu yo. *(You are talking to a division*

   manager at your company.)

ANSWER KEY
1. ご兄弟 Gokyoodai; 2. 兄弟 kyoodai; 3. 両親 ryooshin; 4. ご両親 Goryooshin; 5. おでんわ
Odenwa.

✎ Drive It Home

A. Complete the following sentences by inserting the appropriate particles.

1. ニューヨーク _____ むすめ _____ います。

   Nyuuyooku _____ musume _____ imasu.

   My daughter is in New York.

2. ながの _____ 両親 _____ います。

   Nagano _____ ryooshin _____ imasu.

   My parents are in Nagano.

3. 家内 _____ うち _____ います。

   Kanai _____ uchi _____ imasu.

   My wife is at home.

4. 子ども _____がっこう _____います。

Kodomo _____ gakkoo _____ imasu.

My children are at school.

B. Insert the appropriate honorific prefix.

1. _____ 兄弟   3. _____ 両親

_____kyoodai   _____ryooshin

siblings   *parents*

2. _____ なまえ   4. _____ 夫婦

_____namae   _____fuufu

name   *married couple*

ANSWER KEY
A: 1. に ni, が ga; 2. に ni, が ga; 3. は wa, に ni; 4. は wa, に ni
B. 1. ご go; 2. お o; 3. ご go; 4. ご go

How Did You Do?

Let's see how you did! By now, you should be able to:

☐ describe the location of subjects using the particle に ni (Still unsure? Jump back to page 68)

☐ use the honorific prefixes お o- and ご go- (Still unsure? Jump back to page 75)

✎ Word Recall

1. <ruby>三人兄弟<rt>さんにんきょうだい</rt></ruby> sannin kyoodai   a. *house, one's home, one's family*

2. アメリカ<ruby>人<rt>じん</rt></ruby> amerikajin   b. *company*

3. かいしゃ kaisha   c. *parents*

4. <ruby>両親<rt>りょうしん</rt></ruby> ryooshin   d. *three children in a family*

5. それじゃまた。 Sore ja mata.   e. *child (someone else's)*

6. きゅうりょう kyuuryoo   f. *salary*

7. <ruby>子<rt>こ</rt></ruby>どもさん kodomosan   g. *cousin*

8. うち uchi   h. *See you then.*

9. いとこ itoko   i. *Yes, it is. / Let me see.*

10. そうですね。 Soo desu ne.   j. *American (person)*

ANSWER KEY
1. d; 2. j; 3. b; 4. c; 5. h; 6. f; 7. e; 8. a; 9. g; 10. i

Don't forget to practice and reinforce what you've learned by visiting **www.livinglanguage.com/languagelab** for flashcards, games, and quizzes for Unit 1!

Unit 1 Essentials

Vocabulary Essentials

Test your knowledge of the key material in this unit by filling in the blanks in the following charts. Once you've completed these pages, you'll have tested your retention, and you'll have your own reference for the most essential vocabulary.

FAMILY

	father (one's own)
	father (someone else's)
	mother (one's own)
	mother (someone else's)
	older brother (one's own)
	older brother (someone else's)
	older sister (one's own)
	older sister (someone else's)
	younger sister (one's own)
	younger sister (someone else's)
	younger brother (one's own)
	younger brother (someone else's)
	grandfather (one's own)
	grandfather (someone else's)
	grandmother (one's own)
	grandmother (someone else's)
	husband (one's own)

	husband (someone else's)
	wife (one's own)
	wife (someone else's)
	child
	child (someone else's)
	son (one's own)
	son (someone else's)
	daughter (one's own)
	daughter (someone else's)
	cousin
	family
	parents
	siblings
	married couple
	relatives
	house, one's home, one's family
	place of origin, hometown

OCCUPATION

	junior high school
	high school
	university, college
	teacher
	mathematics
	economy

	economics
	housewife
	job, work
	company
	company employee
	bank clerk
	web designer
	engineer
	electrical engineer
	(business) administration, accounting
	salary
	place of origin, hometown

HONORIFIC PREFIXES

	family (polite)
	siblings (polite)
	name (polite)
	telephone (polite)
	job, work (polite)
	parents (polite)
	married couple (polite)
	relatives (polite)
	salary (polite)

QUESTION WORDS

	When?
	Where? (neutral)
	Where? (polite)
	Who? (neutral)
	Who? (polite)
	What kind?
	Why?
	How much? (neutral)
	How much? (polite)
	How many? (neutral)
	How many? (polite)
	How many people?
	How many books?
	What nationality?

VERBS

	to be
	to exist, to have, there is/are (animate)

Grammar Essentials

Here is a reference of the key grammar that was covered in Unit 1. Make sure you understand the summary and can use all of the grammar it covers before moving on to the next unit.

PARTICLES

が ga

FUNCTION	EXAMPLE
Marks a subject	やまださんがいます。 **Yamada san ga imasu.** *Mr./Ms. Yamada is there.*

は wa

FUNCTION	EXAMPLE
Marks a topic	やまださんは弟^{おとうと}さんがいます。 **Yamada san wa otootosan ga imasu.** *Mr./Ms. Yamada has (a) younger brother(s).*
Replaces が *ga in a question and a negative sentence*	弟^{おとうと}さんはいますか。 **Otootosan wa imasu ka.** *Is there a younger brother? / Do you have a younger brother?* 弟^{おとうと}はいません。 **Otooto wa imasen.** *There isn't a younger brother. / I don't have a younger brother.*

の no

FUNCTION	EXAMPLE
Connects nouns	やまださんのお父^{とう}さんのかいしゃ **Yamada san no otoosan no kaisha** *Mr./Ms. Yamada's father's company* こうこうのすうがくのせんせい **kookoo no suugaku no sensee** *high school mathematics teacher*

も mo

FUNCTION	EXAMPLE
Corresponds to English too, also, or both ... and	<ruby>弟<rt>おとうと</rt></ruby> もがくせいです。 **Otooto mo gakusee desu.** *My younger brother is also a student.* <ruby>妹<rt>いもうと</rt></ruby> も <ruby>弟<rt>おとうと</rt></ruby>もがくせいです。 **Imooto mo otooto mo gakusee desu.** *Both my younger sister and younger brother are students.*

に ni

FUNCTION	EXAMPLE
Marks a location	<ruby>父<rt>ちち</rt></ruby>と<ruby>母<rt>はは</rt></ruby>はとうきょうにいます。 **Chichi to haha wa tookyoo ni imasu.** *The father and mother are in Tokyo.*

か ka

FUNCTION	EXAMPLE
Marks a question	だいがくのせんせいですか。 **Daigaku no sensee desu ka.** *Are you a college professor?*
Used to express surprise (with falling intonation)	だいがくのせんせいですか（あ）。 **Daigaku no sensee desu ka(a).** *College professor? Really?*

ね ne

FUNCTION	EXAMPLE
Used to seek agreement	おいしいですね。 **Oishii desu ne.** *It's delicious, isn't it?*
Used to express agreement	そうですね。 **Soo desu ne.** *Yes, it is.*
Used to confirm information	それからフットボールもしますね。 **Sorekara futtobooru mo shimasu ne.** *And you also play football, right?*

よ yo

FUNCTION	EXAMPLE
Used to make an assertion	わたしは五人家族ですよ。 **Watashi wa gonin kazoku desu yo.** *There are five people in my family. (I assure you.)*

て Te-Form

VERB	て TE-FORM	EXAMPLE
です desu	で de	父はいしゃで、母は主婦です。 **Chichi wa isha de, haha wa shufu desu.** *My father is a doctor, and my mother is a housewife.*

Unit 1 Quiz

Let's put the most essential Japanese words and grammar points you've learned so far to practice in a few exercises. It's important to be sure that you've mastered this material before you move on. Score yourself at the end of the review and see if you need to go back for more practice, or if you're ready to move on to Unit 2.

A. Complete the following phrases and sentences by inserting appropriate particles.

1. 子ども _____ いません。

   Kodomo _____ imasen.

   I don't have any child.

2. かいしゃ _____ おきゅうりょう _____ たんとう

   kaisha _____ okyuuryoo _____ tantoo

   being in charge of salary at the company

3. とうきょう _____ 親せきがいます。

   Tookyoo _____ shinseki ga imasu.

   I have my relatives in Tokyo.

4. けいざいがくのせんせいです _____。

   Keezaigaku no sensee desu _____.

   You are an economics professor? Really?

5. むすめはかいしゃいんです _____。 (asserting)

   Musume wa kaishain desu _____.

   My daughter is a company employee。

6. むす子さんはエンジニアです _____。

   Musuko san wa enginia desu _____.

   Your son is an engineer, right?

7. 姉 _____ 妹 _____ 主婦です。

   Ane _____ imooto _____ shufu desu.

   Both my older sister and younger sister are housewives.

B. Complete the following questions by inserting appropriate question words.

1. ご主人は _____ ですか。

   Goshujin wa _____ desu ka.

   Where is your husband?

2. いとこは_____ いますか。

   Itoko wa _____ imasu ka.

   How many cousins do you have?

3. ミラーさんは _____ ですか。

   Miraa san wa _____ desu ka.

   What nationality is Mr. Miller?

4. このジャケットは _____ ですか。

   Kono jaketto wa _____ desu ka.

   How much is this jacket?

5. あのおとこの人<ruby>人<rt>ひと</rt></ruby>は _____ ですか。

   Ano otoko no hito wa _____ **desu ka.**

   Who is that man?

6. パーティーは _____ ですか。

   Paatii wa _____ **desu ka.**

   When is the party?

7. おなまえは _____ ですか。

   Onamae wa _____ **desu ka.**

   What is your name?

C. Insert appropriate honorific prefixes.

1. _____ <ruby>家族<rt>か ぞ く</rt></ruby>

   _____ kazoku

   family

2. _____ しごと

   _____ shigoto

   job, work

D. Connect sentences using て te-form of the copula です desu.

1. *a.* すずきさんのお父さんはぎんこういんです。Suzuki san no otoosan wa ginkooin desu.

   b. すずきさんのお母さんは主婦です。Suzuki san no okaasan wa shufu desu.

   _____

2. *a.* コリンズさんはアメリカ人です。Korinzu san wa amerikajin desu.

   b. コリンズさんはえいごのせんせいです。Korinzu san wa eego no sensee desu.

   _____

E. Translate the following sentences into Japanese.

1. *Both my older brother and older sister are in the U.S.*

   _____

2. *My math teacher has a daughter.*

   _____

ANSWER KEY

A. 1. は wa; 2. の no, の no; 3. に ni; 4. か ka; 5. よ yo; 6. ね ne; 7. も mo, も mo

B. 1. どこ doko or どちら dochira; 2. なん人 nannin; 3. なに人 nanijin; 4. いくら ikura or おいくら oikura; 5. だれ dare or どなた donata; 6. いつ itsu; 7. なん nan

C. 1. ご go; 2. お o

D. 1. すずきさんのお父さんはぎんこういんで、お母さんは主婦です。Suzuki san no otoosan wa ginkooin de, okaasan wa shufu desu. 2. コリンズさんはアメリカ人で、えいごのせんせいです。Korinzu san wa amerikajin de, eego no sensee desu.

E. 1. 兄も姉もアメリカにいます。Ani mo ane mo amerika ni imasu. 2. わたしのすうがくのせんせいは (むすめさん / おじょうさん) がいます。Watashi no suugakuno sensee wa (musumesan/ojoosan) ga imasu.

How Did You Do?

Give yourself a point for every correct answer, then use the following key to tell whether you're ready to move on:

0-7 points: It's probably a good idea to go back through the lesson again. You may be moving too quickly, or there may be too much "down time" between your contact with Japanese. Remember that it's better to spend 30 minutes with Japanese three or four times a week than it is to spend two or three hours just once a week. Find a pace that's comfortable for you, and spread your contact hours out as much as you can.

8-12 points: You would benefit from a review before moving on. Go back and spend a little more time on the specific points that gave you trouble. Re-read the Grammar Builder sections that were difficult, and do the work out one more time. Don't forget about the online supplemental practice material, either. Go to **www. livinglanguage.com/languagelab** for games and quizzes that will reinforce the material from this unit.

13-17 points: Good job! There are just a few points that you could consider reviewing before moving on. If you haven't worked with the games and quizzes on **www.livinglanguage.com/languagelab**, please give them a try.

18-20 points: Great! You're ready to move on to the next unit.

☐☐ points

Unit 2:
Everyday life

Welcome to Unit 2! Here you will learn how to talk about your daily life; you'll be able to describe what you do every day, where you live, and your likes and dislikes. By the end of the unit, you'll be able to:

☐ use key vocabulary related to time and frequency

☐ use counters to count different types of objects around the home

☐ use key vocabulary to describe your house or apartment

☐ use the copula です desu in different tense forms

☐ use the static verb あります arimasu

☐ express quantity of items in sentences

☐ express your likes and dislikes

☐ use the particle が ga as an object marker

☐ use the plain form of copula

☐ conjugate different classes of verbs

☐ use the conjunctions *and* and *but*

が Ga as object marker

The basics of Japanese verbs:
Verb forms, classes, and tense

だ Da: The plain form of the
copula です desu

Conjunctions から kara, ので node,
けど kedo, and が ga

Lesson 5: Words

In this lesson you'll learn how to:

☐ use key vocabulary related to time and frequency

☐ use counters to count different types of objects around the home

☐ use key vocabulary to describe your house or apartment

☐ use the copula です desu in different tense forms

Word Builder 1

▶ 5A Word Builder 1 (CD 4, Track 19)

毎日	mainichi	*every day*
今日	kyoo	*today*
明日	ashita	*tomorrow*
昨日	kinoo	*yesterday*
あさって	asatte	*the day after tomorrow*
おととい	ototoi	*the day before yesterday*
平日	heejitsu	*weekday*
週末	shuumatsu	*weekend*
今週	konshuu	*this week*
来週	raishuu	*next week*
先週	senshuu	*last week*

あさ 朝	asa	morning
ひる 昼	hiru	noon, afternoon
ゆうがた 夕方	yuugata	early evening
よる　ばん 夜、晩	yoru or ban	evening, night
ご ご 午後	gogo	afternoon, p.m.
ご ぜん 午前	gozen	morning, a.m.
あさ　はん　ちょうしょく 朝ご飯、朝食	asagohan or chooshoku	breakfast
ひる　はん　ちゅうしょく 昼ご飯、昼食	hirugohan or chuushoku	lunch
ばん　はん　ゆうはん 晩ご飯、夕飯、 ゆうしょく 夕食	bangohan or yuuhan or yuushoku	dinner
よく	yoku	often
ときどき 時々	tokidoki	sometimes
たまに	tamani	once in a while
あ（ん）まり	a(n)mari (+ negative)	not so often, not so much

Take It Further

You just saw the word **tokidoki** (*sometimes*) written in as 時々. The second
character 々 is an iteration mark indicating that the previous kanji should be
repeated. Without using the iteration mark, the word **tokidoki** is written as 時時.
However, it is almost never written that way; the iteration mark 々 is normally
used. Keep in mind that 々 itself does not have any inherent reading assigned
to it; its reading is completely dependent on the previous kanji. Note that the
repeated character might not have the same pronunciation as the first kanji;

が Ga as object marker

The basics of Japanese verbs:
Verb forms, classes, and tense

だ Da: The plain form of the
copula です desu

Conjunctions から kara, ので node,
けど kedo, and が ga

sometimes the first repeated consonant becomes voiced as in 時々 tokidoki (i.e.
[t] becomes [d]). The following are some more word examples with 々.

しょうしょう 少々	shooshoo	*a few, a little*
そうそう　はやばや 早々 or 早々	soosoo or hayabaya	*promptly*
ひさびさ 久々	hisabisa	*long-absence*
むかしむかし 昔々	mukashimukashi	*once upon a time*

✎ Word Practice 1

Translate the following words into Japanese.

1. *every day* _____

2. *yesterday* _____

3. *the day after tomorrow* _____

4. *the day before yesterday* _____

5. *weekday* _____

6. *last week* _____

7. *early evening* _____

8. *often* _____

9. *sometimes* _____

10. *once in a while* _____

ANSWER KEY

1. 毎日 mainichi; 2. 昨日 kinoo; 3. あさって asatte; 4. おととい ototoi; 5. 平日 heejitsu; 6. 先週 senshuu; 7. 夕方 yuugata; 8. よく yoku; 9. 時々 tokidoki; 10. たまに tamani

Grammar Builder 1
COUNTERS

▶ 5B Grammar Builder 1 (CD 4, Track 20)

In *Essential Japanese*, you learned measure words to count people (人 nin), books (冊 satsu), machines (台 dai), and glasses/cups of drinks (杯 hai). You also learned handy native Japanese numbers, which you can use to count furniture, small round objects, abstract concepts, etc. *Measure words* are also called *counters*, which is a more formal term. Don't worry if you feel you've forgotten some of the counters. In this section, you'll review the counters from *Essential Japanese* as well as adding a few new ones.

Japanese has many different types of counters and they are classified according to the physical properties of the object a noun represents. For instance, 枚 mai is used when thin flat objects, such as *paper*, *handkerchiefs*, *T-shirts* and *blankets*, are counted; 本 hon is used when long cylindrical objects, such as *pens*, *pencils* and *umbrellas*, are counted.

紙十枚
kami (*paper*) juumai
ten pieces of paper

ハンカチ三枚
hankachi (*handkerchief*) sanmai
three handkerchiefs

が Ga as object marker

The basics of Japanese verbs:
Verb forms, classes, and tense

だ Da: The plain form of the
copula です desu

Conjunctions から kara, ので node,
けど kedo, and が ga

えんぴつ に ほん
鉛筆二本

enpitsu (*pencil*) **nihon**

two pencils

ペン五本
ご ほん

pen gohon

five pens

Note that a counter usually follows a noun. The position of a counter will be discussed more in Lesson 10. The following chart gives counters for several different types of objects in combination numbers from one to ten. The counters 人 nin, 冊 satsu, 台 dai, and 杯 hai are reviewed for you.

	にん 人 **nin**	さつ 冊 **satsu**	だい 台 **dai**	はい 杯 **hai**	まい 枚 **mai**	ほん 本 **hon**	ひき 匹 **hiki**
	people	bound objects	mechanical items	liquid in cups/ glasses/ bowls	thin flat objects	long cylindrical objects	animals
1	ひとり 一人 **hitori**	いっさつ 一冊 **issatsu**	いちだい 一台 **ichidai**	いっぱい 一杯 **ippai**	いちまい 一枚 **ichimai**	いっぽん 一本 **ippon**	いっぴき 一匹 **ippiki**
2	ふたり 二人 **futari**	にさつ 二冊 **nisatsu**	に だい 二台 **nidai**	に はい 二杯 **nihai**	に まい 二枚 **nimai**	に ほん 二本 **nihon**	に ひき 二匹 **nihiki**
3	さんにん 三人 **sannin**	さんさつ 三冊 **sansatsu**	さんだい 三台 **sandai**	さんばい 三杯 **sanbai**	さんまい 三枚 **sanmai**	さんぼん 三本 **sanbon**	さんびき 三匹 **sanbiki**
4	よんにん 四人 **yonin**	よんさつ 四冊 **yonsatsu**	よんだい 四台 **yondai**	よんはい 四杯 **yonhai**	よんまい 四枚 **yonmai**	よんほん 四本 **yonhon**	よんひき 四匹 **yonhiki**
5	ごにん 五人 **gonin**	ごさつ 五冊 **gosatsu**	ご だい 五台 **godai**	ご はい 五杯 **gohai**	ご まい 五枚 **gomai**	ご ほん 五本 **gohon**	ご ひき 五匹 **gohiki**

The static verb あります arimasu (to exist)

Conjugation of the copula です desu

Expressing quantity using あ
arimasu/います imasu

	人 nin	冊 satsu	台 dai	杯 hai	枚 mai	本 hon	匹 hiki
	people	bound objects	mechanical items	liquid in cups/ glasses/ bowls	thin flat objects	long cylindrical objects	animals
6	六人 rokunin	六冊 roku-satsu	六台 rokudai	六杯 roppai	六枚 roku-mai	六本 roppon	六匹 roppiki
7	七人 nananin or 七人 shichi-nin	七冊 nana-satsu	七台 nana-dai	七杯 nana-hai	七枚 nana-mai	七本 nana-hon	七匹 nana-hiki
8	八人 hachinin	八冊 hassatsu	八台 hachidai	八杯 happai	八枚 hachi-mai	八本 happon or 八本 hachi-hon	八匹 happiki
9	九人 kyuunin	九冊 kyuu-satsu	九台 kyuudai	九杯 kyuu-hai	九枚 kyuu-mai	九本 kyuu-hon	九匹 kyuu-hiki
10	十人 juunin	十冊 jussatsu	十台 juudai	十杯 juppai	十枚 juumai	十本 juppon	十匹 juppiki

が Ga as object marker

The basics of Japanese verbs:
Verb forms, classes, and tense

だ Da: The plain form of the
copula です desu

Conjunctions から kara, ので node,
けど kedo, and が ga

Notice that there are some irregularities and variations in the form of numbers and counters. For instance, *one (long cylindrical object)* and *three (long cylindrical object)* are not いちほん ichihon and さんほん sanhon, but いっぽん ippon and さんぼん sanbon.

In *Essential Japanese*, you also learned native Japanese numbers. Let's review them here.

1	一つ hitotsu	6	六つ muttsu
2	二つ futatsu	7	七つ nanatsu
3	三つ mittsu	8	八つ yattsu
4	四つ yottsu	9	九つ kokonotsu
5	五つ itsutsu	10	十 too

Native Japanese numbers only exist for numbers from one to ten, so you have to use numbers of Chinese origin from eleven on up (i.e. 十一 juuichi, 十二 juuni, 十三 juusan and so on). These numbers are often used to count round objects such as balls, apples, oranges, and eggs as well as objects that are not clearly categorized such as pieces of furniture, boxes, mountains, or stars. Also, when counting some abstract things, such as ideas, questions, and problems, the native Japanese numbers are used.

りんごを一つ食べます。
Ringo (*apple*) o hitotsu tabemasu.
I eat one apple.

オレンジも三つ食べます。
Orenji (*orange*) mo mittsu tabemasu.
I eat three oranges, too.

ソファーを一つ買います。
<ruby>一<rt>ひと</rt></ruby>つ<ruby>買<rt>か</rt></ruby>います。

Sofaa (*sofa*) **o hitotsu kaimasu.**

I will buy one sofa.

<ruby>質問<rt>しつもん</rt></ruby>が<ruby>二<rt>ふた</rt></ruby>つあります。

Shitsumon (*question*) **ga futatsu arimasu.**

I have two questions.

<ruby>問題<rt>もんだい</rt></ruby>が<ruby>一<rt>ひと</rt></ruby>つあります。

Mondai (*problem*) **ga hitotsu arimasu.**

There's one problem.

✎ Work Out 1

A. Which counter should you use when counting the following items? Match the right counter with the noun.

1. 学生 gakusee   a. 台 dai

2. 雑誌 zasshi (*magazine*)   b. 本 hon

3. 犬 inu   c. 杯 hai

4. ティーシャツ T-shatsu (*T-shirt*)   d. 匹 hiki

5. ペン pen   e. 冊 satsu

6. 車 kuruma   f. 枚 mai

7. コーヒー koohii   g. 人 nin

が Ga as object marker

The basics of Japanese verbs:
Verb forms, classes, and tense

だ Da: The plain form of the
copula です desu

Conjunctions から kara, ので node,
けど kedo, and が ga

B. Fill in the blanks with the appropriate number and counter combination.

Ex. 子供が三人います。Kodomo ga sannin imasu. (three)

1. 車が＿＿＿＿＿＿＿＿あります。(four)

   Kuruma ga ＿＿＿＿＿＿＿＿ arimasu.

2. 本が＿＿＿＿＿＿＿ あります。(six)

   Hon ga ＿＿＿＿＿＿＿＿ arimasu.

3. 鉛筆が ＿＿＿＿＿＿ あります。(three)

   Enpitsu (pencil) ga ＿＿＿＿＿ arimasu.

4. 紙が＿＿＿＿＿＿＿ あります。(twenty)

   Kami ga ＿＿＿＿＿＿＿＿ arimasu.

5. 学生が ＿＿＿＿＿＿ います。(fifteen)

   Gakusee ga ＿＿＿＿＿＿＿ imasu.

6. 犬が ＿＿＿＿＿＿＿＿います。(one)

   Inu ga ＿＿＿＿＿＿＿＿ imasu.

7. りんごが ＿＿＿＿＿＿あります。(ten)

   Ringo ga ＿＿＿＿＿＿＿＿ arimasu.

8. コーヒーが ＿＿＿＿＿ あります。(two)

   Koohii ga ＿＿＿＿＿＿＿＿ arimasu.

ANSWER KEY

A: 1. g; 2. e; 3. d; 4. f; 5. b; 6. a; 7. c

B: 1. 四台 yondai; 2. 六冊 rokusatsu; 3. 三本 sanbon; 4. 二十枚 nijuumai; 5. 十五人 juugonin;
6. 一匹 ippiki; 7. 十 too; 8. 二杯 nihai

Word Builder 2

▶ 5C Word Builder 2 (CD 4, Track 21)

せいかつ 生活	seekatsu	*life*
じゅぎょう 授業	jugyoo	*class*
りょうり 料理	ryoori	*cooking, cuisine*
しょうせつ 小説	shoosetsu	*novel*
しんぶん 新聞	shinbun	*newspaper*
ざっし 雑誌	zasshi	*magazine*
へや 部屋	heya	*room*
いま 居間	ima	*living room*
しんしつ 寝室	shinshitsu	*bedroom*
だいどころ 台所	daidokoro	*kitchen*
せんめんじょ 洗面所	senmenjo	*area with a wash stand*
よくしつ 浴室	yokushitsu	*bathroom*
て あら お手洗い、トイレ	otearai or toire	*toilet*
げんかん 玄関	genkan	*entrance hall*
かいだん 階段	kaidan	*stairs*
にわ 庭	niwa	*garden, yard*
ソファー	sofaa	*sofa*
つくえ 机	tsukue	*desk*
ベッド	beddo	*bed*
たんす	tansu	*chest of drawers*

が Ga as object marker

The basics of Japanese verbs:
Verb forms, classes, and tense

だ Da: The plain form of the
copula です desu

Conjunctions から kara, ので node,
けど kedo, and が ga

冷蔵庫 (れいぞうこ)	reezooko	refrigerator
電子レンジ (でんし)	denshirenji	microwave oven
洗濯機 (せんたくき)	sentakuki	washing machine
大変 (たいへん)	taihen	hard
忙しい (いそが)	isogashii	busy
楽しい (たの)	tanoshii	enjoyable
狭い (せま)	semai	narrow
広い (ひろ)	hiroi	spacious
リラックスします	rirakkusushimasu	to relax
洗います (あら)	araimasu	to wash
入ります (はい)	hairimasu	to enter
磨きます (みが)	migakimasu	to brush, to polish
話します (はな)	hanashimasu	to speak
嫌い (きら)	kirai	to dislike
僕 (ぼく)	boku (*used only by male speakers*)	I
友達 (ともだち)	tomodachi	friend
法律 (ほうりつ)	hooritsu	law
弁護士 (べんごし)	bengoshi	lawyer
フランス語 (ご)	furansugo	French (language)

Counters

The static verb あります arimasu (to exist)

┤- - - - - - - - - - - ┤- - - - - - - - - - - - - ┤- - - -

Conjugation of the copula です desu

Expressing quantity using あ
arimasu/います imasu

Take It Further

In Unit 1, you learned to express nationalities by saying "country name + 人 jin."
To refer to languages, use the formula "country name + 語 go." 語 Go is a suffix
that means *language*.

COUNTRY		LANGUAGE	
日本 nihon	*Japan*	日本語 nihongo	*Japanese* *(language)*
フランス furansu	*France*	フランス語 furansugo	*French (language)*
スペイン supein	*Spain*	スペイン語 supeingo	*Spanish* *(language)*
中国 chuugoku	*China*	中国語 chuugokugo	*Chinese* *(language)*
ドイツ doitsu	*Germany*	ドイツ語 doitsugo	*German* *(language)*
イギリス igirisu	*England*	英語 eego	*English* *(language)*

Please note that *English (language)* in Japanese is 英語 eego, not イギリス語
igirisugo.

✎ Word Practice 2

Translate the following words into Japanese.

1. *cooking, cuisine* _____

が Ga as object marker

The basics of Japanese verbs:
Verb forms, classes, and tense

- - - - - - - - - ┼ - - - - - - - - - - ┼ - - - - - - - - - - ┼ - - - - - - - - -

だ Da: The plain form of the
copula です desu

Conjunctions から kara, ので node,
けど kedo, and が ga

2. *newspaper* _____

3. *living room* _____

4. *busy* _____

5. *narrow* _____

6. *spacious* _____

7. *to speak* _____

8. *to wash* _____

9. *friend* _____

10. *bedroom* _____

ANSWER KEY
1. 料理 ryoori; 2. 新聞 shinbun; 3. 居間 ima; 4. 忙しい isogashii; 5. 狭い semai; 6. 広い hiroi;
7. 話します hanashimasu; 8. 洗います araimasu; 9. 友達 tomodachi; 10. 寝室 shinshitsu

Grammar Builder 2
CONJUGATION OF THE COPULA です DESU

(▶) 5D Grammar Builder 2 (CD 4, Track 22)

You already learned about the copula です desu in *Essential Japanese* and its

て te-form で de in Lesson 3. Now let's look at the different forms of です desu.

Since Japanese does not distinguish between the present and the future tense, the

term "non-past" is used in the following chart to refer to both concepts.

NON-PAST		PAST		
Affirmative	Negative	Affirmative	Negative	て Te-form
です desu	ではありません de wa arimasen ではないです de wa nai desu じゃありません ja arimasen じゃないです ja nai desu	でした deshita	ではありませんでした de wa arimasen deshita ではなかったです de wa nakatta desu じゃありませんでした ja arimasen deshita じゃなかったです ja nakatta desu	で de

Note that there are four different forms for the negative of the copula です desu. In *Essential Japanese*, you learned one of them: ではありません de wa arimasen, but now you're ready to study the rest. Negative expressions with じゃ ja are more colloquial than those with では de wa. The difference between ありません arimasen and ないです nai desu, and ありませんでした arimasen deshita and なかったです nakatta desu are more subtle; some people feel that ありません arimasen sounds softer, but both forms are equally acceptable at all situations.

Let's look some sentences with affirmative, negative, non-past, and past forms of です desu.

が Ga as object marker

The basics of Japanese verbs:
Verb forms, classes, and tense

だ Da: The plain form of the
copula です desu

Conjunctions から kara, ので node,
けど kedo, and が ga

私は日本人です。

Watashi wa nihonjin desu.

I am Japanese.

私は日本人ではありません。/ 私は日本人ではないです。

Watashi wa nihonjin de wa arimasen./Watashi wa nihonjin de wa nai desu.

私は日本人じゃありません。/ 私は日本人じゃないです。

Watashi wa nihonjin ja arimasen./Watashi wa nihonjin ja nai desu.

I am not Japanese.

料理が好きです。

Ryoori ga suki desu.

I like cooking.

料理は好きではありません。料理は好きではないです。

Ryoori wa suki de wa arimasen./Ryoori wa suki de wa nai desu.

料理は好きじゃありません。料理は好きじゃないです。

Ryoori wa suki ja arimasen./Ryoori wa suki ja nai desu.

I don't like cooking.

私は学生でした。

Watashi wa gakusee deshita.

I was a student.

私は学生ではありませんでした。私は学生ではなかったです。

Watashi wa gakusee de wa arimasen deshita./Watashi wa gakusee de wa nakatta desu.

私は学生じゃありませんでした。私は学生じゃなかったです。

Watashi wa gakusee ja arimasen deshita./Watashi wa gakusee ja nakatta desu.

I was not a student.

✎ Work Out 2

Give the negative form of the following sentences.

1. 私はアメリカ人です。

   Watashi wa amerikajin desu.

   _____

2. 田中さんは大学生でした。

   Tanaka san wa daigakusee deshita.

   _____

3. 佐藤さんは医者です。

   Satoo san wa isha desu.

   _____

4. 妹 はテニスが好きです。

   Imooto wa tenisu ga suki desu.

   _____

5. 兄は英語の授業が好きでした。

   Ani wa eego no jugyoo ga suki deshita.

   _____

ANSWER KEY

1. 私はアメリカ人 (では/じゃ) (ありません/ないです)。Watashi wa amerikajin (de wa/ja)(arimasen/
nai desu)。2. 田中さんは大学生 (では/じゃ) (ありませんでした/なかったです)。Tanaka san wa
daigakusee (de wa/ja) (arimasen deshita/nakatta desu)。3. 佐藤さんは医者 (では/じゃ) (ありませ
ん/ないです)。Satoo san wa isha (de wa/ja)(arimasen/nai desu)。4. 妹はテニスが好き (では/じゃ)
(ありません/ないです)。Imooto wa tenisu ga suki (de wa/ja)(arimasen/nai desu)。5. 兄は英語の授
業が好き (では/じゃ) (ありませんでした/なかったです)。Ani wa eego no jugyoo ga suki (de wa/ja)
(arimasen deshita/nakatta desu)。

✎ Drive It Home

A. Fill in the blanks with the appropriate number and counter combination.

1. 本が _____あります。(one)

   Hon ga _____ arimasu.

2. ペンが _____あります。(one)

   Pen ga _____ arimasu.

3. コーヒーが _____あります。(one)

   Koohii ga _____ arimasu.

4. 車が _____あります。(one)

   Kuruma ga _____ arimasu.

5. 紙が_____あります。(one)

   Kami ga _____ arimasu.

6. テーブルが _____あります。(one)

   Teeburu ga _____ arimasu.

7. 猫が_____います。(one)

   Neko ga _____ imasu.

B. Fill in each of the blanks with the appropriate form of です desu based on the English translation provided.

1. 学生_____。

   Gakusee_____.

   I am not a student.

2. 学生^{がくせい} _____ 。

Gakusee _____ .

I was a student.

3. 学生^{がくせい} _____ 。

Gakusee _____ .

I was not a student.

ANSWER KEY

A: 1. 一冊 issatsu; 2. 一本 ippoon; 3. 一杯 ippai; 4. 一台 ichidai; 5. 一枚 ichimai; 6. 一つ hitotsu;
7. 一匹 ippiki

B. 1. (では/じゃ) (ありません/ないです) (de wa/ja)(arimasen/nai desu); 2. でした deshita;
3. (では/じゃ) (ありませんでした/なかったです) (de wa/ja) (arimasen deshita/nakatta desu)

Take It Further

Practice counters by counting things around your house. Open the refrigerator
and check how many oranges, apples, cucumbers, or other fruits or vegetables
you have in it. Make a list in Japanese using appropriate counters. Next, go to
the bookshelf and count in Japanese how many books are there. Because you
can count only up to twenty for now, you can stop counting once you reach that
number. Then, check the pen and pencil holder and count how many ballpoint
pens, pencils, etc., you have there. Also, check the computer printer and see how
many sheets of papers are left in the paper feeder. Feel free to continue with
other objects around the house in a similar way.

が Ga as object marker

The basics of Japanese verbs:
Verb forms, classes, and tense

- -

だ Da: The plain form of the
copula です desu

Conjunctions から kara, ので node,
けど kedo, and が ga

How Did You Do?

Let's see how you did! By now, you should be able to:

□ use key vocabulary related to time and frequency
(Still unsure? Jump back to page 93)

□ use counters to count different types of objects around the home
(Still unsure? Jump back to page 96)

□ use key vocabulary to describe your house or apartment
(Still unsure? Jump back to page 102)

□ use the copula です desu in different tense forms
(Still unsure? Jump back to page 105)

✎ Word Recall

1. お嬢さん ojoosan   a. *bank clerk*

2. 夫婦 fuufu   b. *however, but*

3. 高校 kookoo   c. *high school*

4. 経済学 keezaigaku   d. *(business) administration,*
                                       accounting

5. 主婦 shufu   e. *housewife*

6. 銀行員 ginkooin   f. *economics*

7. 技師 gishi   g. *being in charge*

8. 経理 keeri   h. *married couple*

9. 担当 tantoo   i. *engineer*

10. でも demo   j. *daughter (someone else's)*

Unit 2 Lesson 5: Words   111

ANSWER KEY
1. j; 2. h; 3. c; 4. f; 5. e; 6. a; 7. i; 8. d; 9. g; 10. b

Lesson 6: Phrases

In this lesson you'll learn how to:

☐ use the static verb あります arimasu

☐ express quantity of items in sentences

Phrase Builder 1

▶ 6A Phrase Builder 1 (CD 4, Track 23)

どうですか。	Doo desu ka.	*How is it?*
東京の生活	tookyoo no seekatsu	*life in Tokyo*
日本語の授業	nihongo no jugyoo	*Japanese class*
小説や雑誌	shoosetsu ya zasshi	*novel, magazine, and so on*
ちょっと大変	chotto taihen	*a little hard*
とても忙しい	totemo isogashii	*very busy*
月曜日から	getsuyoobi kara	*from Monday*
金曜日まで	kin-yoobi made	*until Friday*
お昼まで	ohiru made	*until noon*
セミナーに出ます	seminaa ni demasu	*attend the seminar*
先週の日曜日	senshuu no nichiyoobi	*last Sunday*

が Ga as object marker

The basics of Japanese verbs:
Verb forms, classes, and tense

だ Da: The plain form of the
copula です desu

Conjunctions から kara, ので node,
けど kedo, and が ga

顔を洗います	kao o araimasu	to wash face
歯を磨きます	ha o migakimasu	to brush teeth
シャワーを浴びます	shawaa o abimasu	to take a shower
お風呂に入ります	ofuro ni hairimasu	to take a bath (lit. to enter a bath)

Take It Further

There is a distinction between と to and や ya, which in English are both translated as *and*. A と to B means *A and B*, but A や ya B means *A and B, among other things*. For instance, if you are asked what is on the desk, you can just mention a couple of things on the desk, among others, by using や ya, whereas you have to enumerate everything on the desk when using と to.

The verb 入ります hairimasu means *enter*. The English verb *enter* takes a direct object, which means that you don't need a preposition for the place you enter. For example, you say *I enter the room*, but not *I enter in the room*. In Japanese, however, the verb 入ります hairimasu cannot take a direct object. So you have to attach the particle に ni (corresponding the English *in* or *to*) to the place. For example, to say *I enter the room* in Japanese, say 部屋に入ります heya ni hairimasu. Likewise, the verb 出ます demasu does not take a direct object, unlike the English verb *attend*. Therefore, you need to say セミナーに出ます seminaa ni demasu (*I attend the seminar*).

✎ Phrase Practice 1

Translate the expressions below.

1. *How is it?*

2. *life in Tokyo*

3. *Japanese class*

4. *novel, magazine, and so on*

5. *until noon*

6. *last Sunday*

7. *to wash face*

8. *to brush teeth*

9. *to take a shower*

10. *attend the seminar*

ANSWER KEY

1. どうですか。 Doo desu ka.; 2. 東京の生活 tookyoo no seekatsu; 3. 日本語の授業 nihongo no jugyoo; 4. 小説や雑誌 shoosetsu ya zasshi; 5. お昼まで ohiru made; 6. 先週の日曜日 senshuu no nichiyoobi; 7. 顔を洗います kao o araimasu; 8. 歯を磨きます ha o migakimasu; 9. シャワーを浴びます shawaa o abimasu; 10. セミナーに出ます seminaa ni demasu

Grammar Builder 1

THE STATIC VERB あります ARIMASU (TO EXIST)

▶ 6B Grammar Builder 1 (CD 4, Track 24)

Let's review another static verb, あります arimasu (*to exist*). Whereas the subject of います imasu must be animate—a person or an animal—the subject of あります

が Ga as object marker

The basics of Japanese verbs:
Verb forms, classes, and tense

だ Da: The plain form of the
copula です desu

Conjunctions から kara, ので node,
けど kedo, and が ga

arimasu must be an inanimate object—a book, a room or a table, for example. あ
ります Arimasu is used in the following structures.

X があります。(affirmative)
X ga arimasu.

X はありません。(negative)
X wa arimasen.

X はありますか。(question)
X wa arimasu ka.

As noted in Lesson 1, Japanese often uses the particle は wa in place of the
particle が ga or を o in yes/no questions and negative sentences. Although this is
not an absolute rule, it is good practice at this level to use the particle は wa in all
yes/no questions and negative sentences.

<ruby>本<rt>ほん</rt></ruby>があります。
Hon ga arimasu.
There is a book./There are books. (lit., Book(s) exist.)

<ruby>机<rt>つくえ</rt></ruby> はありません。
Tsukue wa arimasen.
There isn't any desk.

ソファーはありますか。
Sofaa wa arimasu ka.
Is there any sofa?

Just like います imasu, あります arimasu can express possession.

じゅぎょう
授業があります。

Jugyoo ga arimasu.

I have a class./I have classes.

えいご きょうかしょ
英語の教科書はありますか。

Eego no kyookasho (*textbook*) wa arimasu ka.

Do you have an English textbook?

はい、あります。

Hai, arimasu.

Yes, we have.

The location of inanimate subjects can be specified in the same way as the location of animate subjects, as discussed in Lesson 4.

いま
居間にソファーがあります。

Ima ni sofaa ga arimasu.

There's a sofa in the living room.

だいどころ れいぞうこ
台所に冷蔵庫があります。

Daidokoro ni reezooko ga arimasu.

There's a refrigerator in the kitchen.

As pointed out in Lesson 4, these sentences are describing what exists at a certain location. So, for instance, the first sentence above can be the answer to the following question.

いま なに
Q: 居間に何がありますか。

Ima ni nani ga arimasu ka.

What's in the living room?

A: (居間に) ソファーがあります。

(Ima ni) sofaa ga arimasu.

There's a sofa in the living room.

As pointed out in Lesson 4, in the answer, 居間に ima ni (*in the living room*) can be dropped because it is understood from the context. Just as with います imasu, if you want to describe where something is, use the structure X は Y にあります X wa Y ni arimasu.

新聞は居間にあります。

Shinbun wa ima ni arimasu.

The newspaper is in the living room. (lit., As for the newspaper, it is in the living room.)

電子レンジは台所にあります。

Denshirenji wa daidokoro ni arimasu.

The microwave oven is in the kitchen. (lit., As for the microwave oven, it is in the kitchen.)

For instance, the first sentence above can be the answer to the following question.

Q: 新聞はどこにありますか。

Shinbun wa doko ni arimasu ka.

Where is the newspaper?

A: (新聞は) 居間にあります。

(Sinbun wa) ima ni arimasu.

The newspaper is in the living room.

Here, 新聞は shinbun wa can be dropped from the answer because it is understood from the context.

✎ Work Out 1

A. Answer the following questions with sentences using the structures Y に X があ ります Y ni X ga arimasu and Y に X がいます Y ni X ga imasu as appropriate, X being what you see in the parentheses.

1. 洗面所に何がありますか。(洗濯機)

   Senmenjo ni nani ga arimasu ka. (sentakuki)

   _____

2. 居間に何がありますか。(ソファーやテーブル)

   Ima ni nani ga arimasu ka. (sofaa ya teeburu)

   _____

3. 台所に何がありますか。(冷蔵庫や電子レンジ)

   Daidokoro ni nani ga arimasu ka. (reezooko ya denshirenji)

   _____

4. 玄関に誰がいますか。(父)

   Genkan ni dare ga imasu ka. (chichi)

   _____

5. 部屋に何がありますか。(たんすや机や椅子)

   Heya ni nani ga arimasu ka. (tansu ya tsukue ya isu)

   _____

B. Answer the following questions with sentences using the structures X は Y にあ ります X wa Y ni arimasu and X は Y にいます X wa Y ni imasu as appropriate. The location noun is provided in parentheses.

1. ベッドはどこですか。(寝室)

   Beddo wa doko desu ka. (shinshitsu)

   _____

2. テレビはどこですか。(居間)

   Terebi wa doko desu ka. (ima)

   _____

3. 電子レンジはどこですか。(台所)

   Denshirenji wa doko desu ka. (daidokoro)

   _____

4. 日本語の本はどこですか。(大学)

   Nihongo no hon wa doko desu ka. (daigaku)

   _____

5. 鈴木さんのお兄さんはどこですか。(アパート)

   Suzuki san no oniisan wa doko desu ka. (apaato)

   _____

ANSWER KEY

A: 1. 洗面所に洗濯機があります。Senmenjo ni sentakuki ga arimasu. 2. 居間にソファーやテーブ ルがあります。Ima ni sofaa ya teeburu ga arimasu. 3. 台所に冷蔵庫や電子レンジがあります。 Daidokoro ni reezooko ya denshirenji ga arimasu. 4. 玄関に父がいます。Genkan ni chichi ga imasu. 5. 部屋にたんすや机や椅子があります。Heya ni tansu ya tsukue ya isu ga arimasu.
B: 1. ベッドは寝室にあります。Beddo wa shinshitsu ni arimasu. 2. テレビは居間にあります。 Terebi wa ima ni arimasu. 3. 電子レンジは台所にあります。Denshirenji wa daidokoro ni

arimasu. 4. 日本語の本は大学にあります。Nihongo no hon wa daigaku ni arimasu. 5. 鈴木さんの お兄さんはアパートにいます。Suzuki san no oniisan wa apaato ni imasu.

Phrase Builder 2

▶ 6C Phrase Builder 2 (CD 4, Track 25)

ウィルソンさんの アパート	Wiruson san no apaato	*Ms. Wilson's apartment*
まあまあ	maa maa	*so so*
料理が好きです。	Ryoori ga suki desu.	*I like cooking.*
料理が嫌いです。	Ryoori ga kirai desu.	*I dislike cooking.*
部屋が二つと台所	heya ga futatsu to daidokoro	*two rooms and a kitchen*
居間と寝室	ima to shinshitsu	*a living room and a bedroom*
居間に	ima ni	*in the living room*
寝室に	shinshitsu ni	*in the bedroom*
ソファーとテーブルとテレビ	sofaa to teeburu to terebi	*a sofa, a table, and a television*
ベッドと机	beddo to tsukue	*a bed and a desk*
ちょっと狭い	chotto semai	*a little small (lit., narrow)*

Take It Further

The adjective 広い hiroi means *roomy, spacious,* or *wide*. The adjective 狭い semai means *limited in space,* or *narrow*. In Japanese, rooms and spaces are normally described with 広い hiroi or 狭い semai, instead of 大きい ookii (*big*)

が Ga as object marker

だ Da: The plain form of the
copula です desu

The basics of Japanese verbs:
Verb forms, classes, and tense

Conjunctions から kara, ので node,
けど kedo, and が ga

or 小さい chiisai (*small*). Thus, to say *big room* in Japanese, say 広い部屋 hiroi heya. *Small room* will be 狭い部屋 semai heya.

✎ Phrase Practice 2

Complete the following by inserting appropriate particles.

1. ウィルソンさん _____ アパート

   Wiruson san _____ apaato

   Ms. Wilson's apartment

2. 料理 _____ 好きです。

   Ryoori _____ suki desu.

   I like cooking.

3. 料理 _____ 嫌いです。

   Ryoori _____ kirai desu.

   I dislike cooking.

4. 部屋 _____ 二つ _____ 台所

   heya _____ futatsu _____ daidokoro

   two rooms and a kitchen

5. 居間 _____ 寝室

   ima _____ shinshitsu

   a living room and a bedroom

6. 居間 _____
   <ruby>居間<rt>い ま</rt></ruby>

   ima _____

   in the living room

7. ソファー _____ テーブル _____ テレビ

   sofaa _____ teeburu _____ terebi

   a sofa, a table, and a television

   ANSWER KEY
   1. の no; 2. が ga; 3. が ga; 4. が ga, と to; 5. と to; 6. に ni; 7. と to, と to

Grammar Builder 2
EXPRESSING QUANTITY USING あります ARIMASU/います IMASU

▶ 6D Grammar Builder 2 (CD 4, Track 26)

To specify the number of items, the number accompanied by an appropriate counter is placed just before the verb as seen in the following formula:

X が ga *numeral + counter* あります arimasu/います imasu.

The following sentences illustrate how this structure is used.

部屋が三つあります。

Heya ga mittsu arimasu.

There are three rooms.

ソファーが一つあります。

Sofaa ga hitotsu arimasu.

There is one sofa.

が Ga as object marker

The basics of Japanese verbs:
Verb forms, classes, and tense

だ Da: The plain form of the
copula です desu

Conjunctions から kara, ので node,
けど kedo, and が ga

本が五冊あります。

Hon ga gosatsu arimasu.

There are five books.

鉛筆が六本あります。

Enpitsu ga roppon arimasu.

There are six pencils.

犬が三匹います。

Inu ga sanbiki imasu.

There are three dogs./I have three dogs.

子供が三人います。

Kodomo ga sannin imasu.

There are three children./I have three children.

Note that the *numeral + counter* phrase in this structure isn't followed by a particle. The location of items can be expressed in the same way as illustrated in Lesson 4 and the Grammar Builder 1 section of this lesson.

居間に椅子が五つあります。

Ima ni isu ga itsutsu arimasu.

There are five chairs in the living room.

寝室にたんすが一つあります。

Shinshitsu ni tansu ga hitotsu arimasu.

There's one chest of drawers in the bedroom.

庭に子供が三人います。

Niwa ni kodomo ga sannin imasu.

There are three children in the garden.

✎ Work Out 2

A. Translate into English.

1. ペンが一本あります。 **Pen ga ippon arimasu.**

_____

2. ティーシャツが五枚あります。 **T-shatsu ga gomai arimasu.**

_____

3. 姉が二人います。 **Ane ga futari imasu.**

_____

4. ノートが十冊あります。 **Nooto (*notebook*) ga jussatsu arimasu.**

_____

5. 部屋が五つあります。 **Heya ga itsutsu arimasu.**

_____

B. Match each sentence to its correct translation.

1. *There are two cups of black tea.*   a. ペンが三本あります。

                                             Pen ga sanbon arimasu.

2. *There are two rooms.*   b. 紙が五枚あります。

                                             Kami ga gomai arimasu.

3. *There are three pens.*

c. 紅茶が二杯あります。
<ruby>紅茶<rt>こうちゃ</rt></ruby> <ruby>二杯<rt>に はい</rt></ruby>

Koocha ga nihai arimasu.

4. *There are eight dogs.*

d. 部屋が二つあります。
<ruby>部屋<rt>へ や</rt></ruby> <ruby>二<rt>ふた</rt></ruby>

Heya ga futatsu arimasu.

5. *There are five sheets of paper.*

e. 犬が八匹います。
<ruby>犬<rt>いぬ</rt></ruby> <ruby>八匹<rt>はっぴき</rt></ruby>

Inu ga happiki imasu.

ANSWER KEY

A: 1. *There's one pen.* 2. *There are five T-shirts.* 3. *I have two older sisters.* 4. *There are ten notebooks.*
5. *There are five rooms.*
B: 1. c; 2. d; 3. a; 4. e; 5. b

✎ Drive It Home

Complete each of the following sentences by inserting the appropriate particle or particles.

1. 机_____あります。
   <ruby>机<rt>つくえ</rt></ruby>

   Tsukue _____ arimasu.

   There is a desk.

2. 机_____ありますか。
   <ruby>机<rt>つくえ</rt></ruby>

   Tsukue _____ arimasu ka.

   Is there a desk?

3. 机_____ありません。
   <ruby>机<rt>つくえ</rt></ruby>

   Tsukue _____ arimasen.

   There isn't any desk.

4. 居間＿＿＿＿ ソファー ＿＿＿＿ あります。

Ima ＿＿＿＿ sofaa ＿＿＿＿ arimasu.

There's a sofa in the living room.

5. 台所＿＿＿ 電子レンジ ＿＿＿＿ あります。

Daidokoro ＿＿＿＿ denshirenji ＿＿＿＿ arimasu.

There's a microwave oven in the kitchen.

6. 寝室 ＿＿＿＿ベッド ＿＿＿＿あります。

Shinshitsu ＿＿＿＿ beddo ＿＿＿＿ arimasu.

There's a bed in the bedroom.

7. ソファー ＿＿＿＿居間 ＿＿＿＿あります。

Sofaa ＿＿＿＿ ima ＿＿＿＿ arimasu.

The sofa is in the living room.

8. 電子レンジ ＿＿＿＿台所＿＿＿＿あります。

Denshirenji ＿＿＿＿ daidokoro ＿＿＿＿ arimasu.

The microwave oven is in the kitchen.

9. ベッド ＿＿＿＿寝室 ＿＿＿＿あります。

Beddo ＿＿＿＿ shinshitsu ＿＿＿＿ arimasu.

The bed is in the bedroom.

ANSWER KEY

1. が ga; 2. は wa; 3. は wa; 4. に ni, が ga; 5. に ni, が ga; 6. に ni, が ga; 7. は wa, に ni; 8. は wa, に ni; 9. は wa, に ni

ⁱ Ga as object marker

The basics of Japanese verbs:
Verb forms, classes, and tense

だ Da: The plain form of the
copula です desu

Conjunctions から kara, ので node,
けど kedo, and が ga

How Did You Do?

Let's see how you did! By now, you should be able to:

☐ use the static verb あります **arimasu** (Still unsure? Jump back to page 114)

☐ express quantity of items in sentences (Still unsure? Jump back to page 122)

✎ Word Recall

1. 祖父 **sofu**

2. おじいさん **ojiisan**

3. 祖母 **sobo**

4. おばあさん **obaasan**

5. 夫 **otto**

6. 子供さん **kodomosan**

7. 家内 **kanai**

8. いとこ **itoko**

9. 両親 **ryooshin**

10. 家族 **kazoku**

a. *cousin*

b. *husband (one's own)*

c. *grandmother (someone else's)*

d. *child (someone else's)*

e. *family*

f. *parents*

g. *grandmother (one's own)*

h. *wife (one's own)*

i. *grandfather (one's own)*

j. *grandfather (someone else's)*

ANSWER KEY

1. i; 2. j; 3. g; 4. c; 5. b; 6. d; 7. h; 8. a; 9. f; 10. e

Lesson 7: Sentences

In this lesson you'll learn how to:

☐ express your likes and dislikes

☐ use the particle が ga as an object marker

☐ use the plain form of the copula です desu (だ da)

Sentence Builder 1

▶ 7A Sentence Builder 1 (CD 4, Track 27)

東京の生活はどうですか。

Tookyoo no seekatsu wa doo desu ka.

How's your life in Tokyo?

ちょっと大変です。

Chotto taihen desu.

It's a bit hard.

楽しいです。

Tanoshii desu.

It's fun.

平日は毎日とても忙しいです。

Heejitsu wa mainichi totemo isogashii desu.

On weekdays, I am very busy every day.

が Ga as object marker

The basics of Japanese verbs:
Verb forms, classes, and tense

だ Da: The plain form of the
copula です desu

Conjunctions から kara, ので node,
けど kedo, and が ga

<ruby>週末<rt>しゅうまつ</rt></ruby>は<ruby>何<rt>なに</rt></ruby>をしますか。

Shuumatsu wa nani o shimasu ka.

What do you do on weekends?

<ruby>法律<rt>ほうりつ</rt></ruby>のセミナーに<ruby>出<rt>で</rt></ruby>ます。

Hooritsu no seminaa ni demasu.

I attend a law seminar.

<ruby>日曜日<rt>にちようび</rt></ruby>はリラックスします。

Nichiyoobi wa rirakkusushimasu.

I relax on Sunday.

<ruby>授業<rt>じゅぎょう</rt></ruby>が<ruby>月曜日<rt>げつようび</rt></ruby>から<ruby>金曜日<rt>きんようび</rt></ruby>まであります。

Jugyoo ga getsuyoobi kara kin-yoobi made arimasu.

I have classes from Monday to Friday.

たまにお<ruby>昼<rt>ひる</rt></ruby>まで<ruby>寝<rt>ね</rt></ruby>ます

Tamani ohiru made nemasu.

Once in a while, I sleep until noon.

<ruby>午後<rt>ごご</rt></ruby>は<ruby>時々<rt>ときどき</rt></ruby><ruby>小説<rt>しょうせつ</rt></ruby>や<ruby>雑誌<rt>ざっし</rt></ruby>を<ruby>読<rt>よ</rt></ruby>みます。

Gogo wa tokidoki shoosetsu ya zasshi o yomimasu.

I sometimes read a novel, magazines, and so on, in the afternoon.

Take It Further

In *Essential Japanese*, you learned the expression <ruby>週末<rt>しゅうまつ</rt></ruby>に<ruby>何<rt>なに</rt></ruby>をしますか
Shuumatsu ni nani o shimasu ka (*What are you going to do for the weekend?*).
You may have noticed in the Sentence Builder 1 above that the particle は **wa** is
used instead of に **ni**. If you use the particle は **wa**, 週末 <ruby>週末<rt>しゅうまつ</rt></ruby> **shuumatsu** becomes

the topic, so the literal translation will be *As for the weekend, what are you going to do?* This literal translation may sound a little odd, but the Japanese equivalent sounds natural and is commonly used. Note that 日曜日 nichiyoobi in 日曜日は リラックスします Nichiyoobi wa rirakkusushimasu and 午後 gogo in 午後は 時々小説や雑誌を読みます Gogo wa tokidoki shoosetsu ya zasshi o yomimasu above are also marked by the topic particle は wa instead of に ni. So the literal translation will be, *As for Sunday, I relax,* and *As for in the afternoon, I sometimes read a novel, magazines, and so on,* respectively.

✎ Sentence Practice 1

Fill in the missing words in each of the following sentences.

1. 東京の生活は＿＿＿＿＿＿＿＿＿。

   Tookyoo no seekatsu wa ＿＿＿＿.

   How's your life in Tokyo?

2. ＿＿＿＿＿＿＿＿＿大変です。

   ＿＿＿＿＿＿＿＿＿ **taihen desu.**

   It's a bit hard.

3. ＿＿＿＿＿＿＿＿＿です。

   ＿＿＿＿＿＿＿＿＿ **desu.**

   It's fun.

4. 平日は毎日＿＿＿＿＿＿＿です。

   Heejitsu wa mainichi ＿＿＿ desu.

   On weekdays, I am very busy every day.

が Ga as object marker

The basics of Japanese verbs:
Verb forms, classes, and tense

だ Da: The plain form of the
copula です desu

Conjunctions から kara, ので node,
けど kedo, and が ga

5. 週末は<ruby>週末<rt>しゅうまつ</rt></ruby>は_____。

   Shuumatsu wa _____.

   What do you do on weekends?

6. <ruby>授業<rt>じゅぎょう</rt></ruby>が_____あります。

   Jugyoo ga _____ **arimasu.**

   I have classes from Monday to Friday.

7. _____お<ruby>昼<rt>ひる</rt></ruby>まで<ruby>寝<rt>ね</rt></ruby>ます。

   _____ **ohiru made nemasu.**

   Once in a while, I sleep until noon.

8. <ruby>午後<rt>ご ご</rt></ruby>は<ruby>時々<rt>ときどき</rt></ruby>_____。

   Gogo wa tokidoki _____.

   I sometimes read a novel, magazines, and so on, in the afternoon.

ANSWER KEY

1. どうですか **doo desu ka**; 2. ちょっと **Chotto**; 3. 楽しい **Tanoshii**; 4. とても忙しい **totemo isogashii**;
5. 何をしますか **nani o shimasu ka**; 6. 月曜日から金曜日まで **getsuyoobi kara kin-yoobi made**;
7. たまに **Tamani**; 8. 小説や雑誌を読みます **shoosetsu ya zasshi o yomimasu**

Grammar Builder 1
が GA AS OBJECT MARKER

▶ 7B Grammar Builder 1 (CD 4, Track 28)

You learned earlier that direct objects are marked by the particle を o in
Japanese, while subjects are followed by the particle が ga. When expressing
likes or dislikes in Japanese, な na-adjectives 好き suki (*like*) and 嫌い kirai
(*dislike*) are used and their object being liked or disliked is marked by が ga.

X	は	Y	が	好きです。/嫌いです。
X	wa	Y	ga	suki desu./ kirai desu.

私はテニスが好きです。

Watashi wa tenisu ga suki desu.

I like tennis.

Note that the English subject *I* corresponds to the Japanese topic noun 私 は watashi wa and the English direct object *tennis* corresponds to the Japanese subject noun テニスが tenisu ga. Here are more examples.

父はゴルフが好きです。

Chichi wa gorufu ga suki desu.

My father likes golf.

妹 はケーキが嫌いです。

Imooto wa keeki ga kirai desu.

My younger sister dislikes cake.

A similar construction is used to express understanding using the verb 分かります wakarimasu (*to understand*).

X	は	Y	が	分かります。
X	wa	Y	ga	wakarimasu.

加藤さんは英語が分かります。

Katoo san wa eego ga wakarimasu.

Mr./Ms. Kato understands English.

が Ga as object marker

The basics of Japanese verbs:
Verb forms, classes, and tense

だ Da: The plain form of the
copula です desu

Conjunctions から kara, ので node,
けど kedo, and が ga

私はフランス語が分かります。

Watashi wa furansugo ga wakarimasu.

I understand French.

As you already know, the particle が ga is usually replaced by は wa in yes/no questions and negative sentences.

妹さんはケーキは嫌いですか。

Imootosan wa keeki wa kirai desu ka.

Does your sister dislike cake?

私はテニスは好きではありません。

Watashi wa tenisu wa suki de wa arimasen.

I don't like tennis.

日本語は分かりますか。

Nihongo wa wakarimasu ka.

Do you understand Japanese?

英語は分かりません。

Eego wa wakarimasen.

I don't understand English.

✎ Work Out 1

A. The following people like the item expressed by the noun in parentheses. Form sentences using 好きです **suki desu** to express that.

1. 高橋 Takahashi (テニス tenisu)

2. 川村 Kawamura (小説 shoosetsu)

_____

3. 矢野 Yano (フランス語の授業 furansugo no jugyoo)

_____

B. The following people dislike the item expressed by the noun in parentheses. Form sentences using 嫌いです kirai desu to express that.

1. 渡辺 Watanabe (料理 ryoori)

_____

2. 山田 Yamada (スポーツ supootsu)

_____

3. 小林 Kobayashi (野菜 yasai)

_____

C. The following people understand the language expressed by the noun in parentheses. Form sentences using 分かります wakarimasu to express that.

1. 中村 Nakamura (英語 eego)

_____

2. 小山 Koyama (フランス語 furansugo)

_____

3. ウィルソン Wiruson (日本語 nihongo)

_____

が Ga as object marker

The basics of Japanese verbs:
Verb forms, classes, and tense

だ Da: The plain form of the
copula です desu

Conjunctions から kara, ので node,
けど kedo, and が ga

ANSWER KEY

A: 1. 高橋さんはテニスが好きです。Takahashi san wa tenisu ga suki desu. 2. 川村さんは小説が好きです。Kawamura san wa shoosetsu ga suki desu. 3. 矢野さんはフランス語の授業が好きです。Yano san wa furansugo no jugyoo ga suki desu.

B: 1. 渡辺さんは料理が嫌いです。Watanabe san wa ryoori ga kirai desu. 2. 山田さんはスポーツが嫌いです。Yamada san wa supootsu ga kirai desu. 3. 小林さんは野菜が嫌いです。Kobayashi san wa yasai ga kirai desu.

C: 1. 中村さんは英語が分かります。Nakamura san wa eego ga wakarimasu. 2. 小山さんはフランス語が分かります。Koyama san wa furansugo ga wakarimasu. 3. ウィルソンさんは日本語が分かります。Wiruson san wa nihongo ga wakarimasu.

Sentence Builder 2

▶ 7C Sentence Builder 2 (CD 4, Track 29)

アパートはどうですか。

Apaato wa doo desu ka.

How's your apartment?/What's your apartment like?

アパートが好きです。

Apaato ga suki desu.

I like my apartment.

アパートが大好きです。

Apaato ga daisuki desu.

I like my apartment very much./I love my apartment.

アパートが嫌いです。

Apaato ga kirai desu.

I don't like my apartment. (lit., I dislike my apartment.)

部屋が二つと台所があります。

Heya ga futatsu to daidokoro ga arimasu.

There are two rooms and a kitchen.

部屋は居間と寝室です。

Heya wa ima to shinshitsu desu.

The rooms are a living room and a bedroom.

たくさん家具はありますか。

Takusan kagu wa arimasu ka.

Is there a lot of furniture?

居間にソファーとテーブルとテレビがあります。

Ima ni sofaa to teeburu to terebi ga arimasu.

There are a sofa, a table and a television in the living room.

部屋はちょっと狭いですけど、台所は広いですよ。

Heya wa chotto semai desu kedo, daidokoro wa hiroi desu yo.

The rooms are a bit small (lit., narrow) but the kitchen is spacious.

料理は好きですか。

Ryoori wa suki desu ka.

Do you like cooking?

まあまあです。

Maa maa desu.

So so.

が Ga as object marker

The basics of Japanese verbs:
Verb forms, classes, and tense

だ Da: The plain form of the
copula です desu

Conjunctions から kara, ので node,
けど kedo, and が ga

✎ Sentence Practice 2

Fill in the missing words in each of the following sentences.

1. アパートが ＿＿＿＿＿＿＿＿。

   Apaato ga ＿＿＿＿＿＿＿＿＿＿＿＿.

   I like my apartment.

2. アパートが ＿＿＿＿＿＿＿＿。

   Apaato ga ＿＿＿＿＿＿＿＿＿＿＿＿＿＿.

   I like my apartment very much./I love my apartment.

3. アパートが ＿＿＿＿＿＿＿＿。

   Apaato ga ＿＿＿＿＿＿＿＿＿＿＿＿＿.

   I don't like my apartment. (lit., I dislike my apartment.)

4. ＿＿＿＿＿＿ と台所<ruby>台所<rt>だいどころ</rt></ruby>があります。

   ＿＿＿＿＿＿＿＿＿＿＿＿＿＿＿＿＿＿ **to daidokoro ga arimasu.**

   There are two rooms and a kitchen.

5. 部屋<ruby>部屋<rt>へや</rt></ruby>は ＿＿＿＿＿＿＿ 。.

   Heya wa ＿＿＿＿＿＿＿＿＿＿＿＿＿＿＿＿＿＿.

   The rooms are a living room and a bedroom.

6. ＿＿＿＿＿＿ソファーとテーブルとテレビがあります。

   ＿＿＿＿＿＿＿＿＿＿ **sofaa to teeburu to terebi ga arimasu.**

   There are a sofa, a table and a television in the living room.

7. 部屋は ＿＿＿＿＿＿＿＿ ですけど、台所は広いですよ。

Heya wa ＿＿＿＿＿＿＿＿＿＿＿ desu kedo, daidokoro wa hiroi

desu yo.

The rooms are a bit small (lit., narrow) but the kitchen is spacious.

8. ＿＿＿＿＿＿＿＿ です。

＿＿＿＿＿＿＿＿ desu.

So so.

ANSWER KEY
1. 好きです suki desu; 2. 大好きです daisuki desu; 3. 嫌いです kirai desu; 4. 部屋が二つ Heya ga futatsu; 5. 居間と寝室です ima to shinshitsu desu; 6. 居間に Ima ni; 7. ちょっと狭い chotto semai; 8. まあまあ Maa maa

Grammar Builder 2
だ DA: THE PLAIN FORM OF THE COPULA です DESU

▶ 7D Grammar Builder 2 (CD 4, Track 30)

You are already familiar with the conjugation of です desu and its て te-form, で de. Now, let's look at the conjugation of だ da, the plain form of です desu.

NON-PAST		PAST	
Affirmative	Negative	Affirmative	Negative
だ	ではない/じゃない	だった	ではなかった/じゃなかった
da	de wa nai/ja nai	datta	de wa nakatta/nakatta

As pointed out earlier, じゃ ja is the contracted form of では de wa and more colloquial than では de wa. The plain form だ da is used in casual speech and conversations, where the polite form of です desu is used in formal speech and

が Ga as object marker

The basics of Japanese verbs:
Verb forms, classes, and tense

だ Da: The plain form of the
copula です desu

Conjunctions から kara, ので node,
けど kedo, and が ga

conversations. Please note however, in written language, だ da is commonly used in formal writing, such as newspaper. The following sentences would be more likely to be said among friends and family members.

ロペスさんはメキシコ人だよ。

Ropesu san wa mekishikojin da yo.

Mr./Ms. Lopez is Mexican (I assure you).

林さんは弁護士だよ。

Hayashi san wa bengoshi da yo.

Mr./Ms. Hayashi is a lawyer (I assure you).

今日は日曜日じゃないよ。

Kyoo wa nichiyoobi ja nai yo.

Today is not Sunday (I assure you.)

森さんは先生じゃなかったね?

Mori san wa sensee ja nakatta ne?

Mr./Ms. Mori was not a teacher, right?

昨日は土曜日だったね。

Kinoo wa doyoobi datta ne?

Yesterday was Saturday, wasn't it?

In daily conversations, だ da is usually accompanied by sentential particles ね ne or よ yo. Without them, the expression sounds bookish. Also, note that in questions, だ da and the question particle か ka are both dropped. Instead, rising intonation is used to indicate a question.

林<ruby>はやし</ruby>さんは弁護士<ruby>べんごし</ruby>？

Hayashi san wa bengoshi? (with rising intonation)

Is Mr./Ms. Hayashi a lawyer?

今日<ruby>きょう</ruby>は日曜日<ruby>にちようび</ruby>？

Kyoo wa nichiyoobi? (with rising intonation)

Is it Sunday today?

ロペスさんはメキシコ人<ruby>じん</ruby>？

Ropesu san wa mekishikojin? (with rising intonation)

Is Mr./Ms. Lopez Mexican?

✎ Work Out 2

Rewrite the following sentences using だ da, the plain form of です desu.

Example : 今日<ruby>きょう</ruby>は月曜日<ruby>げつようび</ruby>ですよ。→ 今日<ruby>きょう</ruby>は月曜日<ruby>げつようび</ruby>だよ。

Kyoo wa getsuyoobi desu yo. → Kyoo wa getsuyoobi <u>da</u> yo.

明日<ruby>あした</ruby>は土曜日<ruby>どようび</ruby>(では/じゃ)ありませんよ。→ 明日<ruby>あした</ruby>は土曜日<ruby>どようび</ruby>(では/じゃ)ないよ。

Ashita wa doyoobi (de wa/ja) arimasen yo. → Ashita wa doyoobi <u>(de wa/ja)</u>

<u>nai</u> yo.

1. 林<ruby>はやし</ruby>さんはアメリカ人<ruby>じん</ruby>ではありませんね。

Hayashi san wa amerikajin de wa arimasen ne.

林<ruby>はやし</ruby>さんはアメリカ人<ruby>じん</ruby>_____ね。

Hayashi san wa amerikajin _____ ne.

が Ga as object marker

The basics of Japanese verbs:
Verb forms, classes, and tense

だ Da: The plain form of the
copula です desu

Conjunctions から kara, ので node,
けど kedo, and が ga

2. おとといは木曜日でしたね。

Ototoi wa mokuyoobi deshita ne.
おとといは木曜日 _____ね。

Ototoi wa mokuyoobi _____ ne.

3. 渡辺さんは大学生ですよ。

Watanabe san wa daigakusee desu yo.
渡辺さんは大学生 _____よ。

Watanabe san wa daigakusee _____ yo.

4. 日本語の本じゃありませんね。

Nihongo no hon ja arimasen ne.
日本語の本 _____ね。

Nihongo no hon _____ ne.

5. パーティーは昨日ではありませんでしたよ。

Paatii wa kinoo de wa arimasen deshita yo.
パーティーは昨日 _____よ。

Paatii wa kinoo _____ yo.

ANSWER KEY
1. ではない de wa nai; 2. だった datta; 3. だ da; 4.じゃない ja nai; 5. ではなかった de wa nakatta

✎ Drive It Home

A. Complete the following sentences by inserting the appropriate particles.

1. スポーツ＿＿＿＿＿好きです。

   Supootsu ＿＿＿＿＿＿ suki desu.

   I like sports.

2. 本＿＿＿＿＿＿＿好きです。

   Hon ＿＿＿＿＿＿ suki desu.

   I like books.

3. スポーツ＿＿＿＿＿嫌いです。

   Supootsu ＿＿＿＿＿＿＿＿ kirai desu.

   I dislike sports.

4. 本＿＿＿＿＿嫌いです。

   Hon ＿＿＿＿＿＿ kirai desu.

   I dislike books.

5. 日本語＿＿＿＿＿分かります。

   Nihongo ＿＿＿＿＿＿ wakarimasu.

   I understand Japanese.

6. 英語＿＿＿＿＿分かります。

   Eego ＿＿＿＿＿＿ wakarimasu.

   I understand English.

が Ga as object marker

The basics of Japanese verbs:
Verb forms, classes, and tense

だ Da: The plain form of the
copula です desu

Conjunctions から kara, ので node,
けど kedo, and が ga

B. Fill in each of the blanks with the appropriate plain form of です **desu** based on the English translation provided.

1. 私は学生＿＿＿＿＿＿ よ。

   Watashi wa gakusee ＿＿＿＿＿＿＿ yo.

   I am a student.

2. 私は学生＿＿＿＿＿＿＿＿＿＿＿＿＿＿＿＿＿ よ。

   Watashi wa gakusee ＿＿＿＿＿＿＿＿＿＿＿＿＿＿＿＿＿ yo.

   I am not a student.

3. 私は学生＿＿＿＿＿＿＿＿＿ よ。

   Watashi wa gakusee ＿＿＿＿＿＿＿＿＿ yo.

   I was a student.

4. 私は学生＿＿＿＿＿＿＿＿＿＿＿＿＿＿＿ よ。

   Watashi wa gakusee ＿＿＿＿＿＿＿＿＿＿＿＿＿＿＿＿＿＿ yo.

   I was not a student.

ANSWER KEY
A: 1-6 all が ga
B: 1. だ da; 2. (じゃ/では) ない (ja/de wa) nai; 3. だった datta; 4. (じゃ/では) なかった (ja/de wa) nakatta

⊕ Culture Note

The Japanese word 嫌い **kirai** corresponds to English *to dislike*. However, the expression あ(ん)まり好きじゃ(ありません/ないです) a(n)mari suki ja [arimasen/nai desu] (*don't like so much*) is more often used for this purpose. This is because indirectness is expected given the importance placed on politeness in the Japanese society. Using あ(ん)まり好きじゃありません a(n)mari suki ja arimasen instead of 嫌いです **kirai desu** helps avoid sounding abrupt or impolite. Also, Japanese speakers can just simply say あ(ん)まり **a(n)mari** without even uttering the rest of the sentence. The addressee will understand what the speaker is trying to say from the context.

How Did You Do?

Let's see how you did! By now, you should be able to:

☐ express your likes and dislikes (Still unsure? Jump back to page 128)

☐ use the particle が **ga** as an object marker (Still unsure? Jump back to page 131)

☐ use the plain form of the copula です **desu** (だ **da**)
(Still unsure? Jump back to page 138)

✎ Word Recall

1. 主人 shujin   a. *weekend*

2. 中学校 chuugakkoo   b. *dinner*

3. 今日 kyoo   c. *junior high school*

4. 週末 shuumatsu   d. *this week*

5. 昼 hiru   e. *tomorrow*

6. 奥さん okusan   f. *husband (one's own)*

7. 晩ご飯 bangohan   g. *today*

8. 明日 ashita   h. *noon, afternoon*

9. 娘 musume   i. *wife (someone else's)*

10. 今週 konshuu   j. *daughter (one's own)*

が Ga as object marker

The basics of Japanese verbs:
Verb forms, classes, and tense

だ Da: The plain form of the
copula です desu

Conjunctions から kara, ので node,
けど kedo, and が ga

ANSWER KEY
1. f; 2. c; 3. g; 4. a; 5. h; 6. i; 7. b; 8. e; 9. j; 10. d

Lesson 8: Conversations

In this lesson you'll learn how to:

☐ conjugate different classes of verbs

☐ use the conjunctions *and* and *but*

🎧 Conversation 1

▶ 8A Conversation 1 (Japanese: CD 5, Track 1; Japanese and English: CD 5, Track 2)

Mr. Nakamura and Ms. Davis are talking about their daily life at a university cafeteria.

中村/Nakamura:	デイビスさん、東京の生活はどうですか。
	Deibisu san, tookyoo no seekatsu wa doo desu ka.
デイビス/Deibisu:	日本語の授業が月曜日から金曜日までありますから、ちょっと大変です。でも、楽しいですよ。
	Nihongo no jugyoo ga getsuyoobi kara kin-yoobi made arimasu kara, chotto taihen desu. Demo, tanoshii desu yo.
中村/Nakamura:	僕ぼくも平日は毎日とても忙しいです。
	Boku mo heejitsu wa mainichi totemo isogashii desu.
デイビス/Deibisu:	中村さんは週末は何をしますか。
	Nakamura san wa shuumatsu wa nani o shimasu ka.

なかむら 中村/Nakamura:	土曜日はよく経済学のセミナーに出ますが、日曜日はリラックスします。
	Doyoobi wa yoku keezaigaku no seminaa ni demasu ga, nichiyoobi wa rirakkusushimasu.
デイビス/Deibisu:	リラックス?
	Rirakkusu?
なかむら 中村/Nakamura:	うん、たくさん寝ますよ。たまにお昼まで寝ます。それから午後は時々小説や雑誌を読みます。
	Un. Takusan nemasu yo. Tamani ohiru made nemasu. Sorekara gogo wa tokidoki shoosetsu ya zasshi o yomimasu.
デイビス/Deibisu:	へぇ。いいですね。
	Hee. Ii desu ne.

Nakamura:	*Ms. Davis, how's your life in Tokyo?*
Davis:	*I have Japanese classes from Monday to Friday, so it's a bit hard. But I enjoy it.*
Nakamura:	*I am also very busy every day on weekdays.*
Davis:	*What do you do on weekends, Mr. Nakamura?*
Nakamura:	*I often attend a seminar in economics on Saturday, but I just relax on Sunday.*
Davis:	*Relax?*
Nakamura:	*Yes. I sleep a lot. I sometimes sleep until noon. And then from time to time, I read a novel, magazines, and so on, in the afternoon.*
Davis:	*Oh, that's nice, isn't it?*

✎ Conversation Practice 1

Fill in the blanks in the following sentences with the missing words. If you're unsure of the answer, listen to the conversation one more time.

が Ga as object marker

The basics of Japanese verbs:
Verb forms, classes, and tense

だ Da: The plain form of the
copula です desu

Conjunctions から kara, ので node,
けど kedo, and が ga

1. デイビスさんは日本語の授業が ＿＿＿＿ から ＿＿＿＿ まであります。

   Deibisu san wa nihongo no jugyoo ga ＿＿＿＿＿＿＿＿＿＿＿＿＿＿ kara

   ＿＿＿＿＿＿＿＿＿＿＿＿ made arimasu.

2. デイビスさんの日本語の授業はちょっと＿＿＿＿ です。でも、楽しいです。

   Deibisu san no nihongo no jugyoo wa chotto ＿＿＿＿ desu. Demo, tanoshii

   desu.

3. 中村さんは平日は毎日とても ＿＿＿＿ です。

   Nakamura san wa heejitsu wa mainichi totemo ＿＿＿＿＿＿＿＿＿＿

   desu.

4. 中村さんは土曜日によく ＿＿＿＿＿＿＿＿＿に出ます。

   Nakamura san wa doyoobi ni yoku ＿＿＿＿＿＿＿＿＿＿＿＿＿＿＿＿

   ＿＿＿＿＿＿＿＿＿ ni demasu.

5. 中村さんは日曜日の ＿＿＿＿ は時々小説や雑誌を読みます。

   Nakamura san wa nichiyoobi no ＿＿＿＿＿＿＿ wa tokidoki shoosetsu ya

   zasshi o yomimasu.

ANSWER KEY
1. 月曜日 getsuyoobi, 金曜日 kin-yoobi; 2. 大変 taihen; 3. 忙しい isogashii; 4. 経済学のセミナー keezaigaku no seminaa; 5. 午後 gogo

Grammar Builder 1

THE BASICS OF JAPANESE VERBS: VERB FORMS, CLASSES, AND TENSE

▶ 8B Grammar Builder 1 (CD 5, Track 3)

There are two basic verb forms in Japanese: the ます masu-form and the plain form. You learned the polite ます masu-form in *Essential Japanese*. The plain form is normally used when talking to family members and friends. In written language, the plain form is also used in formal writing, such as newspaper. We'll discuss the plain form of verbs in Lesson 9, but for now, let's go over the ます masu-form of verbs in detail in this lesson.

The ます masu-form is formed by adding ます masu to the verb stem in the case of non-past affirmative verb forms like 食べます tabemasu, あります arimasu, and います imasu. (Remember, the term "non-past" is used here because the present and the future tense are not distinguished in Japanese.)

Japanese verbs can be divided into three different classes. Class I (う u-verbs), Class II (る ru-verbs), and Class III (irregular verbs). There are only two verbs in Class III: the irregular verbs 来ます kimasu (*come*) and します shimasu (*do*). Remember that Japanese verbs, as well as the copula です desu (and its plain form counterpart だ da), only conjugate with respect to tense and affirmative/ negative distinction. The following table represents the non-past tense affirmative form.

NON-PAST TENSE AFFIRMATIVE FORM: STEM + ます MASU		
Class I (う u-verbs)	Class II (る ru-verbs)	Class III (irregular verbs)
話します hanashimasu (*speak*)	出ます demasu (*attend, leave*)	来ます kimasu (*come*)
読みます yomimasu (*read*)	寝ます nemasu (*sleep, go to bed*)	します shimasu (*do*)

が Ga as object marker

The basics of Japanese verbs:
Verb forms, classes, and tense

だ Da: The plain form of the
copula です desu

Conjunctions から kara, ので node,
けど kedo, and が ga

The conjugation of the ます masu-form is very simple because it is the same for all three verb classes. For the non-past tense negative form, ません masen is attached instead of ます masu.

NON-PAST NEGATIVE FORM: STEM + ません MASEN		
Class I Verb (う u-verb)	Class II (る ru-verb)	Class III (irregular)
話しません hanashimasen (do/does not speak)	出ません demasen (do/does not attend, do/does not leave)	来ません kimasen (do/does not come)
読みません yomimasen (do/does not read)	寝ません nemasen (do/does not sleep, do/does not go to bed)	しません shimasen (do/does not do)

For the past tense affirmative form, change ます masu to ました mashita.

PAST AFFIRMATIVE FORM: STEM + ました MASHITA		
Class I Verb (う u-verb)	Class II (る ru-verb)	Class III (irregular)
話しました hanashimashita (spoke)	出ました demashita (attended, left)	来ました kimashita (came)
読みました yomimashita (read)	寝ました nemashita (slept, went to bed)	しました shimashita (did)

For the past tense negative form, just add でした deshita to the non-past tense negative form.

PAST NEGATIVE FORM: STEM + ませんでした MASEN DESHITA		
Class I Verb (う u-verb)	Class II (る ru-verb)	Class III (irregular)
話しませんでした hanashimasen deshita (did not speak)	出ませんでした demasen deshita (did not attend, did not leave)	来ませんでした kimasen deshita (did not come)
読みませんでした yomimasen deshita (did not read)	寝ませんでした nemasen deshita (did not sleep, did not go to bed)	しませんでした shimasen deshita (did not do)

Take It Further

The subject of regular verbs such as those introduced above are usually marked by the particle は wa. For example:

山田さんは英語を話します。

Yamada san wa eego o hanashimasu.

Mr./Ms. Yamada speaks English.

スミスさんは本を読みます。

Sumisu san wa hon o yomimasu.

Mr./Ms. Smith reads books.

However, there are a few verbs whose subjects are normally marked by the particle が ga. The verb 来ます kimasu (*come*) is one such example.

が Ga as object marker

The basics of Japanese verbs:
Verb forms, classes, and tense

だ Da: The plain form of the
copula です desu

Conjunctions から kara, ので node,
けど kedo, and が ga

田中さんが来ます。

Tanaka san ga kimasu.

Mr./Ms. Tanaka comes.

✎ Work Out 1

Fill in the blanks with the appropriate form of verbs given in parentheses.

1. 昨日授業に＿＿＿＿＿＿＿＿か。(出ます)

   Kinoo jugyoo ni ＿＿＿＿＿＿＿＿ ka. (demasu)

   Did you attend the class yesterday?

2. 明日友達が＿＿＿＿＿。(来ます)

   Ashita tomodachi ga ＿＿＿＿＿. (kimasu)

   A friend of mine is coming tomorrow./Friends of mine are coming tomorrow.

3. 先週本は＿＿＿＿＿＿。(読みます)

   Senshuu hon wa ＿＿＿＿＿＿＿＿＿.

   (yomimasu)

   I did not read a book/any books last week.

4. 本田さんはフランス語は＿＿＿＿＿＿。(話します)

   Honda san wa furansugo wa ＿＿＿＿＿＿＿＿.

   (hanashimasu)

   Mr./Ms. Honda does not speak French.

5. 週末にセミナーは＿＿＿＿＿＿＿＿＿＿か。(あります)

   Shuumatsu ni seminaa wa ＿＿＿＿＿＿＿＿＿＿＿ ka. (arimasu)

   Was there a seminar on the weekend?

6. 昨日テニスを＿＿＿＿＿＿＿＿。(します)

   Kinoo tenisu o ＿＿＿＿＿＿＿＿＿＿＿. (shimasu)

   I played tennis yesterday.

7. 昨日＿＿＿＿＿＿＿＿＿。(寝ます)

   Kinoo ＿＿＿＿＿＿＿＿＿＿＿＿＿. (nemasu)

   I didn't sleep yesterday.

ANSWER KEY

1. 出ました demashita; 2. 来ます kimasu; 3. 読みませんでした yomimasen deshita; 4. 話しません hanashimasen; 5. ありました arimashita; 6. しました shimashita; 7. 寝ませんでした nemasen deshita

◖ Conversation 2

▶ 8C Conversation 2 (Japanese: CD 5, Track 4; Japanese and English: CD 5, Track 5)

Ms. Wilson is talking with her Japanese friend Ms. Sato in a university cafeteria.

佐藤/Satoo:　　　　　ウィルソンさんのアパートはどうですか。

　　　　　　　　　　Wiruson san no apaato wa doo desu ka.

ウィルソン/Wiruson:　いいですよ。部屋が二つと台所があります。部屋は居間と寝室です。

　　　　　　　　　　Ii desu yo. Heya ga futatsu to daidokoro ga arimasu.

　　　　　　　　　　Heya wa ima to shinshitsu desu.

佐藤/Satoo:　　　　　そうですか。たくさん家具はありますか。

　　　　　　　　　　Soo desu ka. Takusan kagu wa arimasu ka.

が Ga as object marker

The basics of Japanese verbs:
Verb forms, classes, and tense

だ Da: The plain form of the
copula です desu

Conjunctions から kara, ので node,
けど kedo, and が ga

ウィルソン/Wiruson: いいえ。居間にソファーとテーブルとテレビがあります。そして寝室にベッドとたんすと机があります。ちょっと狭いですけど、台所は広いですよ。

Iie. Ima ni sofaa to teeburu to terebi ga arimasu. Soshite shinshitsu ni beddo to tansu to tsukue ga arimasu. Chotto semai desu kedo, daidokoro wa hiroi desu yo.

佐藤/Satoo: ウィルソンさんは料理は好きですか。

Wiruson san wa ryoori wa suki desu ka.

ウィルソン/Wiruson: ええ、好きですよ。佐藤さんのアパートはどうですか。

Ee, suki desu yo. Sato san no apaato wa doo desu ka.

佐藤/Satoo: えっと、まあまあです。

Etto, maa maa desu.

Sato:	How's your apartment, Ms. Wilson?
Wilson:	It's nice. There are two rooms and a kitchen. The rooms are a living room and a bedroom.
Sato:	I see. Is there a lot of furniture?
Wilson:	No. There is a sofa, a table and a television in the living room. And there is a bed, a chest of drawers and a desk in the bedroom. The rooms are a bit small, but the kitchen is big.
Sato:	Do you like cooking, Ms. Wilson?
Wilson:	Yes, I like it. How's your apartment, Ms. Sato?
Sato:	Well, so-so.

Take It Further

The expression まあまあです maa maa desu (so-so) is often used in daily conversations, and is a convenient expression to remember.

✎ Conversation Practice 2

Fill in the blanks in the following sentences with the missing words. If you're unsure of the answer, listen to the conversation one more time.

1. ウィルソンさんのアパートは部屋が _____ と台所ががあります。

   Wiruson san no apaato wa heya ga _____ to daidokoro ga

   arimasu.

2. ウィルソンさんのアパートは居間に _____ がありま

   す。

   Wiruson san no apaato wa ima ni _____

   _____ ga arimasu.

3. ウィルソンさんのアパートはちょっと狭いですが、_____ は広いで

   す。

   Wiruson san no apaato wa chotto semai desu ga,

   _____ wa hiroi desu.

4. ウィルソンさんは料理が _____。

   Wiruson san wa ryoori ga _____.

5. 佐藤さんのアパートは_____ です。

   Satoo san no apaato wa _____ desu.

ANSWER KEY

1. 二つ futatsu; 2. ソファーとテーブルとテレビ sofaa to teeburu to terebi; 3. 台所 daidokoro; 4. 好きです suki desu; 5. まあまあ maa maa

が Ga as object marker

The basics of Japanese verbs:
Verb forms, classes, and tense

だ Da: The plain form of the
copula です desu

Conjunctions から kara, ので node,
けど kedo, and が ga

Grammar Builder 2
CONJUNCTIONS から KARA, ので NODE, けど KEDO, AND が GA

▶ 8D Grammar Builder 2 (CD 5, Track 6)

The conjunctions から kara (*so*) and ので node (*because, since*) are used to express reason or cause. から Kara and ので node appear at the end of a sentence where the reason is stated; this sentence is followed by a second sentence where the conclusion or the result is stated. から Kara can follow either the polite or the plain form of a verb, copula, or adjective, but ので node usually follows only the plain form. The following sentences show how から kara and ので node are used. Note that だ da, the plain form of the copula です desu, becomes な na before ので node.

明日友達が来ますから、セミナーに出ません。

Ashita tomodachi ga kimasu kara, seminaa ni demasen.

明日友達が来るから、セミナーに出ません。

Ashita tomodachi ga kuru kara, seminaa ni demasen.

明日友達が来るので、セミナーに出ません。

Ashita tomodachi ga kuru node, seminaa ni demasen.

I will not attend the seminar because a friend of mine is coming tomorrow.

学生ですから、勉強します。

Gakusee desu kara, benkyooshimasu.

学生だから、勉強します。

Gakusee da kara, benkyooshimasu.

学生なので、勉強します。

Gakusee na node, benkyooshimasu.

I study because I'm a student.

今日(きょう)は日曜日(にちようび)ですから、お昼(ひる)まで寝(ね)ました。

Kyoo wa nichiyoobi desu kara, ohiru made nemashita.

今日(きょう)は日曜日(にちようび)だから、お昼(ひる)まで寝(ね)ました。

Kyoo wa nichiyoobi da kara, ohiru made nemashita.

今日(きょう)は日曜日(にちようび)なので、お昼(ひる)まで寝(ね)ました。

Kyoo wa nichiyoobi na node, ohiru made nemashita.

Since it is Sunday today, I slept until noon.

Now, let's look at the conjunctions けど kedo (*but*) and が ga (*but*). けど Kedo and が ga appear at the end of the first sentence just like から kara and ので node. けど Kedo and が ga can be used interchangeably.

明日(あした)は日曜日(にちようび)ですけど、セミナーがあります。

Ashita wa nichiyoobi desu kedo, seminaa ga arimasu.

明日(あした)は日曜日(にちよう)ですが、セミナーがあります。

Ashita wa nichiyoobi desu ga, seminaa ga arimasu.

It's Sunday tomorrow, but there is a seminar.

台所(だいどころ)は狭(せま)いですけど、いいですよ。

Daidokoro wa semai desu kedo, ii desu yo.

台所(だいどころ)は狭(せま)いですが、いいですよ。

Daidokoro wa semai desu ga, ii desu yo.

The kitchen is small, but it's good.

Now, let's compare けど kedo and が ga with でも demo (*but*). Note that でも demo appears at the beginning of an independent sentence, whereas けど kedo and が ga appear at the end of a subordinate sentence.

明日(あした)は土曜日(どようび)ですけど、授業(じゅぎょう)があります。

Ashita wa doyoobi desu kedo, jugyoo ga arimasu.

明日は土曜日ですが、授業があります。

Ashita wa doyoobi desu ga, jugyoo ga arimasu.

It is Saturday tomorrow, but there is a class/there are classes.

明日は土曜日です。でも、授業があります。

Ashita wa doyoobi desu. Demo, jugyoo ga arimasu.

It is Saturday tomorrow. But, there is a class/there are classes.

✎ Work Out 2

Connect the two sentences using conjunctions given in parentheses.

1. 今日は日曜日です。リラックスします。(から)

   Kyoo wa nichiyoobi desu. Rirakkusu shimasu. (kara)

   _____

2. 部屋は狭いです。家具がたくさんあります。(けど)

   Heya wa semai desu. Kagu ga takusan arimasu. (kedo)

   _____

3. 明日は土曜日です。授業があります。(が)

   Ashita wa doyoobi desu. Jugyoo ga arimasu. (ga)

   _____

4. 本が好きです。よく本を読みます。(ので)

   Hon ga suki desu. Yoku hon o yomimasu. (node)

   _____

5. 母は東京にいます。父は今ニューヨークにいます。(でも)

Haha wa tookyoo ni imasu. Chichi wa ima nyuuyooku ni imasu. (demo)

___

ANSWER KEY

1. 今日は日曜日ですから、リラックスします。Kyoo wa nichiyoobi desu kara, rirakkusushimasu.
2. 部屋は狭いですけど、家具がたくさんあります。Heya wa semai desu kedo, kagu ga takusan arimasu. 3. 明日は土曜日ですが、授業があります。Ashita wa doyoobi desu ga, jugyoo ga arimasu. 4. 本が好きなので、よく本を読みます。Hon ga suki na node, yoku hon o yomimasu.
5. 母は東京にいます。でも、父は今ニューヨークにいます。Haha wa tookyoo ni imasu. Demo, chichi wa ima nyuuyooku ni imasu.

✎ Drive It Home

A. Fill in the blanks with the appropriate form of verbs in parentheses based on the English translation provided.

1. 昨日山田さんが _____。(来ます)

   Kinoo Yamada san ga _____. (kimasu)

   Mr./Ms. Yamada came yesterday.

2. 昨日山田さんは _____。(来ます)

   Kinoo Yamada san wa _____. (kimasu)

   Mr./Ms. Yamada did not come yesterday.

3. 山田さんは英語を _____。(話します)

   Yamada san wa eego o _____.

   (hanashimasu)

   Mr./Ms. Yamada spoke English.

が Ga as object marker

The basics of Japanese verbs:
Verb forms, classes, and tense

だ Da: The plain form of the
copula です desu

Conjunctions から kara, ので node,
けど kedo, and が ga

4. 山田さんは英語は ＿＿＿＿＿＿＿＿＿＿＿＿＿＿＿＿。(話します)

   Yamada san wa eego wa ＿＿＿＿＿＿＿＿＿＿＿＿＿＿＿＿＿

   ＿＿＿＿＿＿＿＿＿. (hanashimasu)

   Mr./Ms. Yamada did not speak English.

5. 昨日たくさん ＿＿＿＿＿＿＿＿＿＿。(寝ます)

   Kinoo takusan ＿＿＿＿＿＿＿＿＿＿＿＿＿. (nemasu)

   I slept a lot yesterday.

6. 昨日たくさん ＿＿＿＿＿＿＿＿＿＿＿＿。(寝ます)

   Kinoo takusan ＿＿＿＿＿＿＿＿＿＿＿＿＿＿＿. (nemasu)

   I did not sleep a lot yesterday.

B. Complete each of the following sentences by inserting the appropriate
   conjunction from the word bank.
   から kara, なので na node, けど kedo, でも demo

1. 明日は日曜日です。＿＿＿＿＿＿、セミナーがあります。

   Ashita wa nichiyoobi desu＿＿＿＿＿＿, seminaa ga arimasu.

2. 明日は日曜日です。＿＿＿＿＿、セミナーがあります。

   Ashita wa nichiyoobi desu.＿＿＿＿＿＿, seminaa ga arimasu.

3. 学生 ＿＿＿＿＿＿＿ 勉強します。

   Gakusee ＿＿＿＿＿＿＿＿＿ benkyooshimasu.

4. 学生 ＿＿＿＿＿＿＿ 勉強します。

   Gakusee desu＿＿＿＿＿＿＿benkyooshimasu.

ANSWER KEY

A: 1. 来ました kimashita; 2. 来ませんでした kimasen deshita; 3. 話しまし
た hanashimashita; 4. 話しませんでした hanashimasen deshita; 5. 寝ました
nemashita; 6. 寝ませんでした nemasen deshita

B. 1. けど kedo; 2. でも Demo; 3. なので na node; 4. から kara

Tip!

It is very important to practice the key structures in as many ways as possible.
For instance, you can say X があります/います X ga arimasu/imasu by
substituting X with whatever you see in your surroundings. If you are at home,
X can be your family members, furniture, electric appliances, books, food, etc.
If you are at your school, X can be your classmates, teachers, desks, textbooks,
etc. If you are at your office, X can be your boss, colleagues, office supplies,
computers, copy machines, etc. If you don't know the Japanese word for X or for
a location, you can even say in your own language. The most important thing is
to keep repeating the key structures until you stop thinking about how they are
put together.

How Did You Do?

Let's see how you did! By now, you should be able to:

☐ conjugate different classes of verbs (Still unsure? Jump back to page 147)

☐ use the conjunctions *and* and *but* (Still unsure? Jump back to page 155)

が Ga as object marker

The basics of Japanese verbs:
Verb forms, classes, and tense

だ Da: The plain form of the
copula です desu

Conjunctions から kara, ので node,
けど kedo, and が ga

✎ Word Recall

1. 妻 tsuma （つま）

2. 家 uchi （うち）

3. 数学 suugaku （すうがく）

4. 来週 raishuu （らいしゅう）

5. 午前 gozen （ごぜん）

6. 息子 musuko （むすこ）

7. 庭 niwa （にわ）

8. あ(ん)まり a(n)mari

9. 皆さん minasan （みな）

10. 朝 asa （あさ）

a. *everyone*

b. *son (one's own)*

c. *morning*

d. *next week*

e. *garden, yard*

f. *morning, a.m.*

g. *wife (one's own)*

h. *not so often, not so much*

i. *house, one's home, one's family*

j. *mathematics*

ANSWER KEY

1. g; 2. i; 3. j; 4. d; 5. f; 6. b; 7. e; 8. h; 9. a; 10. c

Don't forget to practice and reinforce what you've learned by visiting **www.livinglanguage.com/languagelab** for flashcards, games, and quizzes for Unit 2!

Unit 2 Essentials

Vocabulary Essentials

Test your knowledge of the key material in this unit by filling in the blanks in the following charts. Once you've completed these pages, you'll have tested your retention, and you'll also have your own reference for the most essential vocabulary.

TIME AND FREQUENCY

	every day
	today
	tomorrow
	yesterday
	the day after tomorrow
	the day before yesterday
	weekday
	weekend
	this week
	next week
	last week
	morning
	noon, afternoon
	early evening
	evening, night
	morning, a.m.

	afternoon, p.m.
	often
	sometimes
	once in a while
	not so often, not so much

AROUND THE HOME

	room
	living room
	bedroom
	kitchen
	area with a wash stand
	bathroom
	toilet
	entrance hall
	stairs
	garden, yard
	sofa
	desk
	bed
	chest of drawers
	refrigerator
	microwave oven
	washing machine

EVERYDAY LIFE

	life
	class
	friend
	cooking, cuisine
	breakfast
	lunch
	dinner
	novel
	newspaper
	magazine

ADJECTIVES

	hard
	busy
	enjoyable, fun
	narrow
	spacious

ADVERBS

	a little
	very
	so so

VERBS

	to relax
	to wash
	to enter
	to brush, to polish
	to speak
	to attend
	to take a shower
	to take a bath

QUESTION

	How is it?

COUNTERS

	people
	bound objects
	mechanical items
	liquid in cups/glasses/bowls
	thin flat objects
	long cylindrical objects
	animal

NATIVE JAPANESE NUMBERS

	1
	2

	3
	4
	5
	6
	7
	8
	9
	10

Grammar Essentials

Here is a reference of the key grammar that was covered in Unit 2. Make sure you understand the summary and can use all of the grammar it covers

CONJUGATION OF THE COPULA です DESU

Non-past		Past		
Affirmative	Negative	Affirmative	Negative	て Te-form
です desu	ではありません de wa arimasen ではないです de wa nai desu じゃありません ja arimasen じゃないです ja nai desu	でした deshita	ではありませんでした de wa arimasen deshita ではなかったです de wa nakatta desu じゃありませんでした ja arimasen deshita じゃなかったです ja nakatta desu	で de

EXPRESSING EXISTENCE OF INANIMATE ITEMS

X があります。	X ga arimasu.	*There is X.*
ソファーがあります。	Sofaa ga arimasu.	*There is a sofa.*

Y に X があります。	Y ni X ga arimasu.	*There is X in Y.*
居間にソファーが あります。	Ima ni sofaa ga arimasu.	*There is a sofa in the living room.*

X は Y にあります。	X wa Y ni arimasu	*X is in Y.*
ソファーは居間に あります。	Sofaa wa ima ni arimasu.	*Sofa is in the living room.*

EXPRESSING QUANTITY OF EXISTING ITEMS

X が [number + counter] あります。	X ga [number + counter] arimasu.	*There are [number] X.*
ペンが五本あります。	Pen ga gohon arimasu.	*There are five pens.*

X が [number + counter] います。	X ga [number + counter] imasu.	*There are [number] X.*
猫が五匹います。	Neko ga gohiki imasu.	*There are five cats*

が GA AS OBJECT MARKER

X は Y が好きです。	X wa Y ga suki desu.	*X likes Y.*
田中さんはテニスが 好きです。	Tanaka san wa tenisu ga suki desu.	*Mr./Ms. Tanaka likes tennis.*

X は Y が嫌いです。	X wa Y ga kirai desu.	*X dislikes Y.*
田中さんはゴルフが嫌いです。	Tanaka san wa gorufu ga kirai desu.	*Mr./Ms. Tanaka dislikes golf.*

X は Y が分かります。	X wa Y ga wakarimasu.	*X understands Y.*
田中さんは英語が分かります。	Tanaka san wa eego ga wakarimasu.	*Mr./Ms. Tanaka understands English.*

THE PLAIN FORM OF THE COPULA です DESU

NON-PAST		PAST	
Affirmative	Negative	Affirmative	Negative
だ	ではない/じゃない	だった	ではなかった/じゃなかった
da	de wa nai/ja nai	datta	de wa nakatta/ja nakatta

VERB CLASSES AND NON-PAST AFFIRMATIVE FORM OF VERBS

NON-PAST TENSE AFFIRMATIVE FORM		
Class I (う u-verbs)	Class II (る ru-verbs)	Class III (irregular verbs)
話します **hanashimasu** *(speak)*	出ます **demasu** *(attend, leave)*	来ます **kimasu** *(come)*
読みます **yomimasu** *(read)*	寝ます **nemasu** *(sleep, go to bed)*	します shimasu *(do)*

NON-PAST NEGATIVE FORM OF VERBS

NON-PAST NEGATIVE FORM		
Class I Verb (う u-verb)	Class II (る ru-verb)	Class III (irregular)
話しません hanashimasen (do/does not speak)	出ません demasen (do/does not attend, do/does not leave)	来ません kimasen (do/does not come)
読みません yomimasen (do/does not read)	寝ません nemasen (do/does not sleep, do/does not go to bed)	しません shimasen (do/does not do)

PAST AFFIRMATIVE FORM OF VERBS

PAST AFFIRMATIVE FORM		
Class I Verb (う u-verb)	Class II (る ru-verb)	Class III (irregular)
話しました hanashimashita (spoke)	出ました demashita (attended, left)	来ました kimashita (came)
読みました yomimashita (read)	寝ました nemashita (slept, went to bed)	しました shimashita (did)

PAST NEGATIVE FORM OF VERBS

PAST NEGATIVE FORM		
Class I Verb (う u-verb)	Class II (る ru-verb)	Class III (irregular)
話しませんでした hanashimasen deshita (did not speak)	出ませんでした demasen deshita (did not attend, did not leave)	来ませんでした kimasen deshita (did not come)

PAST NEGATIVE FORM		
Class I Verb (う u-verb)	Class II (る ru-verb)	Class III (irregular)
読_よみませんでした yomimasen deshita (did not read)	寝_ねませんでした nemasen deshita (did not sleep, did not go to bed)	しませんでした shimasen deshita (did not do)

CONJUNCTIONS

から kara (so)

明日友達が来ますから、 セミナーに出ません。	Ashita tomodachi ga kimasu kara, seminaa ni demasen.	I will not attend the seminar because a friend of mine will come tomorrow.
明日友達が来るから、 セミナーに出ません。	Ashita tomodachi ga kuru kara, seminaa ni demasen.	I will not attend the seminar because a friend of mine will come tomorrow.

ので node (because, since)

明日友達が来るので、 セミナーに出ません。	Ashita tomodachi ga kuru node, seminaa ni demasen.	I will not attend the seminar because a friend of mine will come tomorrow.
学生なので、勉強します。	Gakusee na node, benkyooshimasu.	I study because I'm a student.

けど kedo (*but*)

明日は土曜日ですけど、授業があります。	Ashita wa doyoobi desu kedo, jugyoo ga arimasu.	*It is Saturday tomorrow, but there is a class/ there are classes.*

が ga (*but*)

明日は土曜日ですが、授業があります。	Ashita wa doyoobi desu ga, jugyoo ga arimasu.	*It is Saturday tomorrow, but there is a class/ there are classes.*

でも demo (*but*)

明日は土曜日です。でも、授業があります。	Ashita wa doyoobi desu. Demo, jugyoo ga arimasu.	*It is Saturday tomorrow. But, there is a class/ there are classes.*

Unit 2 Quiz

A. Fill in the blanks with the appropriate number and counter combination.

1. 紙が _____ あります。(four)

   Kami ga _____ arimasu.

2. 猫が_____ います。(three)

   Neko ga _____ imasu.

B. Complete the following sentences by inserting the appropriate particles.

1. 居間 _____ ソファー _____ あります。

   Ima _____ sofaa _____ arimasu.

   There's a sofa in the living room.

2. 電子レンジ _____台所 _____あります。

   Denshirenji _____ daidokoro _____ arimasu.

   The microwave oven is in the kitchen.

3. スポーツ_____好きです。

   Supootsu _____ suki desu.

   I like sports.

4. 日本語_____分かります。

   Nihongo _____ wakarimasu.

   I understand Japanese.

C. Fill in each of the blanks with the appropriate polite form of です desu based on the English translation provided.

あに　がくせい
1. 兄は学生 _____ 。

   Ani wa gakusee _____.

   My older brother was a student.

はは　きょうし
2. 母は教師_____ 。

   Haha wa kyooshi _____.

   My mother was not a teacher.

D. Fill in each of the blanks with the appropriate plain form of the copula です desu based on the English translation provided.

ちち　きょうし
1. 父は教師 _____ よ。

   Chichi wa kyooshi _____ yo.

   My father is a teacher.

わたし　がくせい
2. 私 は学生 _____ よ。

   Watashi wa gakusee _____ yo.

   I am not a student.

あに　がくせい
3. 兄は学生_____ よ。

   Ani wa gakusee _____ yo.

   My older brother was a student.

はは　きょうし
4. 母は教師_____ よ。

   Haha wa kyooshi _____ yo.

   My mother was not a teacher.

E. Fill in the blanks with the appropriate form of the verbs given in parentheses based on the English translation provided.

1. 昨日友達が＿＿＿＿＿＿＿＿＿。(来ます)

   Kinoo tomodachi ga ＿＿＿. (kimasu)

   My friend came yesterday.

2. 昨日野球を＿＿＿＿＿＿＿＿＿。(します)

   Kinoo yakyuu o ＿＿＿＿＿. (shimasu)

   I played baseball yesterday.

3. 昨日授業に ＿＿＿＿＿＿＿＿。(出ます)

   Kinoo jugyoo ni ＿＿＿＿＿. (demasu)

   I didn't attend the class yesterday.

4. 昨日本は＿＿＿＿＿＿＿＿＿。(読みます)

   Kinoo hon wa ＿＿＿＿＿. (yomimasu)

   I didn't read a book yesterday.

F. Complete each of the following sentences by inserting the appropriate conjunction from the word bank.

   から kara, なので na node, けど kedo, でも demo

1. 台所は狭いです＿＿＿＿＿＿ 居間は広いですよ。

   Daidokoro wa semai desu ＿＿＿＿＿＿＿＿ ima wa hiroi desu yo.

2. 明日は日曜日＿＿＿＿＿＿＿ 授業がありません。

   Ashita wa nichiyoobi ＿＿＿＿＿＿＿＿＿＿ jugyoo ga arimasen.

3. 学生です _____ 勉強します。
<ruby>学生<rt>がくせい</rt></ruby> <ruby>勉強<rt>べんきょう</rt></ruby>

Gakusee desu _____ benkyooshimasu.

4. 英語を話します。_____ スペイン語は話しません。
<ruby>英語<rt>えいご</rt></ruby> <ruby>話<rt>はな</rt></ruby> <ruby>語<rt>ご</rt></ruby> <ruby>話<rt>はな</rt></ruby>

Eego o hanashimasu. _____ supeingo wa hanashimasen.

ANSWER KEY
A. 1. 四枚 yonmai; 2. 三匹 sanbiki
B. 1. に ni, が ga; 2. は wa, に ni; 3. が ga; 4. が ga
C. 1. でした deshita; 2. (では/じゃ) (ありませんでした/なかったです) (de wa/ja) (arimasen deshita/nakatta desu)
D. 1. だ da; 2. (じゃ/では) ない (ja/de wa) nai; 3. だった datta; 4. (じゃ/では) なかった (ja/de wa) nakatta
E. 1. 来ました kimashita; 2. しました shimashita; 3. 出ませんでした demasen deshita; 4. 読みませんでした yomimasen deshita
F. 1. けど kedo; 2. なので na node; 3. から kara; 4. でも Demo

How Did You Do?

Give yourself a point for every correct answer, then use the following key to tell whether you're ready to move on:

0-7 points: It's probably a good idea to go back through the lesson again. You may be moving too quickly, or there may be too much "down time" between your contact with Japanese. Remember that it's better to spend 30 minutes with Japanese three or four times a week than it is to spend two or three hours just once a week. Find a pace that's comfortable for you, and spread your contact hours out as much as you can.

8-12 points: You would benefit from a review before moving on. Go back and spend a little more time on the specific points that gave you trouble. Re-read the Grammar Builder sections that were difficult, and do the work out one more time. Don't forget about the online supplemental practice material, either. Go to **www.livinglanguage.com/languagelab** for games and quizzes that will reinforce the material from this unit.

13-17 points: Good job! There are just a few points that you could consider reviewing before moving on. If you haven't worked with the games and quizzes on **www.livinglanguage.com/languagelab**, please give them a try.

18-20 points: Great! You're ready to move on to the next unit.

points

Unit 3:
Work and School

Welcome to Unit 3! You've done a great job so far and learned a lot of Japanese words and structures. In Unit 3, you will learn how to talk about such important things such as your school or your work. In this lesson you'll learn how to:

- [ ] use key vocabulary related to school and work
- [ ] use the plain non-past tense form of verbs
- [ ] use the particles へ e, に ni, で de with words expressing places
- [ ] express a purpose using に ni
- [ ] use the て te-form of verbs
- [ ] use the progressive form of verbs
- [ ] use the plain past tense form of verbs
- [ ] use the expression んです n desu to state or ask for a reason

Lesson 9: Words

In this lesson you'll learn how to:

- [ ] use key vocabulary related to school and work
- [ ] use the plain non-past form of verbs

Word Builder 1

▶ 9A Word Builder 1 (CD 5, Track 7)

幼稚園	yoochien	*kindergarten*
小学校	shoogakkoo	*elementary school*
大学院	daigakuin	*graduate school*
大学院生	daigakuinsee	*graduate school student*
図書館	toshokan	*library*
心理学	shinrigaku	*psychology*
経営学	kee-eegaku	*business management*
レポート	repooto	*report*
発表	happyoo	*presentation*
グループ発表	gruupu happyoo	*group presentation*
ミーティング	miitingu	*meeting*
電車	densha	*train*
地下鉄	chikatetsu	*subway*
バス	basu	*bus*
新幹線	shinkansen	*Japanese bullet train*
飛行機	hikooki	*airplane*
紙	kami	*paper*
鉛筆	enpitsu	*pencil*

* From this point on both the ます masu-form and the dictionary form (plain non-past affirmative form) of verbs will be listed in all word lists.

ボールペン	boorupen	*ballpoint pen*
万年筆 まんねんひつ	mannenhitsu	*fountain pen*
勉強します、 べんきょう 勉強する べんきょう	benkyooshimasu (masu-form), benkyoosuru (dictionary form)	*to study*
入学します、 にゅうがく 入学する にゅうがく	nyuugakushimasu, nyuugakusuru	*to enter school*
卒業します、 そつぎょう 卒業する そつぎょう	sotsugyooshimasu, sotsugyoosuru	*to graduate*
行きます、行く い　　　　い	ikimasu, iku	*to go*
来ます、来る き　　　く	kimasu, kuru	*to come*
帰ります、帰る かえ　　　　かえ	kaerimasu, kaeru	*to go back, to return*
戻ります、戻る もど　　　　もど	modorimasu, modoru	*to return*
乗ります、乗る の　　　　の	norimasu, noru	*to ride, to get on*
降ります、降りる お　　　　お	orimasu, oriru	*to get off*
借ります、借りる か　　　　か	karimasu, kariru	*to borrow*
貸します、貸す か　　　か	kashimasu, kasu	*to lend*
一年間 いちねんかん	ichinenkan	*for a year*
半年間 はんとしかん	hantoshikan	*for half a year*

* From this point on both the ます masu-form and the dictionary form (plain non-past affirmative form) of verbs will be listed in all word lists.

Take It Further

As you see more and more kanji in this course, you'll notice that a single kanji can have multiple possible readings. How to read a particular kanji is dependent on which word it is used in. For example, the character 日, which means *day* has multiple possible readings. Let's look at some examples.

<ruby>毎日<rt>まいにち</rt></ruby>	mainichi	*every day*
<ruby>日曜日<rt>にちようび</rt></ruby>	nichiyoobi	*Sunday*
いい<ruby>日<rt>ひ</rt></ruby>	ii hi	*good day*
<ruby>一日<rt>ついたち</rt></ruby>	tsuitachi	*the first day of the month*
<ruby>一日<rt>いちにち</rt></ruby>	ichinichi	*one day*
<ruby>二日<rt>ふつか</rt></ruby>	futsuka	*the second day of the month, two days*
<ruby>今日<rt>きょう</rt></ruby>	kyoo	*today*
<ruby>明日<rt>あした</rt></ruby> or <ruby>明日<rt>あす</rt></ruby>	ashita or asu	*tomorrow*
<ruby>昨日<rt>きのう</rt></ruby>	kinoo	*yesterday*

You see that 日 can be read as にち nichi, ひ hi, び bi, or か ka. Furthermore, there are some words which are assigned with specific readings as a whole but no particular reading is assigned to the individual characters that make up the word, such as <ruby>今日<rt>きょう</rt></ruby> kyoo (*today*), <ruby>明日<rt>あした</rt></ruby> ashita (*tomorrow*), <ruby>明日<rt>あす</rt></ruby> asu (*tomorrow*), and <ruby>昨日<rt>きのう</rt></ruby> kinoo (*yesterday*). But don't worry, 日 is a special character that has many readings, so it is not the case that every kanji character has as many readings as 日 does. However, you do need to learn how to read each kanji at the word level, as opposed to learning a character in isolation; reading of kanji is always dependent on usage.

✎ Word Practice 1

Translate the following words into Japanese.

1. *kindergarten* _____

2. *elementary school* _____

3. *graduate school* _____

4. *library* _____

5. *business management* _____

6. *presentation* _____

7. *train* _____

8. *subway* _____

9. *airplane* _____

10. *for a year* _____

ANSWER KEY

1. 幼稚園 yoochien; 2. 小学校 shoogakkoo; 3. 大学院 daigakuin; 4. 図書館 toshokan; 5. 経営学 kee-eegaku; 6. 発表 happyoo; 7. 電車 densha; 8. 地下鉄 chikatetsu; 9. 飛行機 hikooki; 10. 一年間 ichinenkan

Grammar Builder 1
THE PLAIN NON-PAST FORM OF VERBS

▶ 9B Grammar Builder 1 (CD 5, Track 8)

In Lesson 8, you learned that there are two basic verb forms in Japanese; i.e. the plain form and the ます masu-form. In speech and conversation, the plain form is mostly used in casual settings, whereas the ます masu-form is used in formal settings. Let's look at the plain form of verbs now. Remember that Japanese verbs can be divided into three different groups. The following chart lists some of the verbs in each group.

CLASS I	CLASS II	CLASS III
話します hanashimasu *(to speak)*	食べます tabemasu *(to eat)*	します shimasu *(to do)*
読みます yomimasu *(to read)*	寝ます nemasu *(to sleep, to go to bed)*	来ます kimasu *(to come)*
行きます ikimasu *(to go)*	見ます mimasu *(to see, to watch)*	
買います kaimasu *(to buy)*	教えます oshiemasu *(to teach)*	
あります arimasu *(to exist)*	います imasu *(to exist)*	

Remember that only します shimasu and 来ます kimasu make up the Class III verbs.

Now, let's look at the plain non-past affirmative forms of the above verbs.

CLASS I	CLASS II	CLASS III
Non-past affirmative	Non-past affirmative	Non-past affirmative
話す hanasu	食べる taberu	する suru
読む yomu	寝る neru	来る kuru
行く iku	見る miru	
買う kau	教える oshieru	
ある aru	いる iru	

The plain non-past affirmative form is called "the dictionary form" because verbs are listed in this form in dictionaries. When you compare a ます masu-form and a dictionary form of a Class I verb, you will notice that if you drop -imasu from the ます masu-form and then attach -u, you will get the dictionary form of the verb. Likewise, if you drop the final -u from the dictionary form and attach -imasu, you will get the verb's ます masu-form counterpart. Note that in case of 話します hanashimasu (*to speak*) you need to drop します shimasu in order to get the dictionary form. This rule applies to the verbs whose ます masu-form ends with します shimasu, such as 話します hanashimasu (*to speak*), 探します sagashimasu (*to look for*) and 引っ越します hikkoshimasu (*to move [to a new location]*).

Now, let's look at the conjugation of Class II verbs. The conjugation of Class II verbs is much simpler. If you drop -masu from the ます masu-form of verbs and attach -ru, you will get the dictionary form counterparts of the verbs. It is also useful to remember that the dictionary forms of Class II verbs end with either -iru or -eru, e.g., 食べる taberu (*to eat*) and 見る miru (*to see*), with a few exceptions. Some of the exceptions are 帰る kaeru (*to return*), 入る hairu (*to enter*), 切る kiru (*to cut*), and 走る hashiru (*to run*). These end with -eru or -iru, but they are Class I verbs. It is clear by now that Class I and Class II verbs are also called う u-verbs and る ru-verbs, because their dictionary forms end with -u and -ru respectively. As for the conjugation of Class III verbs, you just have to memorize them, which shouldn't be too difficult for only two verbs.

✎ Work Out 1

A. Class I, Class II or Class III? Put the following verbs in their appropriate class.

1. 食べる taberu (*to eat*) _____

2. 読む yomu *(to read)* _____

3. する suru *(to do)* _____

4. 見る miru *(to see)* _____

5. 来る kuru *(to come)* _____

6. 行く iku *(to go)* _____

7. 寝る neru *(to sleep, to go to bed)* _____

8. 話す hanasu *(to speak)* _____

9. ある aru *(to exist, for inanimate subjects)* _____

10. いる iru *(to exit, for animate subjects)* _____

B. Provide the dictionary forms of the following verbs.

1. します shimasu *(to do)* _____

2. 行きます ikimasu *(to go)* _____

3. 見ます mimasu *(to see)* _____

4. 読みます yomimasu *(to read)* _____

5. 寝ます nemasu *(to sleep, to go to bed)* _____

6. 来ます kimasu *(to come)* _____

7. あります arimasu *(to exist)* _____

8. 食べます tabemasu *(to eat)* _____

9. 探します sagashimasu *(to look for)* _____

10. います imasu *(to exist, for animate subjects)* _____

The て te-form of verbs   The plain past tense form of verbs

The progressive form of verbs   The expression んです n desu

ANSWER KEY

A: 1. Class II; 2. Class I; 3. Class III; 4. Class II; 5. Class III; 6. Class I; 7. Class II; 8. Class I; 9. Class I;
10. Class II
B: 1. する suru; 2. 行く iku; 3. 見る miru; 4. 読む yomu; 5. 寝る neru; 6. 来る kuru; 7. ある aru; 8. 食べる taberu; 9. 探す sagasu; 10. いる iru

Word Builder 2

▶ 9C Word Builder 2 (CD 5, Track 9)

貿易会社	booekigaisha	*trading company*
事務所	jimusho	*office*
法律事務所	hooritsu jimusho	*law firm*
マーケティング	maaketingu	*marketing*
ファックス	fakkusu	*fax*
コピー	kopii	*copy*
ワープロ	waapuro	*word processor*
します、する	shimasu, suru	*to do*
使います、使う	tsukaimasu, tsukau	*to use*
分かります、分かる	wakarimasu, wakaru	*to understand*
働きます、働く	hatarakimasu, hataraku	*to work*
探します、探す	sagashimasu, sagasu	*to look for*
たぶん	tabun	*perhaps*
たくさん	takusan	*many, much*

✎ Word Practice 2

Translate the following words into Japanese.

1. *trading company* _____

2. *office* _____

3. *law firm* _____

4. *marketing* _____

5. *fax* _____

6. *copy* _____

7. *word processor* _____

8. *perhaps* _____

9. *many, much* _____

ANSWER KEY

1. 貿易会社 booekigaisha; 2. 事務所 jimusho; 3. 法律事務所 hooritsu jimusho; 4. マーケティング maaketingu; 5. ファックス fakkusu; 6. コピー kopii; 7. ワープロ waapuro; 8. たぶん tabun; 9. たくさん takusan

Grammar Builder 2
PLAIN NON-PAST NEGATIVE FORMS OF VERBS

▶ 9D Grammar Builder 2 (CD 5, Track 10)

To form the non-past negative plain forms of Class I verbs, drop -u from the dictionary form and attach -anai. Note that in case of 買う kau (*to buy*) you need to attach -wanai instead of -anai in order to get the plain non-past negative form. This rule applies to other verbs whose dictionary forms end with -au, such as 買う kau (*to buy*), 会う au (*to meet*), 使う tsukau (*to use*), and 洗う arau (*to wash*).

Also, it is important to remember that the plain non-past negative form of ある aru (*to exist*) is ない nai.

CLASS I	
Non-past affirmative	Non-past negative
話す hanasu	話さない hanasanai
読む yomu	読まない yomanai
行く iku	行かない ikanai
買う kau	買わない kawanai
ある aru	ない nai

The Class II verbs are far simpler to make negative: just replace -ru in the plain form with -nai.

CLASS II	
Non-past affirmative	Non-past negative
食べる taberu	食べない tabenai
寝る neru	寝ない nenai
見る miru	見ない minai
教える oshieru	教えない oshienai
いる iru	いない inai

As for the conjugation of Class III verbs, again, it's just best to memorize their negative non-past forms.

CLASS III	
Non-past affirmative	Non-past negative
する suru	しない shinai
来る kuru	来ない konai

✎ Work Out 2

Give the plain non-past negative form of the following verbs.

1. 食べる taberu (*to eat*) _____

2. 読む yomu (*to read*) _____

3. する suru (*to do*) _____

4. 見る miru (*to see*) _____

5. 来る kuru (*to come*) _____

6. 行く iku (*to go*) _____

7. 寝る neru (*to sleep, to go to bed*) _____

8. 買う kau (*to buy*) _____

9. ある aru (*to exist, for inanimate subjects*) _____

10. いる iru (*to exist, for animate subjects*) _____

ANSWER KEY

1. 食べない tabenai; 2. 読まない yomanai; 3. しない shinai; 4. 見ない minai; 5. 来ない konai; 6. 行かない ikanai; 7. 寝ない nenai; 8. 買わない kawanai; 9. ない nai; 10. いない inai

✎ Drive It Home

Convert the following verbs into their plain forms.

Ex. 食べます tabemasu → 食べる taberu

食べません tabemasen → 食べない tabenai

1. します shimasu _____

2. 寝ません nemasen _____

3. 買います kaimasu _____

4. 読みません yomimasen _____

5. 行きます ikimasu _____

6. 来ません kimasen _____

7. 見ます mimasu _____

8. 教えません oshiemasen _____

9. います imasu _____

10. ありません arimasen _____

ANSWER KEY

1. する suru; 2. 寝ない nenai; 3. 買う kau; 4. 読まない yomanai; 5. 行く iku; 6. 来ない konai; 7. 見る miru; 8. 教えない oshienai; 9. いる iru; 10. ない nai

💡 Tip!

Mastering the conjugation of the plain form of verbs is key to improving your Japanese. The best way to become comfortable with these forms is to keep reviewing them every day. Even though there are rules you can apply when conjugating verbs, the best way is to repeat the different forms over and over until you can produce them without thinking. For instance, pick five verbs every morning and conjugate them as many times as possible throughout the day. By evening, you will be able to conjugate them easily.

How Did You Do?

Let's see how you did! By now, you should be able to:

☐ use key vocabulary related to school and work
(Still unsure? Jump back to page 178)

☐ use the plain non-past form of verbs (Still unsure? Jump back to page 186)

✎ Word Recall

1. 経済学 keezaigaku   a. *novel*

2. 授業 jugyoo   b. *economics*

3. 会社員 kaishain   c. *kitchen*

4. 親戚 shinseki   d. *company employee*

5. 小説 shoosetsu   e. *class*

6. 部屋 heya   f. *husband (someone else's)*

7. ご主人 goshujin   g. *teacher*

8. 雑誌 zasshi   h. *relatives*

9. 台所 daidokoro   i. *magazine*

10. 教師 kyooshi   j. *room*

ANSWER KEY

1. b; 2. e; 3. d; 4. h; 5. a; 6. j; 7. f; 8. i; 9. c; 10. g

Lesson 10: Phrases

In this lesson you'll learn how to:

☐ use the particles へ e, に ni, で de with words expressing places

☐ express a purpose using に ni

Phrase Builder 1
▶ 10A Phrase Builder 1 (CD 5, Track 11)

<ruby>大学<rt>だいがく</rt></ruby><ruby>で勉強<rt>べんきょう</rt></ruby>します	daigaku de benkyooshimasu	*study at a university*
<ruby>大学<rt>だいがく</rt></ruby> (に/へ) <ruby>行<rt>い</rt></ruby>きます	daigaku (ni/e) ikimasu	*go to a university*
<ruby>大学<rt>だいがく</rt></ruby>に<ruby>入学<rt>にゅうがく</rt></ruby>します	daigaku ni nyuugakushimasu	*enter a university*
<ruby>大学<rt>だいがく</rt></ruby>を<ruby>卒業<rt>そつぎょう</rt></ruby>します	daigaku o sotsugyooshimasu	*graduate from a university*
<ruby>大学院<rt>だいがくいん</rt></ruby> (に/へ) <ruby>戻<rt>もど</rt></ruby>ります	daigakuin (ni/e) modorimasu	*return to a graduate school*
ミーティングに<ruby>出<rt>で</rt></ruby>ます	miitingu ni demasu	*attend a meeting*
<ruby>日本<rt>にほん</rt></ruby> (に/へ) <ruby>留学<rt>りゅうがく</rt></ruby>します	nihon (ni/e) ryuugakushimasu	*study abroad in Japan*
<ruby>日本語<rt>にほんご</rt></ruby>を<ruby>勉強<rt>べんきょう</rt></ruby>しに<ruby>日本<rt>にほん</rt></ruby> (に/へ) <ruby>来<rt>き</rt></ruby>ました	nihongo o benkyooshi ni nihon (ni/e) kimashita	*came to Japan to study Japanese*

電車に乗ります	densha ni norimasu	*get on a train*
電車を降ります	densha o orimasu	*get off a train*
本を借ります	hon o karimasu	*borrow (a) book(s)*
本を貸します	hon o kashimasu	*lend (a) book(s)*
勉強しています	benkyooshite imasu	*am/is/are studying*
小学校から高校まで	shoogakkoo kara kookoo made	*from elementary school to high school*
レポートや発表	repooto ya happyoo	*report and presentation among other things*

Take It Further

The Japanese verb 卒業します sotsugyooshimasu takes a direct object, while the English equivalent, *to graduate*, does not. Thus, in English, you have to say *I graduate from university*, whereas in Japanese you say 大学を卒業します daigaku o sotsugyooshimasu. 大学 Daigaku (*university*) is a direct object, as indicated by the particle を o.

On the other hand, the verb 入学します nyuugakushimasu (*to enter [school]*) does not take a direct object, just like the verb 入ります hairimasu (*to enter*), which was discussed in Lesson 6. Thus, you need to say 大学に入学します daigaku ni nyuugakushimasu (*I enter a university*).

It is also important to note the contrast between 電車に乗ります densha ni norimasu (*to get on a train*) and 電車を降ります densha o orimasu (*to get off a train*); i.e. the former requires the particle に ni, whereas the latter requires the particle を o.

✎ Phrase Practice 1

Complete the following by inserting the appropriate particles.

1. 大学 _____ 勉強します

   daigaku _____ benkyooshimasu

   study at a university

2. 大学 _____ 入学します

   daigaku _____ nyuugakushimasu

   enter a university

3. 大学 _____ 卒業します

   daigaku _____ sotsugyooshimasu

   graduate from a university

4. ミーティング _____ 出ます

   miitingu _____ demasu

   attend a meeting

5. 電車_____ 乗ります

   densha _____ norimasu

   get on a train

6. 電車_____ 降ります

   densha _____ orimasu

   get off a train

7. レポート _____ 発表
はっぴょう

repooto _____ **happyoo**

report and presentation among other things

ANSWER KEY

1. で de; 2. に ni; 3. を o; 4. に ni; 5. に ni; 6. を o; 7. や ya

Grammar Builder 1
PARTICLES へ E, に NI, で DE

▶ 10B Grammar Builder 1 (CD 5, Track 12)

The particle に ni, marking a location of an item that exists, used in the structure X は Y にあります/います X wa Y ni arimasu/imasu was introduced in Lesson 10. Now, let's look at other Japanese particles へ e and で de, as well as に ni. It is important that the particle へ is pronounced [e], but not [he]. This is the only case where the character へ is pronounced [e].

へ e に ni	[PLACE] (へ/に) 行きます、来ます、帰ります、戻ります, etc. [PLACE] (e/ni) ikimasu, kimasu, kaerimasu, modorimasu, *etc.*	*to go, to come, to go back, to return, etc., to [PLACE]*
で de	[PLACE] で de + *action verb*	*[action verb] + at/in [PLACE]*

As shown in the chart above, へ e and に ni correspond to the English preposition *to* and express the direction of the motion.

毎日学校へ行きます。
まいにちがっこう　い

Mainichi gakkoo e ikimasu.

毎日学校に行きます。

Mainichi gakkoo ni ikimasu.

I go to school every day.

本田さんは大学へ来ませんでした。

Honda san wa daigaku e kimasen deshita.

本田さんは大学に来ませんでした。

Honda san wa daigaku ni kimasen deshita.

Mr./Ms. Honda didn't come to the university.

来週日本へ帰ります。

Raishuu nihon e kaerimasu.

来週日本に帰ります。

Raishuu nihon ni kaerimasu.

I will go back to Japan next week.

いつアメリカへ戻りますか。

Itsu amerika e modorimasu ka.

いつアメリカに戻りますか。

Itsu amerika ni modorimasu ka.

When are you returning to the U.S.A.?

As you can see from the examples, へ e and に ni can be used interchangeably when a motion verb follows them.

Note that the translation of に ni doesn't always translate directly as the English preposition *to*: e.g., 電車に乗る densha ni noru (*to get on a train*) ミーティングに出る miitingu ni deru (*to attend a meeting*).

Now, let's look at another particle, で de. As shown in the chart above, で de marks the place where the action takes place.

大学でテニスをします。

Daigaku de tenisu o shimasu.

I play tennis at the university.

家で本を読みます。

Uchi de hon o yomimasu.

I read a book at home.

小野さんは会社で働きます。

Ono san wa kaisha de hatarakimasu.

Mr./Ms. Ono works at a company.

ジョンソンさんは日本で日本語を勉強します。

Jonson san wa nihon de nihongo o benkyooshimasu.

Mr./Ms. Johnson studies Japanese in Japan.

で De is also used when referring to means and instruments, similar to *by* and *with* in English.

バスで学校へ行きます。

Basu de gakkoo e ikimasu.

バスで学校に行きます。

Basu de gakkoo ni ikimasu.

I go to school by bus.

ペンで手紙を書きます。

Pen de tegami o kakimasu.

I write a letter with a pen.

日本語で話します。

Nihongo de hanashimasu.

I speak in Japanese. (lit., using Japanese)

✎ Work Out 1

Fill in the blanks with the particles へ e, に ni or で de.

1. ジョンソンさんは明日ニューヨーク＿＿＿＿帰ります。

   Jonson san wa ashita nyuuyooku ＿＿＿＿ kaerimasu.

   Mr./Ms. Johnson will return to New York tomorrow.

2. 居間＿＿＿＿コンピューターを使いました。

   Ima ＿＿＿＿ konpyuutaa o tsukaimashita.

   I used a computer in the living room.

3. 毎日地下鉄＿＿＿＿大学＿＿＿＿行きます。

   Mainichi chikatetsu ＿＿＿＿ daigaku ＿＿＿＿ ikimasu.

   I go to the university by subway every day.

4. 万年筆＿＿＿＿名前を書きました。

   Mannenhitsu ＿＿＿＿ namae o kakimashita.

   I wrote my name with a fountain pen.

5. 週末は家 _____ 小説を読みました。

Shuumatsu wa uchi _____ shoosetsu o yomimashita.

I read a novel at home on the weekend.

ANSWER KEY

1. へ e or に ni; 2. で de; 3. で de, へ e or に ni; 4. で de; 5. で de

Phrase Builder 2

▶ 10C Phrase Builder 2 (CD 5, Track 13)

弁護士の仕事	bengoshi no shigoto	*lawyer's work*
マーケティングの仕事	maaketingu no shigoto	*marketing job*
アメリカの法律事務所	amerika no hooritsu jimusho	*law firm in the U.S.A.*
日本の会社	nihon no kaisha	*Japanese company*
日本語を使います	nihongo o tsukaimasu	*use Japanese*
仕事で使います	shigoto de tsukaimasu	*use at work*
仕事を探します	shigoto o sagashimasu	*look for a job*
東京で仕事を探します	tookyoo de shigoto o sagashimasu	*look for a job in Tokyo*
会社で働きます	kaisha de hatarakimasu	*work at a company*
あまり使いません	amari tsukaimasen	*don't use so often/much*
よく分かりません	yoku wakarimasen	*don't understand well*
まだ分かりません	mada wakarimasen	*don't know yet*
まだ大学生です	mada daigakusee desu	*still a college student*

Take It Further

まだ **Mada** can be combined with both the negative and the affirmative form of verbs, copula, and adjectives. When used with the affirmative form, it means *still*.

まだ大学生です。
<ruby>大学生<rt>だいがくせい</rt></ruby>

Mada daigakusee desu.

I'm still a college student.

まだ忙しいです。
<ruby>忙<rt>いそが</rt></ruby>

Mada isogashii desu.

I'm still busy.

When used with the negative form, mada means *not yet*.

まだ分かりません。
<ruby>分<rt>わ</rt></ruby>

Mada wakarimasen.

I don't know yet.

まだ家に帰りません。
<ruby>家<rt>うち</rt></ruby> <ruby>帰<rt>かえ</rt></ruby>

Mada uchi ni kaerimasen.

I don't go home yet.

✎ Phrase Practice 2

Fill in the missing words in each of the following sentences.

1. 日本語を _____
<ruby>日<rt>に</rt></ruby> <ruby>本<rt>ほん</rt></ruby> <ruby>語<rt>ご</rt></ruby>

nihongo o _____

use Japanese

2. _____ 使<ruby>使<rt>つか</rt></ruby>います

_____ tsukaimasu

use at work

3. 仕事<ruby>仕事<rt>しごと</rt></ruby>を _____

shigoto o _____

look for a job

4. _____ 仕事<ruby>仕事<rt>しごと</rt></ruby>を探<ruby>探<rt>さが</rt></ruby>します

_____ shigoto o sagashimasu

look for a job in Tokyo

5. 会社<ruby>会社<rt>かいしゃ</rt></ruby>で _____

kaisha de _____

work at a company

6. _____ 使<ruby>使<rt>つか</rt></ruby>いません

_____ tsukaimasen

don't use so often/much

7. _____ 分<ruby>分<rt>わ</rt></ruby>かりません

_____ wakarimasen

don't understand well

8. _____ 分<ruby>分<rt>わ</rt></ruby>かりません

_____ wakarimasen

don't know yet

The progressive form of verbs | The expression んです n desu

ANSWER KEY

1. 使います tsukaimasu; 2. 仕事で shigoto de; 3. 探します sagashimasu; 4. 東京で tookyoo de;
5. 働きます hatarakimasu; 6. あまり amari; 7. よく yoku; 8. まだ mada

Grammar Builder 2
EXPRESSING A PURPOSE USING に NI

▶ 10D Grammar Builder 2 (CD 5, Track 14)

Purpose, as in the English sentence *I went home to eat*, is expressed in Japanese by adding the particle に ni to the conjunctive form of a verb. The conjunctive form of a verb is obtained by taking off ます masu from the ます masu-form of the verb. Take a look at the following examples.

ます MASU-FORM OF THE VERB	CONJUNCTIVE FORM OF THE VERB
勉強します benkyooshimasu (to study)	勉強し benkyooshi
食べます tabemasu (to eat)	食べ tabe
買います kaimasu (to buy)	買い kai
話します hanashimasu (to speak)	話し hanashi

日本語を勉強しに日本へ来ました。

Nihongo o benkyooshi ni nihon e kimashita.

日本語を勉強しに日本に来ました。

Nihongo o benkyooshi ni nihon ni kimashita.

I came to Japan to study Japanese.

昼ご飯を食べに家へ帰ります。

Hirugohan o tabe ni uchi e kaerimasu.

昼ご飯を食べに家に帰ります。

Hirugohan o tabe ni uchi ni kaerimasu.

I go home to eat lunch.

テニスをしに大学へ行きます。

Tenisu o shi ni daigaku e ikimasu.

テニスをしに大学に行きます。

Tenisu o shi ni daigaku ni ikimasu.

I go to the university to play tennis.

映画を見に銀座へ行きました。

Eega o mi ni ginza e ikimashita.

映画を見に銀座に行きました。

Eega o mi ni ginza ni ikimashita.

I went to Ginza to see a movie.

The phrase expressing destination can also precede the phrase expressing purpose.

日本へ日本語を勉強しに来ました。

Nihon e nihongo o benkyooshi ni kimashita.

日本に日本語を勉強しに来ました。

Nihon ni nihongo o benkyooshi ni kimashita.

I came to Japan to study Japanese.

家へ昼ご飯を食べに帰ります。

Uchi e hirugohan o tabe ni kaerimasu.

家に昼ご飯を食べに帰ります。

Uchi ni hirugohan o tabe ni kaerimasu.

I go home to eat lunch.

銀座へ映画を見に 行きました。

Ginza e eega o mi ni ikimashita.

銀座に映画を見に行きました。

<u>**Ginza ni**</u> **eega o mi ni ikimashita.**

I went to Ginza to see a movie.

✎ Work Out 2

Translate the following Japanese sentences into English.

1. 鈴木さんは英語を勉強しにアメリカへ来ました。

   Suzuki san wa eego o benkyooshi ni amerika e kimashita.

   _____

2. 東京に仕事を探しに行きます。

   Tookyoo ni shigoto o sagashi ni ikimasu.

   _____

3. 弟 はコンピューターを買いに秋葉原へ行きました。

   Otooto wa konpyuutaa o kai ni akihabara *(name of the town in Tokyo)* **e**

   ikimashita.

   _____

4. テレビを見に家に帰ります。

   Terebi o mi ni uchi ni kaerimasu.

   _____

Unit 3 Lesson 10: Phrases   203

5. 姉は図書館へ本を借りに行きました。

Ane wa toshokan e hon o kari ni ikimashita.

ANSWER KEY :

1. *Mr./Ms. Suzuki came to the U.S.A. to study English.* 2. *I will go to Tokyo to look for a job.* 3. *My younger brother went to Akihabara to buy a computer.* 4. *I will go home to watch T.V.* 5. *My older sister went to the library to borrow books.*

✎ Drive It Home

Fill in the blanks with the particles へ e, に ni, or で de.

1. 大学 _____ 勉強します。します。

   Daigaku _____ benkyooshimasu.

   I study at university.

2. 家 _____ 本を読みます。

   Uchi _____ hon o yomimasu.

   I read a book at home.

3. バス _____ 学校 _____ 行きます。

   Basu _____ gakkoo _____ ikimasu.

   I go to school by bus.

4. 日本語 _____ 話します。

   Nihongo _____ hanashimasu.

   I speak in Japanese.

5. ペン ＿＿＿＿＿ 手紙を書きます。

Pen ＿＿＿＿＿ tegami o kakimasu.

I write a letter with a pen.

6. 昼ご飯を食べ ＿＿＿＿＿ 家 ＿＿＿＿＿ 帰ります。

Hirugohan o tabe ＿＿＿＿＿ uchi ＿＿＿＿＿ kaerimasu.

I go home to eat lunch.

7. 日本語を勉強し ＿＿＿＿＿ 日本 ＿＿＿＿＿ 来ました。

Nihongo o benkyooshi ＿＿＿＿＿ nihon ＿＿＿＿＿ kimashita.

I came to Japan to study Japanese.

8. 家 ＿＿＿＿＿ 昼ご飯を食べ ＿＿＿＿＿ 帰ります。

Uchi ＿＿＿＿＿ hirugohan o tabe ＿＿＿＿＿ kaerimasu.

I go home to eat lunch.

9. 日本 ＿＿＿＿＿ 日本語を勉強し ＿＿＿＿＿ 来ました。

Nihon ＿＿＿＿＿ nihongo o benkyooshi ＿＿＿＿＿ kimashita.

I came to Japan to study Japanese.

ANSWER KEY

1. で de; 2. で de; 3. で de, へ e or に ni; 4. で de; 5. で de; 6. に ni, へ e or に ni; 7. に ni, へ e or に ni;
8. へ e or に ni, に ni; 9. へ e or に ni, に ni

How Did You Do?

Let's see how you did! By now, you should be able to:

☐ use the particles へ e, に ni, で de with words expressing places (Still unsure?
Jump back to page 194)

☐ express a purpose using に ni (Still unsure? Jump back to page 201)

✎ Word Recall

1. 日本人 nihonjin   a. *chest of drawers*

2. 洗面所 senmenjo   b. *bathroom*

3. 出身 shusshin   c. *Japanese (person)*

4. 浴室 yokushitsu   d. *area with a wash stand*

5. 玄関 genkan   e. *place of origin, hometown*

6. 大変 taihen   f. *being in charge*

7. 給料 kyuuryoo   g. *toilet*

8. たんす tansu   h. *entrance hall*

9. お手洗い otearai   i. *hard*

10. 担当 tantoo   j. *salary*

ANSWER KEY

1. c; 2. d; 3. e; 4. b; 5. h; 6. i; 7. j; 8. a; 9. g; 10. f

Lesson 11: Sentences

In this lesson you'll learn how to:

☐ use the て te-form of verbs

☐ use the progressive form of verbs

Sentence Builder 1

▶ 11A Sentence Builder 1 (CD 5, Track 15)

日本の大学で勉強しましたか。

Nihon no daigaku de benkyooshimashita ka.

Did you study at a university in Japan?

日本の大学を卒業しました。

Nihon no daigaku o sotsugyooshimashita.

I graduated from university in Japan.

それから大学院 (へ/に) 行きました。

Sorekara daigakuin (e/ni) ikimashita.

After that, I went to graduate school.

アメリカの大学を卒業しましたか。

Amerika no daigaku o sotsugyooshimashita ka.

Did you graduate from a university in the U.S.A.?

小学校から高校まではアメリカでした。

Shoogakkoo kara kookoo made wa amerika deshita.

As for elementary school to high school, they were in the U.S.A.

それからイギリスの大学に入学しました。

Sorekara igirisu no daigaku ni nyuugakushimashita.

After that, I started college (lit., entered the university) in England.

大学院で経営学を勉強しています。

Daigakuin de kee-eegaku o benkyooshite imasu.

I am studying business management in graduate school.

一年間日本語を勉強しに日本 (へ/に) 来ましたが、またアメリカの大学院 (へ/に) 戻ります。

Ichinenkan nihongo o benkyooshi ni nihon (e/ni) kimashita ga, mata amerika no daigakuin (e/ni) modorimasu.

I came to Japan to study Japanese for a year, but will return to graduate school in the U.S.A. again.

MBA のクラスはどうですか。

MBA no kurasu wa doo desu ka.

How are MBA classes?

レポートや発表_{はっぴょう}がたくさんありますから、とても大変_{たいへん}です。

Repooto ya happyoo ga takusan arimasu kara, totemo taihen desu.

There are a lot of reports, presentations, and so on, so it is very hard.

グループ発表_{はっぴょう}もありますから、よくミーティングに出_でます。

Guruupu happyoo mo arimasu kara, yoku miitingu ni demasu.

There are also group presentations, so I often attend meetings.

✎ Sentence Practice 1

Fill in the missing words in each of the following sentences.

1. _____ 勉強_{べんきょう}しましたか。

_____benkyooshimashita ka.

Did you study at a university in Japan?

2. _____ 卒業_{そつぎょう}しました。

_____ sotsugyooshimashita.

I graduated from university in Japan.

3. アメリカの大学を_____か。

    Amerika no daigaku o _____ ka.

    Did you graduate from a university in the U.S.A.?

4. _____ はアメリカでした。

    _____

    _____ **wa amerika deshita.**

    As for elementary school to high school, they were in the U.S.A.

5. _____イギリスの大学に入学しました。

    _____ **igirisu no daigaku ni nyuugakushimashita.**

    After that, I started college (lit., entered the university) in England.

6. _____経営学を勉強しています。

    _____ **kee-eegaku o benkyooshite imasu.**

    I am studying business management in graduate school.

7. _____がたくさんありますから、とても大変です。

    _____ **ga takusan arimasu**

    kara, totemo taihen desu.

    There are a lot of reports, presentations, and so on, so it is very hard.

8. グループ発表もありますから、よく _____。

    Guruupu happyoo mo arimasu kara, yoku _____

    _____.

    There are also group presentations, so I often attend meetings.

ANSWER KEY

1. 日本の大学で Nihon no daigaku de; 2. 日本の大学を Nihon no daigaku o; 3. 卒業しました sotsugyooshimashita; 4. 小学校から高校まで Shoogakkoo kara kookoo made; 5. それから Sorekara; 6. 大学院で Daigakuin de; 7. レポートや発表 Repooto ya happyoo; 8. ミーティングに出ます miitingu ni demasu

Grammar Builder 1
THE て TE-FORM OF VERBS

▶ 11B Grammar Builder 1 (CD 5, Track 16)

Every verb has a て te-form, used when connecting two or more verbs, as in the English sentence *I came home, ate dinner, took a shower, and went to bed.* The て te-form of a verb is also used when making a request, as in *Please tell me*, and forming the progressive form, as in *I am studying now.* Since the て te-form of verbs is used frequently in daily conversations, it is very important to remember it. The following chart represents the て te-form of verbs in the three different verb classes.

CLASS I		CLASS II		CLASS III	
Dictionary form	て Te-form	Dictionary form	て Te-form	Dictionary form	て Te-form
話す hanasu	話して hanashite	食べる taberu	食べて tabete	する suru	して shite
読む yomu	読んで yonde	寝る neru	寝て nete	来る kuru	来て kite
行く iku	行って itte	見る miru	見て mite		
ある aru	あって atte	いる iru	いて ite		

First, let's look at the て te-form of Class I verbs. Class I verbs can be divided into four categories based on the formation of their て te-form.

1. If the dictionary form of verbs ends in -ku, like 書く kaku (*to write*) or -gu, like 脱ぐ nugu (*to take off [shoes, clothes]*), drop -ku and -gu and attach -ite and -ide instead. So, you get 書いて kaite and 脱いで nuide. Please note that 行く iku (*to go*) is an exception, and its て te-form is 行って itte.

2. If the dictionary form of verbs ends with -u, -tsu or -ru, like 使う tsukau (*to use*), 立つ tatsu (*to stand up*) and 戻る modoru (*to return*), drop -u, -tsu or -ru and attach -tte. So, you get 使って tsukatte, 立って tatte and 戻って modotte respectively.

3. If the dictionary form of verbs ends with -mu, -nu or -bu, like 読む yomu (*to read*), 死ぬ shinu (*to die*) and 遊ぶ asobu (*to play [a game]*), drop -mu, -nu or -bu and attach -nde. So, you get 読んで yonde, 死んで shinde and 遊んで asonde.

4. If the dictionary form of verbs ends with -su, like 話す hanasu (*to speak*), drop -su and attach -shite. So, you get 話して hanashite.

Next, let's look at the て te-form of Class II verbs. Compared to Class I verbs, the formation of the て te-form of Class II verbs is much simpler. Drop -ru from the dictionary form and attach て te. So, for instance, the て te-form of 食べる taberu (*to eat*), 見る miru (*to see*), 寝る neru (*to sleep*), and いる iru (*to exist*) are 食べて tabete, 見て mite, 寝て nete, and いて ite respectively.

Finally, the て te-form of the two Class III verbs する suru (*to do*) and 来る kuru (*to come*) are して shite and 来て kite respectively.

✎ Work Out 1

A. Give the て te-form of the following Class I verbs.

1. 読む yomu _____

2. 行く iku _____

3. 遊ぶ asobu _____

4. 書く kaku _____

5. 話す hanasu _____

6. 帰る kaeru _____

7. 使う tsukau _____

8. 立つ tatsu _____

9. ある aru _____

10. 戻る modoru _____

B. Now, give the て te-form of the following Class II verbs.

1. 寝る neru _____

2. 食べる taberu _____

3. 見る miru _____

4. 出る deru _____

5. いる iru _____

C. Finally, give the て te-form of the Class III verbs.

1. する suru _____

2. 来る kuru _____

ANSWER KEY

A: 1. 読んで yonde; 2. 行って itte; 3. 遊んで asonde; 4. 書いて kaite; 5. 話して hanashite; 6. 帰って kaette; 7. 使って tsukatte; 8. 立って tatte; 9. あって atte; 10. 戻って modotte

B: 1. 寝て nete; 2. 食べて tabete; 3. 見て mite; 4. 出て dete; 5. いて ite

C: 1. して shite; 2. 来て kite

Sentence Builder 2

⊙ 11C Sentence Builder 2 (CD 5, Track 17)

アメリカの会社で働いています。

Amerika no kaisha de hataraite imasu.

I am working at a company in the U.S.A.

半年間日本で勉強しますが、またアメリカの会社 (へ/に) 戻ります。

Hantoshikan nihon de benkyooshimasu ga, mata amerika no kaisha (e/ni) modorimasu.

I will study in Japan for half a year but will go back to the company in the U.S.A. again.

どうして日本語を勉強しに日本 (へ/に) 来たんですか。

Dooshite nihongo o benkyooshi ni nihon (e/ni) kita n desu ka.

Why did you come to Japan to study Japanese?

貿易会社で日本の担当なので、仕事で日本語を使うんです。

Booekigaisha de nihon no tantoo na node, shigoto de nihongo o tsukau n desu.

It's that I'm in charge of Japan at my trading company, so I use Japanese a lot for my work.

将来どんな仕事をしますか。

Shoorai donna shigoto o shimasu ka.

What kind of job will you do in the future?

まだ分かりませんけど、たぶんマーケティングの仕事をします。

Mada wakarimasen kedo, tabun maaketingu no shigoto o shimasu.

I don't know yet, but perhaps I will take a marketing job.

どうして東京で働かないんですか。

Dooshite tookyoo de hatarakanai n desu ka.

Why won't you work in Tokyo?

家族が神戸にいますから、神戸で仕事を探すんです。

Kazoku ga koobe ni imasu kara, koobe de shigoto o sagasu n desu.

I have a family in Kobe, so I will look for a job in Kobe.

✎ Sentence Practice 2

Fill in the missing words in each of the following sentences.

1. _____ 働いています。

 _____ hataraite imasu.

 I am working at a company in the U.S.A.

2. 半年間 _____が、またアメリカの会社 (へ/に) 戻ります。

 Hantoshikan _____

 _____ ga, mata amerika no kaisha

(e/ni) modorimasu.

I will study in Japan for half a year but will go back to the company in the U.S.A.

again.

3. どうして＿＿＿＿＿＿＿＿＿＿＿＿＿＿＿ 日本 (へ/に) 来たんですか。

　Dooshite ＿＿＿＿＿＿＿＿＿＿＿＿＿＿＿＿＿＿＿＿

　nihon (e/ni) kita n desu ka.

　Why did you come to Japan to study Japanese?

4. 貿易会社で＿＿＿＿＿＿＿＿＿＿＿なので、仕事で日本語を使うんです。

　Booekigaisha de ＿＿＿＿＿＿＿＿＿＿＿＿＿＿＿＿ na node, shigoto

　de nihongo o tsukau n desu.

　It's that I'm in charge of Japan at my trading company, so I use Japanese a lot for

　my work.

5. 将来 ＿＿＿＿＿＿＿ をしますか。

　Shoorai ＿＿＿＿＿＿＿＿＿＿＿＿＿＿＿＿＿＿ o shimasu ka.

　What kind of job will you do in the future?

6. まだ分かりませんけど、＿＿＿＿＿＿＿マーケティングの仕事をします。

　Mada wakarimasen kedo, ＿＿＿＿＿＿＿＿ maaketingu no shigoto o

　shimasu.

　I don't know yet, but perhaps I will take a marketing job.

7. ＿＿＿＿＿＿＿＿＿東京で働かないんですか。

　＿＿＿＿＿＿＿＿＿＿＿＿ tookyoo de hatarakanai n desu ka.

　Why won't you work in Tokyo?

8. 家族が神戸にいますから、＿＿＿＿＿＿＿＿＿＿＿＿＿ 探すんです。

Kazoku ga koobe ni imasu kara, ＿＿＿＿＿＿＿＿＿＿＿＿＿＿＿＿＿＿＿＿

sagasu n desu.

I have a family in Kobe, so I will look for a job in Kobe.

ANSWER KEY

1. アメリカの会社で Amerika no kaisha de; 2. 日本で勉強します nihon de benkyooshimasu; 3. 日本語を勉強しに nihongo o benkyooshi ni; 4. 日本の担当 nihon no tantoo; 5. どんな仕事 donna shigoto; 6. たぶん tabun; 7. どうして Dooshite; 8. 神戸で仕事を koobe de shigoto o

Grammar Builder 2
THE PROGRESSIVE FORM OF VERBS

▶ 11D Grammar Builder 2 (CD 5, Track 18)

Let's look at the progressive form of Japanese verbs. The progressive form corresponds to the English present progressive tense, as in *I'm eating breakfast now*. In Japanese, the progressive form is made using the て te-form of verbs and います imasu.

山田さんは本を読んでいます。

Yamada san wa hon o yonde imasu.

Mr./Ms. Yamada is reading a book.

高橋さんは今寝ています。

Takahashi san wa ima nete imasu.

Mr./Ms. Takahashi is sleeping now.

小山さんはフランス語を勉強しています。

Koyama san wa furansugo o benkyooshite imasu.

Mr./Ms. Koyama is studying French.

Just like the English present progressive, the Japanese progressive form describes the currently ongoing action. For instance, the examples above describe what Takahashi and Koyama are doing at this moment. Depending on the context, the progressive form can also describe a longer term continuous action. For instance, the last example has two different interpretations: one is that Koyama is studying French at this moment, and the other is that she has been studying French for a certain period of time, say, for three years. Also, the negative form of the ています te imasu form can have two different interpretations—to refer to an ongoing action or to an action that hasn't been completed yet.

Q: 今本を読んでいますか。

Ima hon o yonde imasu ka.

Are you reading a book now?

A: いいえ、読んでいません。

Iie, yonde imasen.

No, I am not reading.

Q: この本は読みましたか。

Kono hon wa yomimashita ka.

Did you read this book?

A: いいえ、まだ読んでいません。

Iie, mada yonde imasen.

No, I haven't read it yet.

As you can see from in the fourth example above, (て/で) いません (te/de) imasen can also describe an action that has not been completed yet, which translates into English as the present perfect.

✎ Work Out 2

Translate the following Japanese sentences into English.

1. 今^{いまなに}何をしていますか。

   Ima nani o shite imasu ka.

   _____

2. すしを食^たべています。

   Sushi o tabete imasu.

   _____

3. 毎日^{まいにち}日本語^{にほんご}を勉強^{べんきょう}しています。

   Mainichi nihongo o benkyooshite imasu.

   _____

4. まだ昼^{ひる}ご飯^{はん}は食^たべていません。

   Mada hirugohan wa tabete imasen.

   _____

5. 田中^{たなか}さんは今^{いま}本^{ほん}を読^よんでいます。

   Tanaka san wa ima hon o yonde imasu.

   _____

6. まだ宿題^{しゅくだい}はしていません。

   Mada shukudai wa shite imasen.

   _____

ANSWER KEY

1. *What are you doing now?* 2. *I am eating sushi.* 3. *I am studying Japanese every day.* 4. *I haven't eaten lunch yet.* 5. *Mr./Ms. Tanaka is reading a book now.* 6. *I haven't done the homework yet.*

✎ Drive It Home

A. What are the て te-form of the following verbs?

1. 話す hanasu _____

2. 食べる taberu _____

3. いる iru _____

4. 行く iku _____

5. ある aru _____

6. 使う tsukau _____

B. Complete the following sentences with the progressive form of the verbs in parentheses.

1. 田中さんは英語を _____ 。(話します)

Tanaka san wa eego o _____. (hanashimasu)

Mr./Ms. Tanaka is speaking English.

2. 田中さんは英語を _____ 。(勉強します)

Tanaka san wa eego o _____. (benkyooshimasu)

Mr./Ms. Tanaka is studying English.

3. 田中さんは英語を _____ 。(読みます)

Tanaka san wa eego o _____. (yomimasu)

Mr./Ms. Tanaka is reading English.

Unit 3 Lesson 11: Sentences   **219**

ANSWER KEY

A: 1. 話して hanashite; 2. 食べて tabete; 3. いて ite; 4. 行って itte; 5. あって atte; 6. 使って tsukatte

B: 1. 話しています hanashite imasu; 2. 勉強しています benkyooshite imasu; 3. 読んでいます yonde imasu

⊕ Culture Note

Japanese company employees tend to have a strong sense of loyalty to the company they work for and bond to their co-workers. For example, sometimes, even if people finish their work, they will remain at the office doing other work to show solidarity with their co-workers who are still finishing their job. Also, co-workers often go to a restaurant or a bar together to have dinner or drinks after work. Even though compared to twenty or so years ago individualism is more respected in the workplace, the traditional tendency to consider the company a big family has not completely disappeared yet.

How Did You Do?

Let's see how you did! By now, you should be able to:

☐ use the て te-form of verbs (Still unsure? Jump back to page 210)

☐ use the progressive form of verbs (Still unsure? Jump back to page 216)

✎ Word Recall

1. 人 nin   a. *counter for mechanical items*

2. 冊 satsu   b. *to attend, to leave*

3. 台 dai   c. *counter for bound objects*

4. 杯 hai   d. *to understand*

5. 枚 mai   e. *counter for long cylindrical objects*

6. 本 hon   f. *counter for animal*

7. 匹 hiki   g. *counter for thin flat objects*

8. 分かります wakarimasu   h. *counter for people*

9. 話します hanashimasu   i. *counter for liquid in cups/glasses/bowls*

10. 出ます demasu   j. *to speak*

ANSWER KEY

1. h; 2. c; 3. a; 4. i; 5. g; 6. e; 7. f; 8. d; 9. j; 10. b

Lesson 12: Conversations

In this lesson you'll learn how to:

☐ use the plain past tense form of verbs

☐ use the expression んです n desu to state or ask for a reason

Conversation 1

12A Conversation 1 (Japanese: CD 5, Track 19; Japanese and English: CD 5, Track 20)

Mr. Martin is talking with his Japanese friend Mr. Yamazaki about their education.

マーティン/Maatin: 山崎さんは日本の大学で勉強しましたか。

Yamazaki san wa nihon no daigaku de benkyooshimashita ka.

山崎/Yamazaki:	はい、日本の大学を卒業しました。それから、大学院に行って、心理学を勉強しました。
	Hai. Nihon no daigaku o sotsugyooshimashita. Sorekara, daigakuin ni itte, shinrigaku o benkyooshimashita.
マーティン/Maatin:	そうですか。
	Soo desu ka.
山崎/Yamazaki:	マーティンさんはアメリカの大学を卒業しましたか。
	Maatin san wa amerika no daigaku o sotsugyooshimashita ka.
マーティン/Maatin:	僕は小学校から高校まではアメリカでしたが、イギリスの大学に入学しました。今はアメリカの大学院で経営学を勉強しています。
	Boku wa shoogakkoo kara kookoo made wa amerika deshita ga, igirisu no daigaku ni nyuugakushimashita. Ima wa amerika no daigakuin de kee-eegaku wo benkyooshite imasu.
山崎/Yamazaki:	MBA ですね。
	MBA desu ne.
マーティン/Maatin:	ええ。一年間日本語を勉強しに日本へ来ましたが、またアメリカの大学院に戻ります。
	Ee. Ichinenkan nihongo o benkyooshi ni nihon e kimashita ga, mata amerika no daigakuin ni modorimasu.
山崎/Yamazaki:	そうですか。MBA のクラスはどうですか。
	Soo desu ka. MBA no kurasu wa doo desu ka.

マーティン/Maatin: レポートや発表がたくさんありますから、とても大変です
よ。グループ発表もありますから、よくミーティングに出
ます。

Repooto ya happyoo ga takusan arimasu kara, totemo
taihen desu yo. Guruupu happyoo mo arimasu kara,
yoku miitingu ni demasu.

山崎/Yamazaki: そうですか。大変ですね。
Soo desu ka. Taihen desu ne.

Martin:	Mr. Yamazaki, did you study at a Japanese university?
Yamazaki:	Yes. I graduated from the Japanese university and then went to graduate school and studied psychology.
Martin:	I see.
Yamazaki:	Mr. Martin, did you graduate from a university in the United States?
Martin:	From elementary school to high school, I went to school in the United States, but I started college (lit., entered the university) in England. Now, I am studying business management at graduate school in the United States.
Yamazaki:	MBA, right?
Martin:	Yes. I came to Japan to study Japanese for one year but will go back to graduate school in the United States again.
Yamazaki:	I see. How are MBA classes?
Martin:	There are many papers, presentations and so on, so it's very hard. There are also group presentations, so I often attend meetings.
Yamazaki:	I see. It's hard, isn't it?

Take It Further

To say (*I*) *know* in Japanese, the ています te imasu form of the verb 知っています shitte imasu is used. So, when asking someone, *Do you know?*, say 知っていますか Shitte imasu ka, instead of 知りますか Shirimasu ka. In case of the negative form, say 知りません Shirimasen (*I don't know*).

✎ Conversation Practice 1

Fill in the blanks in the following sentences with the missing words. If you're unsure of the answer, listen to the conversation one more time.

1. 山崎さんは日本の大学を _____。

   Yamazaki san wa nihon no daigaku o _____.

2. 山崎さんは大学院で_____ を勉強しました。

   Yamazaki san wa daigakuin de _____ o
   benkyooshimashita.

3. マーティンさんはアメリカの大学院で _____ を勉強しています。

   Maatin san wa amerika no daigakuin de _____ o
   benkyooshite imasu.

4. マーティンさんは _____ 日本語を勉強しに日本へ来ました。

   Maatin san wa _____ nihongo o benkyooshi ni
   nihon e kimashita.

5. MBA のクラスでグループ発表^{はっぴょう}がありますから、マーティンさんはよく

_____ に出^でます。

MBA no kurasu de guruupu happyoo ga arimasu kara, Maatin san wa yoku

_____ **ni demasu.**

ANSWER KEY

1. 卒業^{そつぎょう}しました sotsugyooshimashita; 2. 心理学^{しんりがく} shinrigaku; 3. 経営学^{けいえいがく} kee-eegaku; 4. 一年間^{いちねんかん} ichinenkan; 5. ミーティング miitingu

Grammar Builder 1
THE PLAIN PAST TENSE FORM OF VERBS

▶ 12B Grammar Builder 1 (CD 5, Track 21)

The plain non-past tense form of verbs was introduced in Lesson 9. First, let's look at the plain past tense form of Class I verbs.

CLASS I				
Dictionary form	Non-past negative	て Te-form	Past affirmative	Past negative
話^{はな}す hanasu (to speak)	話^{はな}さない hanasanai	話^{はな}して hanashite	話^{はな}した hanashita	話^{はな}さなかった hanasanakatta
読^よむ yomu (to read)	読^よまない yomanai	読^よんで yonde	読^よんだ yonda	読^よまなかった yomanakatta
行^いく iku (to go)	行^いかない ikanai	行^いって itte	行^いった itta	行^いかなかった ikanakatta

CLASS I				
Dictionary form	Non-past negative	て Te-form	Past affirmative	Past negative
ある aru (to have, there is)	ない nai	あって atte	あった atta	なかった nakatta

As you can see in the chart, the plain past affirmative form of Class I verbs has the same pattern as the て te-form. Since you are already familiar with the te-form of verbs, you just need to remember to replace て te/で de of the て te-form with た ta/だ da in order to get the plain past affirmative form. As for the plain past negative form, just replace the ない nai ending of the plain non-past negative form with the ending なかった nakatta. Next, let's look at the plain past tense form of Class II verbs.

CLASS II				
Dictionary form	Non-past negative	て Te-form	Past affirmative	Past negative
食べる taberu (to eat)	食べない tabenai	食べて tabete	食べた tabeta	食べなかった tabenakatta
寝る neru (to sleep)	寝ない nenai	寝て nete	寝た neta	寝なかった nenakatta
見る miru (to see)	見ない minai	見て mite	見た mita	見なかった minakatta
いる iru (to be)	いない inai	いて ite	いた ita	いなかった inakatta

As shown in the chart, you just need to drop る ru on the dictionary form and attach た ta in order to get the plain past affirmative form. For the plain past negative form, just like in the case of Class I verbs, you just need to change ない nai of the plain non-past negative form to なかった nakatta. Finally, let's look at the plain past form of Class III verbs.

CLASS III				
Dictionary form	Non-past negative	て Te-form	Past affirmative	Past negative
する suru (to do)	しない shinai	して shite	した shita	しなかった shinakatta
来る kuru (to come)	来ない konai	来て kite	来た kita	来なかった konakatta

It is best to just memorize the conjugation of Class III verbs because there are only two verbs in this class. Note that you just need to replace て te in the て te-form of the verbs with た ta in order to get their plain past tense form. Also, as for the plain past negative form, just like Class I and II verbs, you just need to change ない nai of the plain non-past negative form to なかった nakatta.

✎ Work Out 1

Give the plain past tense form of the following verbs.

Ex. 話す hanasu → 話した hanashita
話さない hanasanai → 話さなかった hanasanakatta

1. 食べる taberu _____

2. 読まない yomanai _____

3. する suru _____

4. 来ない konai _____

5. 書く kaku _____

6. 使わない tsukawanai _____

7. 出る deru _____

8. 帰る kaeru _____

9. いない inai _____

10. ある aru _____

ANSWER KEY

1. 食べた tabeta; 2. 読まなかった yomanakatta; 3. した shita; 4. 来なかった konakatta; 5. 書いた kaita; 6. 使わなかった tsukawanakatta; 7. 出た deta; 8. 帰った kaetta; 9. いなかった inakatta; 10. あった atta

Conversation 2

▶ 12C Conversation 2 (Japanese: CD 5, Track 22; Japanese and English: CD 5, Track 23)

Ms. Lee and her Japanese friend Ms. Kawamura are talking about their work.

川村/Kawamura:　リーさんはアメリカの会社で働いていますか。

Rii san wa amerika no kaisha de hataraite imasu ka.

リー/Rii:　ええ、貿易会社で働いています。私は半年間日本で日本語を勉強しますが、またアメリカの会社に戻ります。

Ee, booekigaisha de hataraite imasu. Watashi wa hantoshikan nihon de nihongo o benkyooshimasu ga, mata amerika no kaisha ni modorimasu.

川村/Kawamura:　そうですか。どうして日本語を勉強しに来たんですか。

Soo desu ka. Dooshite nihongo o benkyooshi ni kita n desu ka.

リー/Rii: 貿易会社で日本の担当なので、仕事で日本語を使うんです。

Booekigaisha de nihon no tantoo na node, shigoto de nihongo o tsukau n desu.

川村/Kawamura: そうですか。

Soo desu ka.

リー/Rii: 川村さんはまだ大学生ですけど、将来どんな仕事をしますか。

Kawamura san wa mada daigakusee desu kedo, shoorai donna shigoto o shimasu ka.

川村/Kawamura: まだ分かりませんけど、たぶんマーケティングの仕事をします。

Mada wakarimasen kedo, tabun maaketingu no shigoto o shimasu.

リー/Rii: 東京で働きますか。

Tookyoo de hatarakimasu ka.

川村/Kawamura: いいえ。

Iie.

リー/Rii: どうして東京で働かないんですか。

Dooshite tookyoo de hatarakanai n desu ka.

川村/Kawamura: 家族が神戸にいますから、神戸で仕事を探すんです。

Kazoku ga koobe ni imasu kara, koobe de shigoto o sagasu n desu.

リー/Rii: そうですか。

Soo desu ka.

Kawamura: *Ms. Lee, are you working at a company in the U.S.A.?*

Lee: *Yes, I'm working at a trading company. I will study Japanese in Japan for half a year, but will go back to the company in the U.S.A. again.*

Unit 3 Lesson 12: Conversations　**229**

Kawamura:	I see. Why did you come to study Japanese?
Lee:	Because I'm in charge of Japan at my trading company, so I use Japanese for my work.
Kawamura:	I see.
Lee:	Ms. Kawamura, you are still a college student, but what kind of work will you do in the future?
Kawamura:	I don't know yet, but perhaps I will take a marketing job.
Lee:	Will you work in Tokyo?
Kawamura:	No.
Lee:	Why won't you work in Tokyo?
Kawamura:	Because I have a family in Kobe, so I will look for a job in Kobe.
Lee:	I see.

Take It Further

In a casual setting, such as when you are talking with your family and close friends, you will use the plain form instead of the ます masu-form of verbs. Also, when asking questions in informal speech, you don't usually attach the question marker か ka to the end of the questions; instead, ask a question using rising intonation. For example, if you want to ask your close friend if he/she wants to eat something, you will just say 食べる？ Taberu? with a rising intonation.

When 会社 kaisha (company) is combined with another word such as 貿易 booeki (trading) or 製薬 seeyaku (pharmaceutical), it becomes 会社 gaisha. So, a trading company is 貿易会社 booekigaisha, and a pharmaceutical company is 製薬会社 seeyakugaisha.

✎ Conversation Practice 2

Fill in the blanks in the following sentences with the missing words. If you're unsure of the answer, listen to the conversation one more time.

1. リーさんは ＿＿＿＿＿＿＿＿＿＿の会社で働いています。

   Rii san wa ＿＿＿＿＿＿＿＿＿＿ no kaisha de hataraite imasu.

2. リーさんはで半年間日本で ＿＿＿＿＿＿＿＿＿＿ します。

   Rii san wa hantoshikan nihon de ＿＿＿＿＿＿＿＿＿＿

   ＿＿＿＿＿＿＿＿＿＿ shimasu.

3. リーさんは貿易会社で日本の ＿＿＿＿＿＿＿＿＿＿ です。

   Rii san wa booekigaisha de nihon no ＿＿＿＿＿＿＿＿＿＿ desu.

4. 川村さんはたぶん ＿＿＿＿＿＿＿＿＿＿ の仕事をします。

   Kawamura san wa tabun ＿＿＿＿＿＿＿＿＿＿ no shigoto o shimasu.

5. 川村さんは神戸で仕事を ＿＿＿＿＿＿＿＿＿＿。

   Kawamura san wa koobe de shigoto o ＿＿＿＿＿＿＿＿＿＿.

ANSWER KEY
1. アメリカ amerika; 2. 日本語を勉強 nihongo o benkyoo; 3. 担当 tantoo; 4. マーケティング maaketingu; 5. 探します sagashimasu

Grammar Builder 2
THE EXPRESSION んです N DESU

▶ 12D Grammar Builder 2 (CD 5, Track 24)

Let's learn about the expression んです n desu. It is a colloquial expression used when stating a reason or asking for an explanation. Remember that the plain form of verbs appears before んです n desu and that んです n desu always remains the same—that is, んです n desu doesn't change its form for tense or affirmative/negative distinction. These features are expressed in the main verb preceding んです n desu.

A: どうして日本へ行くんですか。

Dooshite nihon e iku n desu ka.

Why do you go to Japan?

B: 日本語を勉強するんです。

Nihongo o benkyoosuru n desu.

Because I will study Japanese.

A: どうして大学へ来なかったんですか。

Dooshite daigaku e konakatta n desu ka.

Why didn't you come to the university?

B: アメリカから友達が来たんです。

Amerika kara tomodachi ga kita n desu.

Because my friend(s) came from the U.S.A.

Note that you can ask for a reason or explanation without using んです n desu, but if you use it, the speaker's desire to be given an explanation will be emphasized. Compare the following sentences.

どうして大学へ来ませんでしたか。

Dooshite daigaku e kimasen deshita ka.

Why didn't you come to the university?

どうして大学へ来なかったんですか。

Dooshite daigaku e konakatta n desu ka.

Why didn't you come to the university?

Since there's no English equivalent for んです **n desu**, these sentences have the same English translation. んです **n desu** expresses a nuance of meaning. For instance, suppose a teacher is asking a student for a reason of his/her absence. If a teacher asks for a reason using んです **n desu**, it sounds like he/she cares about a student and really wants to know the reason for his or her absence.

✎ Work Out 2

A. Give the plain form counterpart of the following ます **masu**-form verbs.

Ex. 見ます **mimasu** (*non-past/affirmative*) → 見る **miru**

読みました **yomimashita** (*past/affirmative*) → 読んだ **yonda**

1. 食べました **tabemashita** (*non-past/affirmative*) _____

2. 書きました **kakimashita** (*past/affirmative*) _____

3. 来ませんでした **kimasen deshita** (*past/negative*) _____

4. 出ません **demasen** (*non-past/negative*) _____

5. 寝ました **nemashita** (*past/affirmative*) _____

6. しました **shimashita** (*past/affirmative*) _____

7. 読みませんでした **yomimasen deshita** (*past/negative*) _____

8. 来ました **kimashita** (*past/affirmative*) _____

9. 見ません **mimasen** (*non-past/negative*) _____

10. ある aru *(non-past/negative)* _____

B. Change the verbs given in parentheses to their appropriate form (if necessary) to complete each sentence.

1. *A:* どうしてアメリカ (へ/に) _____ んですか。(行く)

   Dooshite amerika (e/ni) _____ n desu ka. (iku)

   Why did you go to the U.S.A.?

   B: 英語を _____ んです。(勉強する)

   Eego o _____ n desu. (benkyoosuru)

   Because I studied English.

2. *A:* どうして _____ んですか。(寝る)

   Dooshite _____ n desu ka. (neru)

   Why don't you go to bed?

   B: 宿題がたくさん _____ んです。(ある)

   Shukudai ga takusan _____ n desu. (aru)

   Because there is a lot of homework.

3. *A:* どうしてスペイン語を _____ んですか。(話す)

   Dooshite supeingo o _____ n desu ka. (hanasu)

   Why do you speak Spanish?

   B: スペインに十年 _____ んです。(いる)

   Supein ni juunen _____ n desu. (iru)

   Because I was in Spain for ten years.

4. *A:* どうしてテレビを _____ んですか。(見る)

Dooshite terebi o _____ n desu ka. (miru)

Why don't you watch T.V.?

B: 日本語が _____ んです。(分かる)

Nihongo ga _____ n desu. (wakaru)

Because I don't understand Japanese.

5. *A:* どうしてセミナーに _____ んですか。(出る)

Dooshite seminaa ni _____ n desu ka. (deru)

Why didn't you attend the seminar?

B: メキシコから家族が _____ んです。(来る)

Mekishiko kara kazoku ga _____ n desu. (kuru)

Because my family came from Mexico.

ANSWER KEY

A: 1. 食べる taberu; 2. 書いた kaita; 3. 来なかった konakatta; 4. 出ない denai; 5. 寝た neta; 6. した shita; 7. 読まなかった yomanakatta; 8. 来た kita; 9. 見ない minai; 10. ない nai
B: 1. 行った itta, 勉強した benkyooshita; 2. 寝ない nenai, ある aru; 3. 話す hanasu, いた ita; 4. 見ない minai, 分からない wakaranai; 5. 出なかった denakatta, 来た kita

✎ Drive It Home

A. Convert each of the following verbs into the form specified in parentheses.

1. 見ます mimasu (*plain non-past/affirmative*) _____

2. 見ます mimasu (*plain non-past/negative*) _____

3. 見ます mimasu (*plain past/affirmative*) _____

4. 見ます mimasu (*plain past/negative*) _____

5. 勉強します benkyooshimasu *(plain non-past/affirmative)* _____

6. 勉強します benkyooshimasu *(plain non-past/negative)* _____

7. 勉強します benkyooshimasu *(plain past/affirmative)* _____

8. 勉強します benkyooshimasu *(plain past/negative)* _____

B. Complete the following sentences by inserting the んです n desu form of verbs.

1. *A:*どうして日本へ _____ か。(行く)

   Dooshite nihon e _____ **ka. (iku)**

   Why are you going to Japan?

2. *B:* 日本語を _____。(勉強する)

   Nihongo o _____.

   (benkyoosuru)

   Because I'm going to study Japanese.

3. *A:*どうしてアメリカへ _____ か。(行く)

   Dooshite amerika e _____ **ka. (iku)**

   Why are you going to the U.S.A.?

4. *B:* 英語を _____。(勉強する)

   Eego o _____. **(benkyoosuru)**

   Because I'm going to study English.

ANSWER KEY

A: 1. 見る miru; 2. 見ない minai; 3. 見た mita; 4. 見なかった minakatta; 5. 勉強する benkyoosuru;
6. 勉強しない benkyooshinai; 7. 勉強した benkyooshita; 8.勉強しなかった benkyooshinakatta
B: 1. 行くんです iku n desu, 勉強するんです benkyoosuru n desu; 2. 行くんです iku n desu, 勉強するんです benkyoosuru n desu

Tip!

A good way to memorize the て te-form of Class I and Class III verbs is to remember it while singing a song, such as *Mary Had a Little Lamb*. Try singing the following to the tune of the song: く-いて ku-ite ぐ-いで gu-ide う u, つ tsu, る-って ru-tte む mu, ぬ nu, ぶ-んで bu-nde す su, する-して suru-shite 来る-来て kuru-kite 行く-行って iku-itte. For instance, く-いて ku-ite means that if the dictionary form of Class I verbs ends with く ku, like 書く kaku (*to write*) and 聞く kiku (*to listen*), you need to replace く ku with いて ite in order to get the て te-form of the verbs, 書いて kaite and 聞いて kiite respectively. Likewise, す su, する-して suru-shite means that in the case of Class I verbs, whose dictionary forms end in す su, like 話す hanasu (*to speak*), and the Class III verb する suru (*to do*), you replace す su and する suru with して shite in order to get the て te-form of the verbs. So, in the case of 話す hanasu and する suru, you get 話して hanashite and して shite respectively.

How Did You Do?

Let's see how you did! By now, you should be able to:

☐ use the plain past tense form of verbs (Still unsure? Jump back to page 225)

☐ use the expression んです n desu to state or ask for a reason (Still unsure? Jump back to page 231)

✎ Word Recall

1. 電気技師 denkigishi   a. *enjoyable*

2. 冷蔵庫 reezooko   b. *bank clerk*

3. 法律 hooritsu   c. *son (someone else's)*

4. 大学 daigaku   d. *lawyer*

5. 階段 kaidan   e. *refrigerator*

6. 洗濯機 sentakuki   f. *stairs*

7. 銀行員 ginkooin   g. *washing machine*

8. 楽しい tanoshii   h. *law*

9. 息子さん musukosan   i. *electrical engineer*

10. 弁護士 bengoshi   j. *university, college*

ANSWER KEY

1. i; 2. e; 3. h; 4. j; 5. f; 6. g; 7. b; 8. a; 9. c; 10. d

Don't forget to practice and reinforce what you've learned by visiting **www.livinglanguage.com/languagelab** for flashcards, games, and quizzes for Unit 3!

Unit 3 Essentials

Vocabulary Essentials

Test your knowledge of the key material in this unit by filling in the blanks in the following charts. Once you've completed these pages, you'll have tested your retention, and you'll have your own reference for the most essential vocabulary.

SCHOOL & WORK

	kindergarten
	elementary school
	graduate school
	graduate school student
	library
	psychology
	business management
	report
	presentation
	group presentation
	meeting
	paper
	pencil
	ballpoint pen
	trading company
	office
	law firm

	marketing
	facsimile
	copy
	word processor

TRANSPORTATION

	train
	subway
	bus
	Japanese bullet train
	airplane

ADJECTIVES & ADVERBS

	for a year
	for half a year
	perhaps
	many, much
	not so often/much
	well
	yet, still

VERBS

	to study
	to enter school
	to graduate

	to go
	to come
	to go back, to return
	to return
	to ride, to get on
	to get off
	to borrow
	to lend
	to do
	to use
	to understand
	to work
	to look for
	to study abroad

Grammar Essentials

Here is a reference of the key grammar that was covered in Unit 3. Make sure you understand the summary and can use all of the grammar it covers.

THE PLAIN NON-PAST TENSE OF VERBS

CLASS I		CLASS II		CLASS III	
Non-past affirmative	Non-past negative	Non-past affirmative	Non-past negative	Non-past affirmative	Non-past negative
話す hanasu	話さない hanasanai	食べる taberu	食べない tabenai	する suru	しない shinai

CLASS I		CLASS II		CLASS III	
読む yomu	読まない yomanai	寝る neru	寝ない nenai	来る kuru	来ない konai
行く iku	行かない ikanai	見る miru	見ない minai		
買う kau	買わない kawanai	教える oshieru	教えない oshienai		
ある aru	ない nai	いる iru	いない inai		

THE PLAIN PAST TENSE OF VERBS

CLASS I				
Dictionary form	Non-past negative	て Te-form	Past affirmative	Past negative
話す hanasu (to speak)	話さない hanasanai	話して hanashite	話した hanashita	話さなかった hanasanakatta
読む yomu (to read)	読まない yomanai	読んで yonde	読んだ yonda	読まなかった yomanakatta
行く iku (to go)	行かない ikanai	行って itte	行った itta	行かなかった ikanakatta
ある aru (to have, there is)	ない nai	あって atte	あった atta	なかった nakatta

CLASS II

Dictionary form	Non-past negative	て Te-form	Past affirmative	Past negative
食べる taberu (to eat)	食べない tabenai	食べて tabete	食べた tabeta	食べなかった tabenakatta
寝る neru (to sleep)	寝ない nenai	寝て nete	寝た neta	寝なかった nenakatta
見る miru (to see)	見ない minai	見て mite	見た mita	見なかった minakatta
いる iru (to be)	いない inai	いて ite	いた ita	いなかった inakatta

CLASS III

Dictionary form	Non-past negative	て Te-form	Past affirmative	Past negative
する suru (to do)	しない shinai	して shite	した shita	しなかった shinakatta
来る kuru (to come)	来ない konai	来て kite	来た kita	来なかった konakatta

THE て TE-FORM OF VERBS

CLASS I		CLASS II		CLASS III	
Dictionary form	て *Te-form*	*Dictionary form*	て *Te-form*	*Dictionary form*	て *Te-form*
話す hanasu	話して hanashite	食べる taberu	食べて tabete	する suru	して shite
読む yomu	読んで yonde	寝る neru	寝て nete	来る kuru	来て kite
行く iku	行って itte	見る miru	見て mite		
ある aru	あって atte	いる iru	いて ite		

THE PROGRESSIVE FORM OF VERBS

The て te-form of verbs + います imasu

AFFIRMATIVE		
山田さんは本を読んでいます。	Yamada san wa hon o yonde imasu.	*Mr./Ms. Yamada is reading a book.*
NEGATIVE 1		
山田さんは本は読んでいません。	Yamada san wa hon wa yonde imasen.	*Mr./Ms. Yamada is not reading a book. or Mr./Ms. Yamada hasn't read the book.*
NEGATIVE 2		
山田さんはまだ本は読んでいません。	Yamada san wa mada hon wa yonde imasen.	*Mr./Ms. Yamada hasn't read the book yet.*

Intermediate Japanese

THE EXPRESSION んです N DESU

The plain form of verbs + んです n desu

Stating a reason or asking for a reason or an explanation

どうして日本へ行くんですか。	Dooshite nihon e iku n desu ka.	*Why do you go to Japan?*
日本語を勉強するんです。	Nihongo o benkyoosuru n desu.	*It's that I will study Japanese.*

PARTICLES

へ e

[PLACE]へ 行きます、来ます、帰ります、戻ります, etc.

[PLACE] e ikimasu, kimasu, kaerimasu, modorimasu, etc.

to go, to come, to go back, to return, etc., to [PLACE]

毎日学校へ行きます。	Mainichi gakkoo e ikimasu.	*I go to school every day.*

に ni

[PLACE]に行きます、来ます、帰ります、戻ります, etc.

[PLACE] ni ikimasu, kimasu, kaerimasu, modorimasu, etc.

to go, to come, to go back, to return, etc., to [PLACE]

毎日学校に行きます。	Mainichi gakkoo ni ikimasu.	*I go to school every day.*

Conjunctive form of the verb + に ni

(in order) to ...

日本語を勉強しに日本 (へ/に) 来ました。	Nihongo o benkyooshi ni nihon (e/ni) kimashita.	*I came to Japan to study Japanese.*

日本 (へ/に) 日本語を勉強しに来ました。	Nihon (e/ni) nihongo o benkyooshi ni kimashita.	*I came to Japan to study Japanese.*

で de

[PLACE] で de+ action verb

action verb + *at/in* [PLACE]

大学でテニスをします。	Daigaku de tenisu o shimasu.	*I play tennis at the university.*

[MEANS/INSTRUMENT] で de+ action verb

action verb + *by/with* [MEANS/INSTRUMENT]

バスで学校 (へ/に) 行きます。	Basu de gakkoo (e/ni) ikimasu.	*I go to school by bus.*
ペンで手紙を書きます。	Pen de tegami o kakimasu.	*I write a letter with a pen.*
日本語で話します。	Nihongo de hanashimasu.	*I speak in Japanese.*

Unit 3 Quiz

A. Convert the following verbs into their plain forms.

Ex. 食^たべます tabemasu → 食^たべる taberu
食^たべません tabemasen → 食^たべない tabenai

1. します shimasu _____

2. 寝^ねません nemasen _____

3. 話^{はな}します hanashimasu _____

4. 読^よみません yomimasen _____

B. Fill in the blanks with the particles へ e, に ni, or で de.

1. 大学^{だいがく} _____ 勉強^{べんきょう}します。

   Daigaku _____ benkyooshimasu.

   I study at a university.

2. 大学^{だいがく} _____行^いきます。

   Daigaku _____ ikimasu.

   I go to a university.

3. ミーティング _____出^でます。

   Miitingu _____ demasu.

   I attend a meeting.

4. 日本語を勉強し＿＿＿＿＿ 日本 ＿＿＿＿＿ 来ました。

Nihongo o benkyooshi ＿＿＿＿＿ nihon ＿＿＿＿＿ kimashita.

I came to Japan to study Japanese.

C. Give the て te-form of the following verbs.

1. する suru ＿＿＿

2. 見る miru ＿＿＿

3. 来る kuru ＿＿＿

4. ある aru ＿＿＿

D. Complete the following sentences by inserting verbs in the appropriate form based on the English translation.

1. 田中さんは英語を ＿＿＿＿＿＿＿＿＿＿＿＿＿＿＿＿。

Tanaka san wa eego o ＿＿＿＿＿＿＿＿＿＿＿＿＿＿＿＿＿＿＿＿＿＿＿＿＿＿＿.

Mr./Ms. Tanaka is speaking English.

2. 川村さんは ＿＿＿＿＿＿＿＿＿＿＿＿＿＿。

Kawamura san wa ＿＿＿＿＿＿＿＿＿＿＿＿＿＿＿＿＿＿＿＿＿.

Mr./Ms. Kawamura is sleeping.

3. 渡辺さんはまだケーキは ＿＿＿＿＿＿＿＿＿＿＿＿＿＿＿＿＿＿＿。

Watanabe san wa mada keeki wa ＿＿＿＿＿＿＿＿＿＿＿＿＿＿＿＿＿＿＿＿＿＿＿.

Mr./Ms. Watanabe hasn't eaten the cake yet.

E. Convert each of the following verbs into the specified form.

1. 行きます ikimasu (*plain non-past/affirmative*) _____

2. います imasu (*plain non-past/negative*) _____

3. 働きます hatarakimasu (*plain past/affirmative*) _____

4. 食べます tabemasu (*plain past/negative*) _____

F. Complete the following sentences by inserting the んです n desu form of verbs.

1. *A:*どうしてへ 日本へ _____ か。(行く) Dooshite nihon e _____

   _____ ka. (iku)

   Why are you going to Japan?

   B: 日本語を _____ 。(勉強する) Nihongo o

   _____. (benkyoosuru)

   It's that I'm going to study Japanese.

ANSWER KEY

A. 1. する suru; 2. 寝ない nenai; 3. 話す hanasu; 4. 読まない yomanai

B. 1. で de; 2. へ e or に ni; 3. に ni; 4. に ni, へ e or に ni

C. 1. して shite; 2. 見て mite; 3. 来て kite; 4. あって atte

D. 1. 話しています hanashite imasu; 2. 寝ています nete imasu; 3. 食べていません tabete imasen

E. 1. 行く iku; 2. いない inai; 3. 働いた hataraita; 4. 食べなかった tabenakatta

F. 1. 行くんです iku n desu, 勉強するんです benkyoosuru n desu

How Did You Do?

Give yourself a point for every correct answer, then use the following key to tell whether you're ready to move on:

0-7 points: It's probably a good idea to go back through the lesson again. You may be moving too quickly, or there may be too much "down time" between your contact with Japanese. Remember that it's better to spend 30 minutes with Japanese three or four times a week than it is to spend two or three hours just once a week. Find a pace that's comfortable for you, and spread your contact hours out as much as you can.

8-12 points: You would benefit from a review before moving on. Go back and spend a little more time on the specific points that gave you trouble. Re-read the Grammar Builder sections that were difficult, and do the work out one more time. Don't forget about the online supplemental practice material, either. Go to **www.livinglanguage.com/languagelab** for games and quizzes that will reinforce the material from this unit.

13-17 points: Good job! There are just a few points that you could consider reviewing before moving on. If you haven't worked with the games and quizzes on **www.livinglanguage.com/languagelab**, please give them a try.

18-20 points: Great! You're ready to move on to the next unit.

points

Unit 4:
Using the Telephone and Making Appointments

Welcome to Unit 4! In this unit you will learn how to make an appointment on the phone. Key expressions used in telephone conversations and when making an appointment, such as telling time and date or making a request, will be introduced. By the end of the unit, you'll be able to:

☐ use key vocabulary related to making an appointment

☐ tell time and date

☐ express when things happen using the particle に ni

☐ express probability and conjecture

☐ make requests

☐ use some basic polite expressions

☐ express wants and desires

☐ use the *when*-clause

Telling time, days of the week and months

Expressing probability and conjecture—
でしょう deshoo

The particle に ni

Expressing probability and conj
かもしれません kamoshirema

Lesson 13: Words

☐ use key vocabulary related to making an appointment

☐ tell time and date

☐ express when things happen using the particle に ni

Word Builder 1

▶ 13A Word Builder 1 (CD 5, Track 25)

びょういん 美容院	biyooin	beauty salon
びようし 美容師	biyooshi	hair dresser
よやく 予約	yoyaku	reservation, appointment
カット	katto	haircut
カラー	karaa	hair dye, hair color
パーマ	paama	perm
でんわばんごう (お)電話番号	(o)denwabangoo (polite with o)	telephone number
ごがつ 五月	gogatsu	May
みっか 三日	mikka	third (day of the month)
よろしい	yoroshii	good (polite)
しばらく	shibaraku	for a while
だいじょうぶ 大丈夫	daijoobu	all right
たいへん 大変	taihen	hard, very

いっぱい 一杯	ippai	*full*
でんわ でんわ 電話します、電話する	denwashimasu, denwasuru	*to make a phone call*
よやく よやく 予約します、予約する	yoyakushimasu, yoyakusuru	*to make a reservation, to make an appointment*
おく おく 遅れます、遅れる	okuremasu, okureru	*to be late*
かかります、かかる	kakarimasu, kakaru	*to take (time)*

Take It Further

Numbers in time and dates are commonly written in Arabic numerals (e.g. 1, 2, 3...etc.) instead of kanji (e.g. 一、二、三 ... etc.). Thus, you'll see time written as, for example, 5 時 9 分 goji kyuufun, 午前 8 時半 gozen hachiji han, 7 月 23 日 shichigatsu nijuusannichi, 12 月 20 日 juunigatsu hatsuka etc. In *Complete Japanese*, however, we'll continue to use kanji instead of Arabic numerals in these lessons so that you'll have more practice with the characters.

✎ Word Practice 1
Translate the following words into Japanese.

1. *beauty salon* _____

2. *hair dresser* _____

3. *reservation, appointment* _____

4. *haircut* _____

5. *perm* _____

Telling time, days of the week and months

Expressing probability and conjecture—
でしょう deshoo

The particle に ni

Expressing probability and conj
かもしれません kamoshirema

6. *telephone number* _____

7. *good (polite)* _____

8. *for a while* _____

9. *all right* _____

10. *full* _____

ANSWER KEY

1. 美容院 biyooin; 2. 美容師 biyooshi; 3. 予約 yoyaku; 4. カット katto; 5. パーマ paama;
6. (お)電話番号 (o)denwabangoo; 7. よろしい yoroshii; 8. しばらく shibaraku; 9. 大丈夫 daijoobu;
10. 一杯 ippai

Grammar Builder 1
TELLING TIME, DAYS OF THE WEEK AND MONTHS

▶ 13B Grammar Builder 1 (CD 5, Track 26)

First, let's review how to ask and tell time.

今何時ですか。

Ima nanji desu ka.

What time is it now?

九時二十五分です。

Kuji nijuugofun desu.

It's nine twenty-five.

Let's review how to say *one o'clock* to *twelve o'clock* by looking at the chart below.
Remember that there are a few variations in the numbers when used to tell time.

For instance, *four o'clock* is よじ **yoji**, which is modified from the number four: 四 **yon**.

one o'clock	two o'clock	three o'clock	four o'clock	five o'clock	six o'clock
いちじ 一時 ichiji	にじ 二時 niji	さんじ 三時 sanji	よじ 四時 yoji	ごじ 五時 goji	ろくじ 六時 rokuji
seven o'clock	eight o'clock	nine o'clock	ten o'clock	eleven o'clock	twelve o'clock
しちじ 七時 shichiji	はちじ 八時 hachiji	くじ 九時 kuji	じゅうじ 十時 juuji	じゅういちじ 十一時 juuichiji	じゅうにじ 十二時 juuniji

Next, let's review how to say the minutes. Please remind yourself that *minute* can be 分 **fun** or 分 **pun** depending on what number comes before it. Numbers also sometimes assigned special pronunciations. For instance, *one minute* is いっぷん **ippun**.

one minute	two minutes	three minutes	four minutes	five minutes
いっぷん 一分 ippun	にふん 二分 nifun	さんぷん 三分 sanpun	よんぷん 四分 yonpun or よんふん 四分 yonfun	ごふん 五分 gofun
six minutes	seven minutes	eight minutes	nine minutes	ten minutes
ろっぷん 六分 roppun	ななふん 七分 nanafun	はっぷん 八分 happun or はちふん 八分 hachifun	きゅうふん 九分 kyuufun	じゅっぷん 十分 juppun

It is important to note that *thirty minutes past the hour* can be 三十分 さんじゅっぷん sanjuppun or 半 はん han. (Think of this as being the same as how you might say *one thirty* or half *past one* in English.) So, for instance, 1:30 is 一時三十分 ichiji sanjuppun or 一時半 ichiji han.

To distinguish between *a.m.* and *p.m.*, use 午前 gozen for *a.m.* and 午後 gogo for *p.m.* So, *1:30 a.m.* is 午前一時半 gozen ichiji han, and *1:30 p.m.* is 午後一時半 gogo ichiji han. Note the position of 午前 gozen and 午後 gogo. Unlike English *a.m.* and *p.m.*, 午前 gozen and 午後 gogo appear before the time. It is also important to remember that 何時 nanji corresponds to the English *what time*, and 何分 nanpun corresponds to the English *what minute(s)*.

Now, let's learn how to ask and tell the date.

今日は何月何日ですか。

Kyoo wa nangatsu nannichi desu ka.

What month and what day is it today?

五月三日です。

Gogatsu mikka desu.

It is May 3rd.

As shown in the examples above, you just need to attach 月 gatsu to a number in order to tell months. *April*, *July*, and *September* require a special attention because they are 四月 shigatsu, 七月 shichigatsu, and 九月 kugatsu.

一月 ichigatsu	January
二月 nigatsu	February
三月 sangatsu	March
四月 shigatsu	April

五月 gogatsu	*May*
六月 rokugatsu	*June*
七月 shichigatsu	*July*
八月 hachigatsu	*August*
九月 kugatsu	*September*
十月 juugatsu	*October*
十一月 juuichigatsu	*November*
十二月 juunigatsu	*December*

To say the day of the month, you have to memorize the terms from the *first day of the month* to *tenth day of the month*.

一日 tsuitachi	*first*
二日 futsuka	*second*
三日 mikka	*third*
四日 yokka	*fourth*
五日 itsuka	*fifth*
六日 muika	*sixth*
七日 nanoka	*seventh*
八日 yooka	*eighth*
九日 kokonoka	*ninth*
十日 tooka	*tenth*

From the eleventh day of the month on, 日 nichi is attached to a number, as in 十一日 juuichinichi (*eleventh day*), 二十三日 nijuusannichi (*twenty-*

Telling time, days of the week
and months

Expressing probability and conjecture—
でしょう deshoo

The particle に ni

Expressing probability and con
かもしれません kamoshirema

さんじゅういちにち
third day) or 三十一日 sanjuuichinichi (thirty-first day), but the numbers

fourteenth, twentieth, and twenty-fourth require special attention. Fourteenth is

じゅうよっか   は つ か   にじゅうよっか
十四日 juuyokka, twentieth is 二十日 hatsuka, and twenty-fourth is 二十四日

nijuuyokka. It is also important to remember that 何月 nangatsu corresponds to
                                           なんがつ
                                   なんにち
English what month, and 何日 nannichi corresponds to English what day.

✎ Work Out 1

A. Tell the following times in Japanese.

1. *7:10* _____

2. *8:05 a.m.* _____

3. *12:30 p.m.* _____

4. *4:20* _____

5. *6:48* _____

6. *9:16* _____

7. *11:55* _____

8. *3:29* _____

9. *1:11 a.m.* _____

10. *2:53 p.m.* _____

B. Give the following dates in Japanese.

1. *January 1st* _____

2. *December 31st* _____

3. *April 3rd* _____

4. *May 5th* _____

5. *November 20th* _____

6. *February 14th* _____

7. *June 6th* _____

8. *August 10th* _____

9. *March 7th* _____

10. *September 8th* _____

11. *July 4th* _____

12. *October 9th* _____

ANSWER KEY

A: 1. 七時十分 shichiji juppun; 2. 午前八時五分 gozen hachiji gofun; 3. 午後十二時三十分 gogo juuniji sanjuppun or 午後十二時半 gogo juuniji han; 4. 四時二十分 yoji nijuppun; 5. 六時四十八分 rokuji yonjuuhappun or 六時四十八分 yonjuuhachifun; 6. 九時十六分 kuji juuroppun; 7. 十一時五十五分 juuichiji gojuugofun; 8. 三時二十九分 sanji nijuukyuufun; 9. 午前一時十一分 gozen ichiji juuippun; 10. 午後二時五十三分 gogo niji gojuusanpun

B: 1. 一月一日 ichigatsu tsuitachi; 2. 十二月三十一日 juunigatsu sanjuuichinichi; 3. 四月三日 shigatsu mikka; 4. 五月五日 gogatsu itsuka; 5. 十一月二十日 juuichigatsu hatsuka; 6. 二月十四日 nigatsu juuyokka; 7. 六月六日 rokugatsu muika; 8. 八月十日 hachigatsu tooka; 9. 三月七日 sangatsu nanoka; 10. 九月八日 kugatsu yooka; 11. 七月四日 shichigatsu yokka; 12. 十月九日 juugatsu kokonoka

Word Builder 2

▶ 13C Word Builder 2 (CD 5, Track 27)

きゅうじん 求人	kyuujin	*job posting*
こうこく 広告	kookoku	*advertisement*

人事部	jinjibu	human resources department
受付	uketsuke	reception desk, information desk
受付係	uketsukegakari	receptionist
ソフト、ソフトウェア	sofuto or sofutowea	software
経験	keeken	experience
五階	gokai	fifth floor
履歴書	rirekisho	curriculum vitae, resume
面接	mensetsu	interview
誕生日	tanjoobi	birthday
休み	yasumi	day off, holiday, vacation
今年	kotoshi	this year
来年	rainen	next year
去年	kyonen	last year
春	haru	spring
夏	natsu	summer
秋	aki	fall, autumn
冬	fuyu	winter
夏休み	natsu yasumi	summer vacation
他	hoka	other
五年間	gonenkan	for five years
少々	shooshoo	a little
一度	ichido	once
代わります、代わる	kawarimasu, kawaru	to transfer (a phone line)

待ちます、待つ	machimasu, matsu	to wait
待たせます、待たせる	matasemasu, mataseru	to keep someone waiting

✎ Word Practice 2
Translate the following words into Japanese.

1. *job posting* _____

2. *advertisement* _____

3. *reception desk, information desk* _____

4. *experience* _____

5. *curriculum vitae, resume* _____

6. *interview* _____

7. *birthday* _____

8. *last year* _____

9. *summer* _____

10. *once* _____

ANSWER KEY
1. 求人 kyuujin; 2. 広告 kookoku; 3. 受付 uketsuke; 4. 経験 keeken; 5. 履歴書 rirekisho; 6. 面接 mensetsu; 7. 誕生日 tanjoobi; 8. 去年 kyonen; 9. 夏 natsu; 10. 一度 ichido

Telling time, days of the week
and months

Expressing probability and conjecture—
でしょう deshoo

The particle に ni

Expressing probability and conj
かもしれません kamoshirema

Grammar Builder 2
THE PARTICLE に NI

▶ 13D Grammar Builder 2 (CD 5, Track 28)

The particle に ni was already discussed in Lessons 6 and 10. It is used when describing a location of a person or a thing and when describing a direction of a movement. It is also used to express purpose. Now, let's go over another function of に ni, which is to mark the time at which, month in which, or day on which something occurs.

七時半に起きます。

Shichiji han ni okimasu.

I wake up/get up at 7:30.

八月に日本 (へ/に) 行きます。

Hachigatsu ni nihon (e/ni) ikimasu.

I will go to Japan in August.

一月一日にパーティーをします。

Ichigatsu tsuitachi ni paatii o shimasu.

We will have a party on January 1.

何曜日に学校 (へ/に) 行きますか。

Nan-yoobi ni gakkoo (e/ni) ikimasu ka.

What day(s) of the week do you go to school?

Note that に ni is not used with expressions such as 今日 kyoo (*today*), 明日 ashita (*tomorrow*), 昨日 kinoo (*yesterday*), 今週 konshuu (*this week*), 去年 kyonen (*last year*), or 来年 rainen (*next year*), as shown in the following examples.

明日京都 (へ/に) 行きます。

Ashita kyooto (e/ni) ikimasu.

I will go to Kyoto tomorrow.

去年大学を卒業しました。

Kyonen daigaku o sotsugyooshimashita.

I graduated from the university last year.

It is also important to remember that the copula です desu does not combine with に ni as shown in the following examples.

今七時半です。

Ima shichiji han desu.

It's seven thirty now.

今日は五月五日です。

Kyoo wa gogatsu itsuka desu.

Today is May fifth.

明日は金曜日です。

Ashita wa kin-yoobi desu.

Tomorrow is Friday.

✎ Work Out 2

Complete the sentences using the Japanese equivalents of the expressions in parentheses.

The particle に ni

1. 今日は_____ですか。 *(what day of the week)*

   Kyoo wa _____ desu ka.

2. _____ 映画を見ました。 *(on Saturday)*

   _____ eega o mimashita.

3. _____ 弟が日本(へ/に)来ます。 *(on June 20)*

   _____otooto ga nihon (e/ni)

   kimasu.

4. 姉の誕生日は _____ です。 *(February 3)*

   Ane no tanjoobi wa _____desu.

5. _____ 家 (へ/に) 帰ります。 *(at 6:30 p.m.)*

   _____ uchi (e/ni)

   kaerimasu.

6. _____ 寝ますか。 *(what time)*

   _____nemasu ka.

7. _____ アメリカ(へ/に)行きますか。 *(what day)*

   _____amerika (e/ni) ikimasu ka.

8. 今_____です。 *(9:10 a.m.)*

   Ima _____ desu.

ANSWER KEY

1.何曜日 nan-yoobi; 2.土曜日に Doyoobi ni; 3.六月二十日に Rokugatsu hatsuka ni; 4.二月三日 nigatsu mikka; 5.午後六時三十分に Gogo rokuji sanjuppun ni or午後六時半に Gogo rokuji han ni;6.何時に Nanji ni; 7.何日に Nannichi ni; 8.午前九時十分 gozen kuji juppun

✎ Drive It Home

A. Tell the following times in Japanese.

1. *6:06* _____

2. *3:23* _____

3. *7:17* _____

B. Give the following dates in Japanese.

1. *January 1* _____

2. *April 10* _____

3. *September 9* _____

C. Complete the following sentences by inserting the appropriate particle.

1. 六時<ruby>六時<rt>ろくじ</rt></ruby> _____ 起<ruby>起<rt>お</rt></ruby>きます。

   Rokuji _____ **okimasu.**

   I wake up/get up at 6:00.

2. 七月<ruby>七月<rt>しちがつ</rt></ruby> _____日本<ruby>日本<rt>にほん</rt></ruby>へ行<ruby>行<rt>い</rt></ruby>きます。

   Shichigatsu _____ **nihon e ikimasu.**

   I will go to Japan in July.

3. 何曜日<ruby>何曜日<rt>なんようび</rt></ruby>_____学校<ruby>学校<rt>がっこう</rt></ruby>へ 行<ruby>行<rt>い</rt></ruby>きますか。

   Nan-yoobi _____ **gakkoo e ikimasu ka.**

   What day(s) of the week do you go to school?

Telling time, days of the week
and months

Expressing probability and conjecture—
でしょう deshoo

The particle に ni

Expressing probability and conje
かもしれません kamoshiremas

ANSWER KEY

A: 1. 六時六分 rokuji roppun; 2. 三時二十三分 sanji nijuusanpun; 3. 七時十七分 shichiji

juunanafun

B: 1. 一月一日 ichigatsu tsuitachi; 2. 四月十日 shigatsu tooka; 3. 九月九日 kugatsu kokonoka

C: 1. に ni; 2. に ni; 3. に ni

⊕ Culture Note

New Year's is a major holiday in Japan. Traditionally, at the end of December,
people prepare special New Year's food, called おせち料理 osechiryoori, which is
meant to last throughout the holidays, and clean the entire house. On December 31,
the Japanese usually eat そば soba, *buckwheat noodles*, for long and healthy lives.
Usually, people are off from their work for the first several days in January. In
the past, most stores, shops and restaurants were closed for the first three days in
January, but nowadays many major stores and shops are open even on January 1st.

How Did You Do?

Let's see how you did! By now, you should be able to:

☐ use key vocabulary related to making an appointment (Still unsure? Jump back to
page 252)

☐ tell time and date (Still unsure? Jump back to page 254)

☐ use the particle に ni to express when things happen (Still unsure? Jump back to
page 262)

✎ Word Recall

1. 夜 yoru

2. 生活 seekatsu

a. *breakfast*

b. *afternoon, p.m.*

3. 電子レンジ denshirenji　　　　　c. *toilet*

4. 僕 boku　　　　　　　　　　　　d. *child*

5. 朝ご飯 asagohan　　　　　　　　e. *I*

6. 子供 kodomo　　　　　　　　　　f. *French (language)*

7. フランス語 furansugo　　　　　　g. *microwave oven*

8. トイレ toire　　　　　　　　　　h. *siblings*

9. 午後 gogo　　　　　　　　　　　i. *evening, night*

10. 兄弟 kyoodai　　　　　　　　　　j. *life*

ANSWER KEY

1. i; 2. j; 3. g; 4. e; 5. a; 6. d; 7. f; 8. c; 9. b; 10. h

Lesson 14: Phrases

☐ express probability and conjecture

Phrase Builder 1

▶ 14A Phrase Builder 1 (CD 5, Track 29)

もしもし	moshi moshi	*hello (on the phone)*
申し訳ございません。	Mooshiwake gozaimasen.	*I'm very sorry. (lit., I have no excuse.) (polite)*
お待ちください。	Omachi kudasai.	*Please, wait. (polite)*

お待ちしております。	Omachishite orimasu.	I/We will be waiting for you. (polite)
お待たせいたしました。	Omatase itashimashita.	I have kept you waiting. (polite)
かしこまりました。	Kashikomarimashita.	Certainly. (polite)
失礼します。	Shitsureeshimasu.	Good-bye. (polite)
カットとカラー	katto to karaa	hair cut and color
お名前とお電話番号	onamae to odenwabangoo	name and telephone number (polite)
明日の三時頃	ashita no sanji goro	around three o'clock tomorrow
あさっての午後四時頃	asatte no gogo yoji goro	the day after tomorrow, around four o'clock p.m.
五月三日の三時に	gogatsu mikka no sanji ni	at three o'clock on May 3rd
九月二十日金曜日の四時に	kugatsu hatsuka kin-yoobi no yoji ni	at four o'clock on Friday, September 20th
十五分ぐらい	juugofun gurai	for about fifteen minutes
どのぐらい	dono gurai	how long, how much
二時間ぐらいかかります。	Nijikan gurai kakarimasu.	It takes about two hours.
遅れるかもしれません	okureru kamoshiremasen	may be late
それでは	sorede wa	then

晴れです。/晴れていま す。	Hare desu./Harete imasu.	*It's sunny.*
雨です。/雨が降ってい ます。	Ame desu./Ame ga futte imasu.	*It's raining.*
曇りです。	Kumori desu.	*It's cloudy.*
雪です。/雪が降ってい ます。	Yuki desu./Yuki ga futte imasu.	*It's snowing.*
風が強いです。	Kaze ga tsuyoi desu.	*The wind is strong.*

Take It Further

失礼 Shitsuree means *impoliteness* or *rudeness*, but the expression 失礼します Shitsureeshimasu is a polite expression and is used as a kind of greeting in a formal setting. For instance, if you're leaving after finishing a conversation with your superior at work, you will say 失礼します Shitsureeshimasu. Also, you can use this phrase as you enter your superior's office: You will knock on the door and wait for your superior to say どうぞ Doozo. After you open the door, say 失礼します Shitsureeshimasu as you enter the office.

頃 Goro and ぐらい gurai both translate as *about*, but 頃 goro is used to indicate the approximate time, e.g., *at about five o'clock*, and the latter is used when telling the approximate duration, e.g., *for about ten minutes*. Please pay attention to the position of these words as it is different from the position of English *about*. 頃 Goro and ぐらい gurai follow the noun expressing time and duration, e.g., 五時頃 goji goro (*around five o'clock*) and 十分ぐらい juppun gurai (*for about ten minutes*).

Telling time, days of the week
and months

Expressing probability and conjecture—
でしょう deshoo

The particle に ni

Expressing probability and conj
かもしれません kamoshiremas

✎ Phrase Practice 1

Translate the expressions below.

1. *hello (on the phone)* _____

2. *I'm very sorry. (polite)* _____

3. *Please, wait. (polite)* _____

4. *I/We will be waiting for you. (polite)* _____

5. *I have kept you waiting. (polite)* _____

6. *Certainly. (polite)* _____

7. *Good-bye. (polite)* _____

8. *name and telephone number (polite)* _____

9. *for about fifteen minutes* _____

10. *how long, how much* _____

ANSWER KEY

1. もしもし **moshi moshi**; 2. 申し訳ございません。**Mooshiwake gozaimasen.**; 3. お待ちください。 **Omachi kudasai.**; 4. お待ちしております。**Omachishite orimasu.**; 5. お待たせいたしました。**Omatase itashimashita.**; 6. かしこまりました。**Kashikomarimashita.**; 7. 失礼します。**Shitsureeshimasu.**; 8. お名前とお電話番号 **onamae to odenwabangoo**; 9. 十五分ぐらい **juugofun gurai**; 10. どのぐらい **dono gurai**

Grammar Builder 1
EXPRESSING PROBABILITY AND CONJECTURE—でしょう DESHOO

▶ 14B Grammar Builder 1 (CD 5, Track 30)

You can express probability and conjecture using でしょう deshoo and かもしれ
ません kamoshiremasen. Let's first look at でしょう deshoo, which corresponds
roughly to English *will probably*.

来年日本へ行くでしょう。
Rainen nihon e iku deshoo.
I will probably go to Japan next year.

It is important to remember that the plain form of verbs and adjectives is used
before でしょう deshoo.

テイラーさんは来年日本へ行くでしょう。
Teiraa san wa rainen nihon e iku deshoo.
Mr./Ms. Taylor will probably go to Japan next year.

テイラーさんは来年日本へ行かないでしょう。
Teiraa san wa rainen nihon e ikanai deshoo.
Mr./Ms. Taylor will probably not go to Japan next year.

テイラーさんは去年日本へ行ったでしょう。
Teiraa san wa kyonen nihon e itta deshoo.
Mr./Ms. Taylor probably went to Japan last year.

テイラーさんは去年日本へ行かなかったでしょう。
Teiraa san wa kyonen nihon e ikanakatta deshoo.
Mr./Ms. Taylor probably didn't go to Japan last year.

Notice that でしょう deshoo doesn't change; the plain form of verbs is conjugated
for tense. Nouns can also appear before でしょう deshoo.

Telling time, days of the week and months

Expressing probability and conjecture—
でしょう deshoo

The particle に ni

Expressing probability and conj⟨
かもしれません kamoshirema⟨

山田さんは先生でしょう。

Yamada san wa sensee deshoo.

Mr./Ms. Yamada is probably a teacher.

山田さんは先生 (じゃ/では) ないでしょう。

Yamada san wa sensee (ja/de wa) nai deshoo.

Mr./Ms. Yamada is probably not a teacher.

山田さんは先生だったでしょう。

Yamada san wa sensee datta deshoo.

Mr./Ms. Yamada was probably a teacher.

山田さんは先生 (じゃ/では) なかったでしょう。

Yamada san wa sensee (ja/de wa) nakatta deshoo.

Mr./Ms. Yamada was probably not a teacher.

Note that in case of the non-past affirmative, the plain form of the copula です desu, だ da, does not appear, and that でしょう deshoo immediately follows a noun.

✎ Work Out 1
Convert the verbs in parentheses into their appropriate forms to fill in the blanks.

1. 明日友達が _____ でしょう。(来ます)

   Ashita tomodachi ga _____ deshoo. (kimasu)

2. ブラウンさんは日本語を _____ でしょう。(話します)

   Buraun san wa nihongo o _____ deshoo. (hanashimasu)

3. 林さんは昨日家に _____ でしょう。(いました)

   Hayashi san wa kinoo uchi ni _____ deshoo. (imashita)

4. スミスさんは今日新聞を _____ でしょう。(読みませんでした)

   Sumisu san wa kyoo shinbun o _____ deshoo.
   (yomimasen deshita)

5. 明日は _____ でしょう。(雨です)

   Ashita wa _____ deshoo. (ame desu)

   ANSWER KEY

   1. 来る kuru; 2. 話す hanasu; 3. いた ita; 4. 読まなかった yomanakatta; 5. 雨 ame

Phrase Builder 2

▶ 14C Phrase Builder 2 (CD 5, Track 31)

新聞の求人広告	shinbun no kyuujin kookoku	a job posting in the newspaper
担当の者	tantoo no mono	a person in charge
担当の者 (に/と) 代わります	tantoo no mono (ni/to) kawarimasu	transfer (a phone line) to a person in charge
人事部の田中	jinjibu no Tanaka	Tanaka in the human resources department
ウェブデザイナーの 仕事の件で	webudezainaa no shigoto no ken de	regarding the job of the web designer
他の会社で	hoka no kaisha de	at another company

Telling time, days of the week
and months

Expressing probability and conjecture—
でしょう deshoo

The particle に ni

Expressing probability and conj
かもしれません kamoshiremas

五階の人事部に	gokai no jinjibu ni	*to the human resources department on the fifth floor*
来る時(に)	kuru toki (ni)	*when you come*
持って来ます、持って来る	motte kimasu, motte kuru	*to bring something (inanimate object)*
持って行きます、持って行く	motte ikimasu, motte iku	*to take something (inanimate object)*
履歴書を持って来てください。	Rirekisho o motte kite kudasai.	*Please bring your resume.*
連れて来ます、連れて来る	tsurete kimasu, tsurete kuru	*to bring someone or an animal (animate object)*
連れて行きます、連れて行く	tsurete ikimasu, tsurete iku	*to take someone or an animal (animate object)*
友達を連れて来てください。	Tomodachi o tsurete kite kudasai.	*Please bring your friends.*

✎ Phrase Practice 2

Complete the following by inserting the appropriate particles.

1. 新聞_____求人広告

shinbun _____ kyuujin kookoku

a job posting in the newspaper

2. 担当_____者

たんとう　もの

tantoo _____ mono

a person in charge

3. 人事部_____田中

じんじ　ぶ　たなか

jinjibu _____ Tanaka

Tanaka in the human resources department

4. ウェブデザイナー _____ 仕事_____ 件_____

しごと　けん

webudezainaa _____ shigoto _____ ken _____

regarding the job of the web designer

5. 他_____ 会社 _____

ほか　かいしゃ

hoka _____ kaisha _____

at another company

6. 五階_____ 人事部 _____

ごかい　じんじ　ぶ

gokai _____ jinjibu _____

to the human resources department on the fifth

7. 来る時_____

く　とき

kuru toki _____

when you come

ANSWER KEY

1. の no; 2. の no; 3. の no; 4. の no, の no, で de; 5. の no, で de; 6. の no, に ni; 7. に ni

Grammar Builder 2
EXPRESSING PROBABILITY AND CONJECTURE—かもしれません KAMOSHIREMASEN

▶ 14D Grammar Builder 2 (CD 5, Track 32)

かもしれません Kamoshiremasen, which corresponds to the English *may*, is also used to express conjecture, and it behaves the same as でしょう deshoo: it takes the plain form if verbs and adjectives, and is not conjugated for tense.

来年日本へ行くかもしれません。

Rainen nihon e iku kamoshiremasen.

I may go to Japan next year.

テイラーさんは来年日本へ行くかもしれません。

Teiraa san wa rainen nihon e iku kamoshiremasen.

Mr./Ms. Taylor may go to Japan next year.

テイラーさんは来年日本へ行かないかもしれません。

Teiraa san wa rainen nihon e ikanai kamoshiremasen.

Mr./Ms. Taylor may not go to Japan next year.

テイラーさんは去年日本へ行ったかもしれません。

Teiraa san wa kyonen nihon e itta kamoshiremasen.

Mr./Ms. Taylor may have been to Japan last year.

テイラーさんは去年日本へ行かなかったかもしれません。

Teiraa san wa kyonen nihon e ikanakatta kamoshiremasen.

Mr./Ms. Taylor may not have been to Japan last year.

Making requests with
てください te kudasai

Expressing wants and desires

- - - - - - - - - ┼ - - - - - - - - - - ┼ - - - - - - - - - - ┼ - - - - - - - - - - ┼ - - - - - - - - -

Polite expressions

The 時 toki-clauses

山田さんは先生かもしれません。

Yamada san wa sensee kamoshiremasen.

Mr./Ms. Yamada may be a teacher.

山田さんは先生 (じゃ/では) ないかもしれません。

Yamada san wa sensee (ja/de wa) nai kamoshiremasen.

Mr./Ms. Yamada may not be a teacher.

山田さんは先生だったかもしれません。

Yamada san wa sensee datta kamoshiremasen.

Mr./Ms. Yamada may have been a teacher.

山田さんは先生 (じゃ/では) なかったかもしれません。

Yamada san wa sensee (ja/de wa) nakatta kamoshiremasen.

Mr./Ms. Yamada may not have been a teacher.

Just as with でしょう **deshoo**, in case of the non-past affirmative, the plain form of the copula です **desu**, だ **da**, does not appear, and かもしれません **kamoshiremasen** immediately follows a noun.

✎ Work Out 2

Answer the following questions using かもしれません **kamoshiremasen** as indicated in parentheses.

1. *A:* 明日パーティーへ行きますか。

   Ashita paatii e ikimasu ka.

   B: _____. *(may not go)*

Telling time, days of the week
and months

Expressing probability and conjecture—
でしょう deshoo

The particle に ni

Expressing probability and conj◖
かもしれません kamoshirema◖

2. *A:* リーさんはおととい京都へ行きましたか。

Rii san wa ototoi kyooto e ikimashita ka.

B: 分かりませんが、_____ ね。

Wakarimasen ga, _____

ne. *(may have gone)*

3. *A:* ウィルソンさんはアメリカへ帰りましたか。

Wiruson san wa amerika e kaerimashita ka.

B: _____ ね。

_____ ne. *(may*

have returned)

4. *A:* 伊藤さんは美容院に電話しましたか。

Itoo san wa biyooin ni denwashimashita ka.

B: _____

_____. *(may not have called)*

5. *A:* ニューヨークは昨日雪でしたか。

Nyuuyooku wa kinoo yuki deshita ka.

B: 分かりませんが、_____ ね。

Wakarimasen ga, _____

_____ ne. *(may have snowed)*

ANSWER KEY

1. 行かないかもしれません Ikanai kamoshiremasen; 2. 行ったかもしれません itta kamoshiremasen;
3. 帰ったかもしれません kaetta kamoshiremasen; 4. 電話しなかったかもしれません
denwashinakatta kamoshiremasen; 5. 雪だったかもしれません yuki datta kamoshiremasen or
雪が降ったかもしれません yuki ga futta kamoshiremasen

✎ Drive It Home

Based on the English translation provided, change the verb 行きます ikimasu
into the appropriate form to fill in each of the blanks.

1. スミスさんは来年日本へ _____ でしょう。

   Sumisu san wa rainen nihon e _____ deshoo.

   Mr./Ms. Smith will probably go to Japan next year.

2. スミスさんは来年日本へ _____ でしょう。

   Sumisu san wa rainen nihon e _____ deshoo.

   Mr./Ms. Smith will probably not go to Japan next year.

3. スミスさんは去年日本へ _____ でしょう。

   Sumisu san wa kyonen nihon e _____ deshoo.

   Mr./Ms. Smith probably went to Japan last year.

4. スミスさんは去年日本へ _____ でしょう。

   Sumisu san wa kyonen nihon e _____ deshoo.

   Mr./Ms. Smith probably didn't go to Japan last year.

5. スミスさんは来年日本へ _____ かもしれません。

   Sumisu san wa rainen nihon e _____ kamoshiremasen.

   Mr./Ms. Smith may go to Japan next year.

6. スミスさんは来年日本へ _____ かもしれません。

   Sumisu san wa rainen nihon e _____ kamoshiremasen.

   Mr./Ms. Smith may not go to Japan next year.

Telling time, days of the week
and months

Expressing probability and conjecture—
でしょう deshoo

The particle に ni

Expressing probability and conj
かもしれません kamoshirema

7. スミスさんは去年日本へ _____ かもしれません。

Sumisu san wa kyonen nihon e _____ kamoshiremasen.

Mr./Ms. Smith may have been to Japan last year.

8. スミスさんは去年日本へ _____ かもしれません。

Sumisu san wa kyonen nihon e _____

kamoshiremasen.

Mr./Ms. Smith may not have been to Japan last year.

ANSWER KEY

1. 行く iku; 2. 行かない ikanai; 3. 行った itta; 4. 行かなかった ikanakatta; 5. 行く iku; 6. 行かない ikanai; 7. 行った itta; 8. 行かなかった ikanakatta

🔆 Tip!

A good way to practice some of the vocabulary you learned in this unit is to check the calendar every morning and say the month, the date, the day of the week in Japanese. Also, whenever you have a chance, you can check your watch and try telling the time in Japanese. This will help you learn to give dates and tell time without thinking.

How Did You Do?

Let's see how you did! By now, you should be able to:

☐ express probability and conjecture (Still unsure? Jump back to pages 270 and 276)

✎ Word Recall

1. 来ます kimasu   a. *to buy*

2. 読^よみます yomimasu

b. *to read*

3. 寝^ねます nemasu

c. *to sleep, to go to bed*

4. します shimasu

d. *to brush, to polish*

5. 行^いきます ikimasu

e. *to do*

6. 見^みます mimasu

f. *to come*

7. 買^かいます kaimasu

g. *to teach*

8. 教^{おし}えます oshiemasu

h. *to enter*

9. 入^{はい}ります hairimasu

i. *to see, to watch*

10. 磨^{みが}きます migakimasu

j. *to go*

ANSWER KEY

1. f; 2. b; 3. c; 4. e; 5. j; 6. i; 7. a; 8. g; 9. h; 10. d

Lesson 15: Sentences

☐ make requests

☐ use some basic polite expressions

Sentence Builder 1

▶ 15A Sentence Builder 1 (CD 6, Track 1)

レモンでございます。

Remon de gozaimasu.

This is Lemon. (polite)

Telling time, days of the week
and months

Expressing probability and conjecture—
でしょう deshoo

The particle に ni

Expressing probability and con
かもしれません kamoshirem

予約<ruby>よやく</ruby>したいんですけど・・・。

Yoyakushitai n desu kedo …

I want to make an appointment, but …

いつがよろしいですか。

Itsu ga yoroshii desu ka.

When is a good time for you?

明日の三時頃がいいんですけど・・・。

Ashita no sanji goro ga ii n desu kedo …

Around three o'clock tomorrow is good, but …

しばらくお待ちください。

Shibaraku omachi kudasai.

Please wait for a moment. (polite)

大変お待たせいたしました。

Taihen omatase itashimashita.

I have kept you waiting for a long time. (polite)

三時は予約が一杯です。

Sanji wa yoyaku ga ippai desu.

There's no opening at three o'clock.

二時半はいかがですか。

Niji han wa ikaga desu ka.

What about two thirty?

カットとカラーをお願いしたいんですけど・・・。

Katto to karaa o onegaishitai n desu kedo ...

I want (to ask for) a hair cut and color, but ...

どのぐらい時間がかかりますか。

Dono gurai jikan ga kakarimasu ka.

How long will it take?

二時間ぐらいでしょう。

Nijikan gurai deshoo.

It will probably take about two hours.

お名前とお電話番号をお願いします。

Onamae to odenwabangoo o onegaishimasu.

Your name and telephone number, please.

明日五月三日の二時半にお待ちしております。

Asu gogatsu mikka no niji han ni omachishite orimasu.

We will be waiting for you at two thirty tomorrow, on May 3rd.

Take It Further

The expression いかがですか **ikaga desu ka** is a polite version of どうですか **doo desu ka**. Both expressions have two meanings: *How is X?* and *What about X?*

Note that 明日 **asu** (*tomorrow*) is a more formal version of 明日 **ashita** you learned earlier.

Please note that the particle が **ga** attaches to the subject of 一杯です **ippai desu** (*to be full*) as in 予約が一杯です **yoyaku ga ippai desu** (*to be full of appointments*).

Telling time, days of the week
and months

Expressing probability and conjecture—
でしょう deshoo

The particle に ni

Expressing probability and conj
かもしれません kamoshirema

The expression かかります kakarimasu (*to take*) is exclusively used for talking about how much time things take. It is important to keep in mind that you don't need a particle when you want to express the specific amount of time it takes. For example, if you want to say *it takes two hours*, say 二時間かかります nijikan kakarimasu; don't attach a particle to 二時間 nijikan (*two hours*). However, you do need a particle when you want to say *it takes time*. You have to say 時間がかかります jikan ga kakarimasu. The particle が ga attaches to the expression 時間 jikan.

✎ Sentence Practice 1

Fill in the missing words in each of the following sentences.

1. レモンで _____。

   Remon de _____.

   This is Lemon. (polite)

2. _____ んですけど・・・。

   _____n desu kedo ...

   I want to make an appointment, but ...

3. いつが _____。

   Itsu ga _____.

   When is a good time for you?

4. _____ お待ちください。

   _____ omachi kudasai.

   Please wait for a moment. (polite)

5. 大変（たいへん）_____。

Taihen _____.

I have kept you waiting for a long time. (polite)

6. 三時（さんじ）は予約（よやく）が_____。

Sanji wa yoyaku ga _____.

There's no opening around three o'clock.

7. 二時半（にじはん）は_____。

Niji han wa _____.

What about two thirty?

8. _____ かかりますか。

_____ kakarimasu ka.

How long will it take?

ANSWER KEY

1.ございます gozaimasu；2.予約（よやく）したい Yoyakushitai；3.よろしいですか yoroshii desu ka；4.しばらく Shibaraku；5.お待（ま）たせいたしました omatase itashimashita；6.一杯（いっぱい）です ippai desu；7.いかがですか ikaga desu ka；8.どのぐらい Dono gurai

Grammar Builder 1
MAKING REQUESTS WITH てください TE KUDASAI

▶ 15B Grammar Builder 1 (CD 6, Track 2)

Making requests in Japanese is very simple. They are made by adding ください kudasai to the て te- form of verbs.

予約してください。

Yoyakushite kudasai.

Please make an appointment/a reservation.

電話してください。

Denwashite kudasai.

Please make a phone call.

名前と電話番号を書いてください。

Namae to denwabangoo o kaite kudasai.

Please write your name and phone number.

家に来てください。

Uchi ni kite kudasai.

Please come to my house.

宿題をしてください。

Shukudai o shite kudasai.

Please do (your) homework.

✎ Work Out 1

A. Make a request using the verbs in parentheses.

1. _____ ください。(来る)

   _____ kudasai. (kuru)

2. _____ ください。(行く)

   _____ kudasai. (iku)

3. _____ ください。(食べる)

_____ kudasai. (taberu)

4. _____ ください。(飲む)

_____ kudasai. (nomu)

5. _____ ください。(聞く)

_____ kudasai. (kiku)

6. _____ ください。(書く)

_____ kudasai. (kaku)

7. _____ ください。(見る)

_____ kudasai. (miru)

8. _____ ください。(買う)

_____ kudasai. (kau)

9. _____ ください。(起きる)

_____ kudasai. (okiru)

10. _____ ください。(話す)

_____ kudasai. (hanasu)

B. Make a request in the following situations.

1. *You want Mr. King to come to the party.*

キングさん、_____。

Kingu san, _____.

Telling time, days of the week
and months

Expressing probability and conjecture—
でしょう deshoo

The particle に ni

Expressing probability and conj
かもしれません kamoshirema

2. *You want Ms. Tanaka, who is fluent in English, to speak English.*

田中さん、＿＿＿＿＿＿＿＿＿＿＿＿＿＿。

Tanaka san, ＿＿＿＿＿＿＿＿＿＿＿＿＿＿＿＿＿

＿＿＿＿＿＿＿＿＿＿.

3. *You want Ms. Lopez to teach you Spanish.*

ロペスさん、＿＿＿＿＿＿＿＿＿＿＿＿＿＿＿。

Ropesu san, ＿＿＿＿＿＿＿＿＿＿＿＿＿＿＿＿

＿＿＿＿＿＿＿＿＿＿.

4. *You want your roommate, Mr. Johnson, to wake up.*

ジョンソンさん、＿＿＿＿＿＿＿＿＿＿＿ 。

Jonson san, ＿＿＿＿＿＿＿＿＿＿＿＿＿＿＿.

5. *You want Ms. Suzuki to call you tomorrow.*

鈴木さん、＿＿＿＿＿＿＿＿＿＿＿＿。

Suzuki san, ＿＿＿＿＿＿＿＿＿＿＿＿＿＿＿＿＿

＿＿＿＿＿＿＿＿＿＿.

ANSWER KEY

A: 1.来て kite; 2.行って itte; 3.食べて tabete; 4.飲んで nonde; 5.聞いて kiite; 6.書いて kaite; 7.見て mite; 8.買って katte; 9.起きて okite; 10.話して hanashite

B: 1.パーティーに来てください paatii ni kite kudasai; 2.英語を話してください eego o hanashite kudasai; 3.スペイン語を教えてください supeingo o oshiete kudasai; 4.起きてください okite kudasai; 5.明日電話してください ashita denwashite kudasai

Sentence Builder 2

▶ 15C Sentence Builder 2 (CD 6, Track 3)

新聞の求人広告を見たんですけど・・・。

Shinbun no kyuujinkookoku o mita n desu kedo …

I saw the job posting in the newspaper, but …

担当の者に代わりますので、少々お待ちください。

Tantoo no mono ni kawarimasu node, shooshoo omachi kudasai.

I will transfer you to the person in charge, so please wait for a moment.

ウェブデザイナーの仕事の件でお電話しているんですが。

Webudezainaa no shigoto no ken de odenwa shiteiru n desu ga.

I am calling you regarding the job of web designer.

経験はありますか。

Keeken wa arimasu ka.

Do you have any work experience?

他の会社で五年間ウェブデザインの仕事をしていました。

Hoka no kaisha de gonenkan webu dezain no shigoto o shite imashita.

I had (lit., was doing) a web-design job at another company for five years.

一度お話ししたいんですけど。

Ichido ohanashishitai n desu kedo.

I want to talk with you, but …

五階の人事部に来てください。

Gokai no jinjibu ni kite kudasai.

Please come to the human resources department on the fifth floor.

来る時に、履歴書を持って来てください。

Kuru toki ni, rirekisho o motte kite kudasai.

Please bring your resume when you come.

二十分ぐらいでしょう。

Nijuppun gurai deshoo.

It will probably be about twenty minutes.

✎ Sentence Practice 2

Fill in the missing words in each of the following sentences.

1. 担当の者に _____ ので、少々お待ちください。

   Tantoo no mono ni _____ node, shooshoo omachi kudasai.

   I will transfer you to the person in charge, so please wait for a moment.

2. ウェブデザイナーの仕事の件で _____ んですが。

   Webudezainaa no shigoto no ken de _____

   _____ n desu ga.

   I am calling you regarding the job of web designer.

3. 経験は _____。

   Keeken wa _____.

   Do you have any work experience?

4. _____五年間ウェブデザインの仕事をしていました。

_____ gonenkan webu dezain no

shigoto o shite imashita.

I had (lit., was doing) a web-design job at another company for five years.

5. 一度_____ んですけど。

Ichido _____ n desu kedo.

I want to talk with you once, but ...

6. 五階の人事部に _____。

Gokai no jinjibu ni _____.

Please come to the human resources department on the fifth floor.

7. 来る時に、履歴書を _____。

Kuru toki ni, rirekisho o _____.

Please bring your resume when you come.

8. 二十分ぐらい _____。

Nijuppun gurai _____.

It will probably be about twenty minutes.

ANSWER KEY

1. 代わります kawarimasu; 2. お電話している odenwa shiteiru; 3. ありますか arimasu ka;
4. 他の会社で Hoka no kaisha de; 5. お話ししたい ohanashishitai; 6. 来てください kite kudasai;
7. 持って来てください motte kite kudasai; 8. でしょう deshoo

Telling time, days of the week
and months

Expressing probability and conjecture—
でしょう deshoo

The particle に ni

Expressing probability and conj
かもしれません kamoshirema

Grammar Builder 2
POLITE EXPRESSIONS

▶ 15D Grammar Builder 2 (CD 6, Track 4)

Japanese polite expressions can be divided into five categories. There is a polite
form of nouns and adjectives, but different degrees of politeness are often
expressed by using different forms of verbs.

In informal situations, such as when talking with close friends and family
members, people use the plain form of verbs and だ da instead of the ます masu-
form of verbs or the copula (です desu). The ます masu-form of verbs and
the copula are used in a variety of more formal social settings, including the
workplace.

Even though the ます masu-form of verbs is considered a polite form, you can
appear even more polite by using an honorific form and a humble form of verbs.
The honorific form of verbs is called 尊敬語 sonkeego, and a humble form of
verbs is called 謙譲語 kenjoogo. An honorific form is used when describing
actions taken by someone you need or want to pay respect to, such as a superior
at work, a teacher or a customer. When describing actions taken by the speaker
himself/herself or members of his/her in-group, such as his/her family members,
a speaker must use a humble form. By humbling yourself or your family member,
you express respect toward the person you're speaking to.

The honorific and humble forms of verbs will be discussed in *Advanced Japanese*,
but for now, let's look at some of the polite expressions that will be used in the
dialogues in Lesson 12 of this unit. We'll call the ます masu-form of verbs and

です **desu**, as well as other expressions with the same level of politeness "the standard form" in order to distinguish them from the more polite expressions.

POLITE FORM	STANDARD FORM	
X でございます。 X de gozaimasu.	X です。 X desu.	*(It) is X.*
お待ちください。 Omachi kudasai.	待ってください。 Matte kudasai.	*Please wait.*
お待たせいたしました。 Omatase itashimashita. *(humble)*	待たせました。 Matasemashita.	*I kept you waiting.*
お待ちしております。 Omachishite orimasu. *(humble)*	待っています。 Matte imasu.	*I'm waiting for you.*
お話ししたいです。 Ohanashishitai desu. *(humble)*	話したいです。 Hanashitai desu.	*I want to talk.*
いらっしゃいます irasshaimasu *(honorific)*	います/行きます/来ます imasu/ikimasu/kimasu	*there is/exist/come/go*
失礼いたします。 Shitsuree itashimasu. *(humble)*	失礼します。 Shitsureeshimasu.	*Good-bye.*
申し訳 (ございません / ありません)。 Mooshiwake (gozaimasen/ arimasen). *(humble)*	ごめんなさい。/ すみません。 Gomennasai./ Sumimasen.	*I am sorry.*

Telling time, days of the week and months

Expressing probability and conjecture—
でしょう deshoo

The particle に ni

Expressing probability and conj
かもしれません kamoshirema

POLITE FORM	STANDARD FORM	
よろしいですか。 Yoroshii desu ka.	いいですか。 Ii desu ka.	*Is it okay?*

At this stage, you should simply concentrate on recognizing these polite expressions rather than worrying about their formation.

✎ Work Out 2

A. Write the polite form of the following expressions.

1. 待っています。

   Matte imasu.

   _____

2. 話したいです。

   Hanashitai desu.

   _____

3. 伊藤さんはいますか。

   Itoo san wa imasu ka.

   _____

4. 待ってください。

   Matte kudasai.

   _____

5. 鈴木です。

   Suzuki desu.

   _____

6. いいですか。

   Ii desu ka.

   _____

7. 待たせました。

   Matasemashita.

   _____

8. ごめんなさい。

   Gomennasai.

   _____

9. 失礼します。

   Shitsureeshimasu.

   _____

B. Choose the appropriate polite expressions from the list below to complete the
   sentences.

   でございます **de gozaimasu**, お待ちください **omachi kudasai**, お待たせいたしま
   した **omatase itashimashita**, お待ちしております **omachishite orimasu**, お話し
   したいです **ohanashishitai desu**, 申し訳ございません **mooshiwake gozaimasen**,
   失礼いたします **shitsuree itashimasu**

Telling time, days of the week
and months

Expressing probability and conjecture—
でしょう deshoo

The particle に ni

Expressing probability and conj
かもしれません kamoshirema

1. *A:* もしもし、田中さんはいらっしゃいますか。

   Moshi moshi, Tanaka san wa irasshaimasu ka.

   B: はい、少々＿＿＿＿＿＿＿＿＿＿＿＿＿＿。

   Hai, shooshoo ＿＿＿＿＿＿＿＿＿＿＿＿＿＿＿＿.

   Please wait for a little moment. (lit., a minute later)

   C: どうも ＿＿＿＿＿＿＿＿＿＿＿＿＿＿。田中です。

   **Doomo ＿＿＿＿＿＿＿＿＿＿＿＿＿＿＿＿＿＿. Tanaka
   desu.**

   I have kept you waiting. This is Tanaka.

2. *A:* 一度 ＿＿＿＿＿＿＿＿＿＿＿から、面接に来てください。

   **Ichido ＿＿＿＿＿＿＿＿＿＿＿＿＿＿＿＿＿ kara, mensetsu
   ni kite kudasai.**

   I want to talk with you once, so please come for an interview.

   B: はい。

   Hai.

   Yes.

3. *A:* はい、レインボーソフト ＿＿＿＿＿＿＿＿＿＿＿＿。

   Hai, Reinboo Sofuto ＿＿＿＿＿＿＿＿＿＿＿＿＿＿.

   Yes, this is Rainbow Soft.

   B: もしもし、田中さんをお願いしたいんですけど。

   Moshi moshi, Tanaka san o onegaishitai n desu kedo.

   Hello, I want to ask for Mr./Ms. Tanaka, but ...

4. A: 明日の三時に予約したいんですけど。
   <ruby>明日<rt>あした</rt></ruby>の<ruby>三時<rt>さんじ</rt></ruby>に<ruby>予約<rt>よやく</rt></ruby>したいんですけど。

   Ashita no sanji ni yoyakushitai n desu kedo.

   I want to make an appointment for three o'clock tomorrow.

   B: _____ が、明日の三時は予約が一杯です。

   _____ ga, ashita

   no sanji wa yoyaku ga ippai desu.

   We're sorry, but there's no opening at three o'clock tomorrow.

5. A: 金曜日の五時に予約したいんですけど。

   Kin-yoobi no goji ni yoyakushitai n desu kedo.

   I want to make an appointment for five o'clock on Friday, but …

   B: はい、かしこまりました。では五時に _____ 。

   Hai, kashikomarimashita. Dewa, goji ni _____

   _____ .

   Yes, certainly. Then, we will be waiting for you at five o'clock.

   ANSWER KEY

   A: 1. お待ちしております。Omachishite orimasu. 2. お話ししたいです。Ohanashishitai desu.
   3. 伊藤さんはいらっしゃいますか。Itoo san wa irasshaimasu ka. 4. お待ちください。Omachi
   kudasai. 5. 鈴木でございます。Suzuki de gozaimasu. 6. よろしいですか。Yoroshii desu ka.
   7. お待たせいたしました。Omatase itashimashita. 8. 申し訳ありません。Mooshiwake arimasen. or
   申し訳ございません。Mooshiwake gozaimasen. 9. 失礼いたします。
   Shitsuree itashimasu.
   B: 1. お待ちください omachi kudasai, お待たせいたしました omatase itashimashita; 2. お話しした
   いです ohanashishitai desu; 3. でございます de gozaimasu; 4. 申し訳ございません Mooshiwake
   gozaimasen; 5. お待ちしております omachishite orimasu

✎ Drive It Home

Make a request using the verbs in parentheses.

1. _____ ください。(食べる)

   _____ kudasai. (taberu)

2. _____ください。(出る)

   _____ kudasai. (deru)

3. _____ ください。(来る)

   _____ kudasai. (kuru)

4. _____ ください。(話す)

   _____ kudasai. (hanasu)

5. _____ ください。(寝る)

   _____ kudasai. (neru)

6. _____ ください。(勉強する)

   _____ kudasai. (benkyoosuru)

7. _____ ください。(読む)

   _____ kudasai. (yomu)

8. _____ ください。(飲む)

   _____ kudasai. (nomu)

ANSWER KEY

1. 食べて tabete; 2. 出て dete; 3. 来て kite; 4. 話して hanashite; 5. 寝て nete; 6. 勉強して benkyooshite; 7. 読んで yonde; 8. 飲んで nonde

Tip!

In order to practice making requests, imagine you have a robot, and you can make five requests to him every day. Tell your robot to do the five things you want him to do using the てください te kudasai structure. Since your vocabulary is still limited, you can make the same requests repeatedly. Alternatively, you can use the same verbs but change the direct objects. If you continue this task for a week or so, you will become comfortable with this structure and will be able to use it in real life situations.

How Did You Do?

Let's see how you did! By now, you should be able to:

☐ make requests (Still unsure? Jump back to page 285)

☐ use some basic polite expressions (Still unsure? Jump back to page 292)

✎ Word Recall

1. 大学院生 daigakuinsee
2. 紙 kami
3. 昼ご飯 hirugohan
4. 心理学 shinrigaku
5. アメリカ人 amerikajin
6. 鉛筆 enpitsu
7. 夕飯 yuuhan
8. 半年間 hantoshikan
9. 嫌い kirai

a. *to dislike*

b. *paper*

c. *psychology*

d. *American (person)*

e. *pencil*

f. *lunch*

g. *for half a year*

h. *ballpoint pen*

i. *graduate school student*

Unit 4 Lesson 15: Sentences   **299**

Telling time, days of the week
and months

Expressing probability and conjecture—
でしょう deshoo

The particle に ni

Expressing probability and conj
かもしれません kamoshirema

10. ボールペン boorupen

j. *dinner*

ANSWER KEY

1. i; 2. b; 3. f; 4. c; 5. d; 6. e; 7. j; 8. g; 9. a; 10. h

Lesson 16: Conversations

☐ express wants and desires

☐ use the *when*-clause

🄰 Conversation 1

▶ 16A Conversation 1 (Japanese: CD 6, Track 5; Japanese and English: CD 6, Track 6)

Ms. Yamamoto is making an appointment with her hairdresser on the phone.

受付係/Uketsukegakari:	レモンでございます。
	Remon de gozaimasu.
山本/Yamamoto:	ああ、もしもし。あのう、予約したいんですけど。
	Aa, moshi moshi. Anoo, yoyakushitai n desu kedo.
受付係/Uketsukegakari:	はい、いつがよろしいですか。
	Hai, itsu ga yoroshii desu ka.
山本/Yamamoto:	明日の三時頃がいいんですけど。
	Ashita no sanji goro ga ii n desu kedo.
受付係/Uketsukegakari:	しばらくお待ちください。
	Shibaraku omachi kudasai.

(One minute later.)

受付係/Uketsukegakari: 大変お待たせいたしました。申し訳ございませんが、三時は予約が一杯です。二時はいかがですか。

Taihen omatase itashimashita. Mooshiwake gozaimasen ga, sanji wa yoyaku ga ippai desu. Niji wa ikaga desu ka.

山本/Yamamoto: 十五分ぐらい遅れるかもしれませんが、大丈夫ですか。

Juugofun gurai okureru kamoshiremasen ga, daijoobu desu ka.

受付係/Uketsukegakari: はい、大丈夫ですよ。

Hai, daijoobu desu yo.

山本/Yamamoto: それじゃあ、二時半にお願いします。

Sore jaa, niji han ni onegai shimasu.

受付係/Uketsukegakari: カットですか。

Katto desu ka.

山本/Yamamoto: カットとカラーをお願いしたいんですけど。

Katto to karaa o onegaishitai n desu kedo.

受付係/Uketsukegakari: はい、かしこまりました。

Hai, kashikomarimashita.

山本/Yamamoto: どのぐらい時間がかかりますか。

Dono gurai jikan ga kakarimasu ka.

受付係/Uketsukegakari: そうですねえ。二時間ぐらいでしょう。よろしいですか。

Soo desu nee. Nijikan gurai deshoo. Yoroshii desu ka.

山本/Yamamoto: はい。

Hai.

受付係/Uketsukegakari: では、お名前とお電話番号をお願いします。

Dewa, onamae to odenwabangoo o onegaishimasu.

Telling time, days of the week and months

Expressing probability and conjecture—
でしょう deshoo

The particle に ni

Expressing probability and conje
かもしれません kamoshiremas

やまもと
山本/Yamamoto:

なまえ やまもと
名前は山本です。

でん わ ばんごう
電話番号は03-3977-5081です。

Namae wa Yamamoto desu. Denwabangoo wa
03-3977-5081 desu.

うけつけがかり
受付係/Uketsukegakari:

あ す ごがつみっか   に じ はん   ま
はい、それでは、明日五月三日の二時半にお待しして
おります。

Hai, sorede wa, asu gogatsu mikka no niji han ni
omachishite orimasu.

やまもと
山本/Yamamoto:

しつれい
じゃ、失礼します。

Ja, shitsureeshimasu.

うけつけがかり
受付係/Uketsukegakari:

しつれい
はい、失礼いたします。

Hai, shitsuree itashimasu.

Receptionist:	This is (the) Lemon (Beauty Salon).
Yamamoto:	Oh, hello. Well, I want to make an appointment …
Receptionist:	Yes, when is a good time for you?
Yamamoto:	Around three o'clock tomorrow is good for me.
Receptionist:	Please wait for a moment.

(One minute later.)

Receptionist:	I'm sorry for keeping you waiting for a long time. We are sorry, but there's no opening at three o'clock. What about two o'clock?
Yamamoto:	I may be about fifteen minutes late, but is it okay?
Receptionist:	Yes, that's fine.
Yamamoto:	Then, at two thirty, please.
Receptionist:	Hair cut?
Yamamoto:	I want (to ask for) a hair cut and color.
Receptionist:	Yes, certainly.
Yamamoto:	Ah, about how long will it take?
Receptionist:	Let me see. It will probably be for about two hours. Is that okay?

Yamamoto:	Yes.
Receptionist:	Then, your name and telephone number, please.
Yamamoto:	My name is Yamamoto, and my phone number is 03-3977-5081.
Receptionist:	Yes, then, we will be waiting for you at two thirty tomorrow, May 3rd.
Yamamoto:	Good-bye then.
Receptionist:	Yes, good-bye.

Take It Further

The conjunctions けど kedo (but) and が ga (but) often appear at the end of unfinished sentences in Japanese. They are used as an indirect and more polite way of turning the conversation to the addressee. In the sentence like お話しし
たいんですけど Ohanashishitai n desu kedo (*I want to talk, but …*), the speaker is waiting to hear the addressee's response without asking overtly whether it is a good time to talk. This style is less direct and, therefore, more polite and used frequently in daily conversations.

When giving a telephone number, you can separate the numbers with の no, which in this case corresponds to the English hyphen, or you can pause for a moment instead of saying の no, just like you would in English. For instance, 03-3954-6782 is ゼロさんの さんきゅうごよんの ろくななはちに zero san no san kyuu go yon no roku nana hachi ni.

Telling time, days of the week
and months

Expressing probability and conjecture—
でしょう deshoo

The particle に ni

Expressing probability and conj●
かもしれません kamoshirema●

✎ Conversation Practice 1

Fill in the blanks in the following sentences with the missing words. If you're unsure of the answer, listen to the conversation one more time.

1. 三時は予約が ＿＿＿＿＿＿＿＿ です。

   Sanji wa yoyaku ga ＿＿＿＿＿＿ desu.

2. 山本さんの予約は ＿＿＿＿時＿＿＿＿ です。

   Yamamoto san no yoyaku wa ＿＿＿＿ji＿＿＿＿ desu.

3. カットとカラーは ＿＿＿＿＿＿＿＿ かかります。

   Katto to karaa wa ＿＿＿＿＿＿＿＿＿＿＿＿ kakarimasu.

4. 山本さんの予約は ＿＿＿＿月＿＿＿＿ です。

   Yamamoto san no yoyaku wa ＿＿＿＿ gatsu ＿＿＿＿＿＿＿ a desu.

ANSWER KEY
1. 一杯 ippai; 2. 二 ni, 半 han; 3. 二時間ぐらい nijikan gurai; 4. 五 go, 三日 mikka

Grammar Builder 1
EXPRESSING WANTS AND DESIRES

▶ 16B Grammar Builder 1 (CD 6, Track 7)

Let's now learn how to express your wants and desires. To do this, you will use the "conjunctive" form of the verb, which you get by dropping the ます masu ending from the ます masu-form of a verb, and attach たいです tai desu.

> *conjunctive form of verbs* (ます **masu**-*form minus* ます **masu**) + たいです **tai**
> **desu**

Polite expressions

The 時 toki-clauses

すしが食べたいです。

Sushi ga tabetai desu.

I want to eat sushi.

コーヒーが飲みたいです。

Koohii ga nomitai desu.

I want to drink coffee.

映画が見たいです。

Eega ga mitai desu.

I want to see a movie.

イタリアへ行きたいです。

Itaria e ikitai desu.

I want to go to Italy.

Notice that the direct object marker を o is replaced by が ga in this construction. However, this is not a rigid rule. Even though が ga is preferred, it is also okay to use を o. The conjugation of たい tai is the same as that of い i-adjectives.

✎ Work Out 1

Change the following sentences using たいです tai desu.

1. コーヒーを飲みます。

   Koohii o nomimasu.

Telling time, days of the week
and months

Expressing probability and conjecture—
でしょう deshoo

The particle に ni

Expressing probability and conje
かもしれません kamoshiremas

2. 京都へ行きます。

   Kyooto e ikimasu.

   _____

3. 中国語を勉強します。

   Chuugokugo o benkyooshimasu.

   _____

4. 本を読みます。

   Hon o yomimasu.

   _____

5. 友達に電話します。

   Tomodachi ni denwashimasu.

   _____

6. 家へ帰ります。

   Uchi e kaerimasu.

   _____

7. 英語を話します。

   Eego o hanashimasu.

   _____

8. 漢字を書きます。

   Kanji o kakimasu.

   _____

9. コンピューターを買います。

Konpyuutaa o kaimasu.

10. 十時半に寝ます。

Juuji han ni nemasu.

11. 日本の映画を見ます。

Nihon no eega o mimasu.

12. 十二時に起きます。

Juuniji ni okimasu.

ANSWER KEY

1. コーヒーが飲みたいです。Koohii ga nomitai desu. 2. 京都へ行きたいです。Kyooto e ikitai desu. 3. 中国語が勉強したいです。Chuugokugo ga benkyooshitai desu. 4. 本が読みたいです。Hon ga yomitai desu. 5. 友達に電話したいです。 Tomodachi ni denwashitai desu. 6. 家へ帰りたいです。Uchi e kaeritai desu. 7. 英語が話したいです。Eego ga hanashitai desu. 8. 漢字が書きたいです。Kanji ga kakitai desu. 9. コンピューターが買いたいです。Konpyuutaa ga kaitai desu. 10. 十時半に寝たいです。Juujihan ni netai desu. 11. 日本の映画が見たいです。Nihon no eega ga mitai desu. 12. 十二時に起きたいです。Juuniji ni okitai desu.

🎧 Conversation 2

▶ 16C Conversation 2 (Japanese: CD 6, Track 8; Japanese and English: CD 6, Track 9)

Mr. Miller is on the phone making an appointment for his job interview at a computer software company.

Telling time, days of the week
and months

Expressing probability and conjecture—
でしょう deshoo

The particle に ni

Expressing probability and conj
かもしれません kamoshirema

受付係/Uketsukegakari: うけつけがかり ABC ソフトでございます。

ABC Sofuto de gozaimasu.

ミラー/Miraa: あのう、新聞の求人広告を見たんですけど。

Anoo, shinbun no kyuujin kookoku o mita n desu
kedo.

受付係/Uketsukegakari: では、担当の者に代わりますから、少々お待ちくだ
さい。

Dewa, tantoo no mono ni kawarimasu kara,
shooshoo omachi kudasai.

(A little later.)

田中/Tanaka: 人事部の田中です。

Jinjibu no Tanaka desu.

ミラー/Miraa: ウェブデザイナーの仕事の件でお電話しているん
ですが。

Webudezainaa no shigoto no ken de odenwa shite
iru n desu ga.

田中/Tanaka: 経験はありますか。

Keeken wa arimasu ka.

ミラー/Miraa: はい。他の会社で五年間ウェブデザインの仕事をして
いました。

Hai. Hoka no kaisha de gonenkan webu dezain no
shigoto o shite imashita.

田中/Tanaka: そうですか。では、一度お話ししたいんですけど。

Soo desu ka. Dewa, ichido ohanashishitai n desu
kedo.

ミラー/Miraa: はい。

Hai.

田中/Tanaka: あさっての午後四時頃はいかがですか。

Asatte no gogo yoji goro wa ikaga desu ka.

ミラー/Miraa:	はい、大丈夫です。
	Hai, daijoobu desu.
田中/Tanaka:	それでは、あさって九月二十日金曜日の四時に五階の人事部に来てください。
	Sorede wa, asatte kugatsu hatsuka kin-yoobi no yoji ni gokai no jinjibu ni kite kudsai.
ミラー/Miraa:	五階ですね。
	Gokai desu ne.
田中/Tanaka:	はい。来る時に、履歴書を持って来てくださいね。
	Hai. Kuru toki ni, rirekisho o motte kite kudasai ne.
ミラー/Miraa:	はい、分かりました。
	Hai, wakarimashita.
田中/Tanaka:	それでは、あさって。
	Sorede wa, asatte.
ミラー/Miraa:	ありがとうございます。失礼いたします。
	Arigatoo gozaimasu. Shitsureeitashimasu.

Receptionist:	*ABC Software.*
Miller:	*Well, I saw your job posting in the newspaper, but…*
Receptionist:	*Then, I will transfer you to the person in charge, so wait a moment, please.*

(A little later.)

Tanaka:	*I'm Tanaka in the human resources department.*
Miller:	*I'm calling regarding the job of web designer.*
Tanaka:	*Do you have any experience?*
Miller:	*Yes. I had (lit., was doing) a web-designing job at another company for five years.*
Tanaka:	*I see. Then, I'd like (lit., want) to talk to you.*
Miller:	*Yes.*

Unit 4 Lesson 16: Conversations

Telling time, days of the week
and months

Expressing probability and conjecture—
でしょう deshoo

The particle に ni

Expressing probability and conj◖
かもしれません kamoshirema◗

Tanaka:	*What about the day after tomorrow around four o'clock?*
Miller:	*Yes, that's fine.*
Tanaka:	*Then, please come to the human resources department on the fifth floor at four o'clock in the afternoon, the day after tomorrow, Friday September twentieth.*
Miller:	*Fifth floor, right?*
Tanaka:	*Yes. When you come, please bring your resume, okay?*
Miller:	*Yes, okay.*
Tanaka:	*Then, I'll see you the day after tomorrow.*
Miller:	*Thank you very much. Good-bye.*

✎ Conversation Practice 2

Fill in the blanks in the following sentences with the missing words. If you're unsure of the answer, listen to the conversation one more time.

1. ミラーさんは _____ を見ました。

   Miraa san wa _____

   _____ o mimashita.

2. ミラーさんは _____の件で電話しました。

   Miraa san wa _____

   _____ no ken de denwashimashita.

3. ミラーさんは _____ でウェブデザインの仕事をしていました。

   Miraa san wa _____ de webudezain no

   shigoto o shite imashita.

4. ミラーさんはあさっての _____ に人事部に行きます。

   Miraa san wa asatte no _____ ni jinjibu ni ikimasu.

5. 人事部は ___ にあります。
   じんじぶ

Jinjibu wa _____ ni arimasu.

ANSWER KEY
1. 新聞の求人広告 shinbun no kyuujin kookoku; 2. ウェブデザイナーの仕事 webudezainaa no
   しんぶん きゅうじんこうこく   しごと
shigoto; 3. 他の会社 hoka no kaisha; 4. 四時 yoji; 5. 五階 gokai
         ほか かいしゃ   よじ   ごかい

Grammar Builder 2
THE 時 TOKI-CLAUSES
       とき

▶ 16D Grammar Builder 2 (CD 6, Track 10)

The 時 toki-clause corresponds to the English *when*-clause, i.e., it is a clause
     とき
describing the time of an action or state. 時 Toki can follow the plain forms of
                                         とき
verbs, nouns followed by の no, い i-adjectives or な na-adjectives followed by な
na. (な na-adjectives will be discussed in Lesson 13.) See the summary below.

> *Plain form of verbs* + 時 toki, …
>   とき
> *Noun* + の no + 時 toki, …
>   とき
> *Plain/Non-past form of* い *i-adjectives* + 時 toki, …
>   とき
> *Stem of* な *na-adjectives* + な na + 時 toki, …
>   とき

Let's look at some sentences containing the 時 toki-clause. Note that the particle
                                        とき
に ni and the topic marker は wa can be added after 時 toki.
                                              とき

The plain form of verbs appears before the 時 toki-clause. Verbs can be either
                                          とき
non-past or past tense and either affirmative or negative. Note that the 時 toki-
                                                                     とき
clause precedes the main clause and is separated from it by a comma.

家に来る時、電話してください。
うち く とき でんわ
Uchi ni kuru toki, denwashite kudasai.
Please call me when you come to my house.

Telling time, days of the week
and months

Expressing probability and conjecture—
でしょう deshoo

The particle に ni

Expressing probability and conj
かもしれません kamoshirema

分からない時は、聞いてください。

Wakaranai toki wa, kiite kudasai.

Please ask me when you don't understand.

勉強していた時に、友達が来ました。

Benkyooshite ita toki ni, tomodachi ga kimashita.

My friend came when I was studying.

分からなかった時、先生に聞きました。

Wakaranakatta toki, sensee ni kikimashita.

When I didn't understand, I asked the teacher.

With nouns, the noun + の no appears before 時 toki regardless of the tense, and
in negative sentences, it is noun + じゃない ja nai instead.

学生の時、たくさん勉強しました。

Gakusee no toki, takusan benkyooshimashita.

When I was a student, I studied a lot.

クラスメートじゃない時は、山田さんの名前を知りませんでした。

Kurasumeeto ja nai toki wa, Yamada san no namae o shirimasen deshita.

When he/she was not a classmate, I didn't know Mr./Ms. Yamada's name.

As with nouns, the non-past tense form of adjectives appears in the 時 toki-
clause regardless of the tense in the main clause.

暑い時、ビーチに行きます。

Atsui (hot) toki, biichi ni ikimasu.

I go to the beach when it's hot.

暑い時、ビーチに行きました。

Atsui toki, biichi ni ikimashita.

I went to the beach when it was hot.

Please also note that the subject in the 時 toki-clause should be marked by the particle が ga instead of は wa, as seen in the examples above.

In case of な na-adjectives, な na is attached to an adjective before 時 toki. This is the special form of な na-adjectives which will be discussed in Lesson 13.

暇な時、よく映画を見ます。

Hima na toki, yoku eega o mimasu.

When I am free, I often see a movie.

暇な時、友達に電話しました。

Hima na toki, tomodachi ni denwashimashita.

I called my friend when I was free.

Now compare the following two sentences.

日本へ行く時、ニューヨークのデパートでカメラを買いました。

Nihon e iku toki, nyuuyooku no depaato de kamera o kaimashita.

I bought a camera at a department store in New York when I was going to Japan.

日本へ行った時、東京のデパートでカメラを買いました。

Nihon e itta toki, tookyoo no depaato de kamera o kaimashita.

I bought a camera at a department store in Tokyo when I went to Japan.

The tense of a verb in a 時 toki-clause indicates a time relative to the event mentioned in the main clause, i.e, it answers the question, "Does the event in the

時<ruby>とき</ruby> toki-clause happen before or after the event in the main clause?" So, if you look at the above two examples, the use of the non-past tense form 行く<ruby>い</ruby> iku in the 時<ruby>とき</ruby> toki-clause in the first example indicates you bought a camera before you went to Japan; the use of the past tense form 行った<ruby>い</ruby> itta in the 時<ruby>とき</ruby> toki-clause in the second example indicates that you bought a camera after you got to Japan.

✎ Work Out 2

Choose the appropriate 時<ruby>とき</ruby> toki-clause from the right-hand column to replace the X in the sentences on the left.

1. X、スペイン語を勉強しました。

   X, supeingo o benkyooshimashita.

2. X、買い物に行きます。

   X, kaimono ni ikimasu.

3. X、富士山を見ました。

   X, fujisan (*Mt. Fuji*) o mimashita.

4. X、五時に家へ帰りました。

   X, goji ni uchi e kaerimashita.

5. X、履歴書を書きました。

   X, rirekisho o kakimashita.

6. X、先生に聞きます。

   X, sensee ni kikimasu.

a. 日本へ行った時

   Nihon e itta toki

b. 面接に行く時

   Mensetsu ni iku toki

c. お金がある時

   Okane ga aru toki

d. 大学生の時

   Daigakusee no toki

e. 分からない時

   Wakaranai toki

f. 先週セミナーに出なかった時

   Senshuu seminaa ni denakatta toki

ANSWER KEY

1. d; 2. c; 3. a; 4. f; 5. b; 6. e

✎ Drive It Home

A. Change the following sentences using たいです **tai desu**.

1. 映画を見ます。

   Eega o mimasu.

   _____

2. テレビを見ます。

   Terebi o mimasu.

   _____

3. イタリアへ行きます。

   Itaria e ikimasu.

   _____

4. フランスへ行きます。

   furansu e ikimasu.

   _____

5. 日本語を話します。

   Nihongo o hanashimasu.

   _____

6. フランス語を話します。

   Furansugo o hanashimasu.

   _____

Telling time, days of the week and months

Expressing probability and conjecture—
でしょう deshoo

The particle に ni

Expressing probability and conj
かもしれません kamoshirema

B. Fill in the blanks by choosing appropriate expressions from the word bank.

学生の Gakusee no, 家に来る Uchi ni kuru, 勉強していた Benkyooshite ita, 分からない Wakaranai

1. ＿＿＿＿＿＿＿＿＿時、電話してください

＿＿＿＿＿＿＿＿＿＿＿＿＿＿ toki, denwashite kudasai.

Please call me when you come to my house.

2. ＿＿＿＿＿＿＿＿＿時は、聞いてください。

＿＿＿＿＿＿＿＿＿＿＿＿ toki wa, kiite kudasai.

Please ask me when you don't understand.

3. ＿＿＿＿＿＿＿＿＿時に、友達が来ました。

＿＿＿＿＿＿＿＿＿＿＿＿＿＿ toki ni, tomodachi ga

kimashita.

My friend came when I was studying.

4. ＿＿＿＿＿時、たくさん勉強しました。

＿＿＿＿＿＿＿＿＿＿＿＿＿ toki, takusan benkyooshimashita.

When I was a student, I studied a lot.

ANSWER KEY

A: 1. 映画が見たいです。Eega ga mitai desu. 2. テレビが見たいです。Terebi ga mitai desu. 3. イタリアへ行きたいです。Itaria e ikitai desu. 4. フランスへ行きたいです。Furansu e ikitai desu. 5. 日本語が話したいです。Nihongo ga hanashitai desu. 6. フランス語が話したいです。Furansugo ga hanashitai desu.

B: 1. 家に来る Uchi ni kuru; 2. 分からない Wakaranai; 3. 勉強していた Benkyooshite ita; 4. 学生の Gakusee no

How Did You Do?

Let's see how you did! By now, you should be able to:

☐ express wants and desires (Still unsure? Jump back to page 304)

☐ use the *when*-clause (Still unsure? Jump back to page 311)

✎ Word Recall

1. 勉強する benkyoosuru   a. *to borrow*

2. 入学する nyuugakusuru   b. *to go back, to return*

3. 行く iku   c. *to study*

4. 帰る kaeru   d. *to enter school*

5. 乗る noru   e. *to return*

6. 借りる kariru   f. *to graduate*

7. 卒業する sotsugyoosuru   g. *to come*

8. 戻る modoru   h. *to ride, to get on*

9. 来る kuru   i. *to get off*

10. 降りる oriru   j. *to go*

ANSWER KEY

1. c; 2. d; 3. j; 4. b; 5. h; 6. a; 7. f; 8. e; 9. g; 10. i

Don't forget to practice and reinforce what you've learned by visiting **www.livinglanguage.com/languagelab** for flashcards, games, and quizzes for Unit 4!

Unit 4 Essentials

Vocabulary Essentials

Test your knowledge of the key material in this unit by filling in the blanks in the following charts. Once you've completed these pages, you'll have tested your retention, and you'll have your own reference for the most essential vocabulary.

BEAUTY SALON APPOINTMENT

	hello (on the phone)
	beauty salon
	hair dresser
	reservation, appointment
	haircut
	hair dye, hair color
	perm
	telephone number

JOB INTERVIEW APPOINTMENT

	job posting
	advertisement
	human resources department
	reception desk, information desk
	receptionist
	software
	experience

	fifth floor
	curriculum vitae, resume
	interview
	other

TIME RELATED EXPRESSIONS

	this year
	next year
	last year
	spring
	summer
	fall, autumn
	winter
	summer vacation
	day off, holiday, vacation
	birthday

ADJECTIVES & ADVERBS

	good (polite)
	for a while
	all right
	hard, very
	full
	for five years
	a little

	once
	strong

VERBS

	to make a phone call
	to make a reservation, to make an appointment
	to be late
	to take (time)
	to replace, to transfer (a phone line)
	to wait
	to keep someone waiting
	to bring something (inanimate object)
	to take something (inanimate object)
	to bring someone or animal (animate object)
	to take someone or animal (animate object)
	It's sunny.
	It's raining.
	It's cloudy.
	It's snowing.

HOURS

	one o'clock
	two o'clock
	three o'clock
	four o'clock
	five o'clock
	six o'clock
	seven o'clock
	eight o'clock
	nine o'clock
	ten o'clock
	eleven o'clock
	twelve o'clock
	around three o'clock
	about two hours

MINUTES

	one minute
	two minutes
	three minutes
	four minutes
	five minutes
	six minutes
	seven minutes
	eight minutes

	nine minutes
	ten minutes
	thirty minutes
	half past the hour
	for about fifteen minutes

MONTHS

	January
	February
	March
	April
	May
	June
	July
	August
	September
	October
	November
	December

DAYS

	first
	second
	third
	fourth

	fifth
	sixth
	seventh
	eighth
	ninth
	tenth
	twentieth

QUESTIONS

	what time
	what minute(s)
	what month
	what day
	how long, how much

Grammar Essentials

Here is a reference of the key grammar that was covered in Unit 4. Make sure you understand the summary and can use all of the grammar it covers.

PARTICLE に NI

Marks time, month, and day

_{しちじはん}_お 七時半に起きます。	Shichiji han ni okimasu.	*I wake up/get up at 7:30.*
_{はちがつ} _{にほん} _い 八月に日本 (へ/に) 行きます。	Hachigatsu ni nihon (e/ni) ikimasu.	*I will go to Japan in August.*
_{いちがつついたち} 一月一日にパーティーをします。	Ichigatsu tsuitachi ni paatii o shimasu.	*We will have a party on January 1.*

323

<ruby>何<rt>なん</rt></ruby><ruby>曜<rt>よう</rt></ruby><ruby>日<rt>び</rt></ruby>に<ruby>学校<rt>がっこう</rt></ruby> (へ/に) <ruby>行<rt>い</rt></ruby>きますか。	Nan-yoobi ni gakkoo (e/ni) ikimasu ka.	*What day(s) of the week do you go to school?*

EXPRESSING PROBABILITY AND CONJECTURE

plain form + でしょう deshoo (probably)

plain form + かもしれません kamoshiremasen (may)

*non-past affirmative だ da does not appear before でしょう deshoo/かもしれません kamoshiremasen

テイラーさんは<ruby>来年<rt>らいねん</rt></ruby><ruby>日本<rt>にほん</rt></ruby>へ<ruby>行<rt>い</rt></ruby>くでしょう。	Teiraa san wa rainen nihon e iku deshoo.	*Mr./Ms. Taylor will probably go to Japan next year.*
テイラーさんは<ruby>来年<rt>らいねん</rt></ruby><ruby>日本<rt>にほん</rt></ruby>へ<ruby>行<rt>い</rt></ruby>かないでしょう。	Teiraa san wa rainen nihon e ikanai deshoo.	*Mr./Ms. Taylor will probably not go to Japan next year.*
テイラーさんは<ruby>去年<rt>きょねん</rt></ruby><ruby>日本<rt>にほん</rt></ruby>へ<ruby>行<rt>い</rt></ruby>ったでしょう。	Teiraa san wa kyonen nihon e itta deshoo.	*Mr./Ms. Taylor probably went to Japan last year.*
テイラーさんは<ruby>去年<rt>きょねん</rt></ruby> <ruby>日本<rt>にほん</rt></ruby>へ<ruby>行<rt>い</rt></ruby>かなかった でしょう。	Teiraa san wa kyonen nihon e ikanakatta deshoo.	*Mr./Ms. Taylor probably didn't go to Japan last year.*
テイラーさんは<ruby>来年<rt>らいねん</rt></ruby><ruby>日本<rt>にほん</rt></ruby>へ<ruby>行<rt>い</rt></ruby>くかもしれません。	Teiraa san wa rainen nihon e iku kamoshiremasen.	*Mr./Ms. Taylor may go to Japan next year.*

テイラーさんは来年 日本へ行かないかも しれません。	Teiraa san wa rainen nihon e ikanai kamoshiremasen.	*Mr./Ms. Taylor may not go to Japan next year.*
テイラーさんは去年 日本へ行ったかも しれません。	Teiraa san wa kyonen nihon e itta kamoshiremasen.	*Mr./Ms. Taylor may have been to Japan last year.*
テイラーさんは去年 日本へ行かなかったかも しれません。	Teiraa san wa kyonen nihon e ikanakatta kamoshiremasen.	*Mr./Ms. Taylor may not have been to Japan last year.*

MAKING REQUESTS WITH てください TE KUDASAI

て te-form of verb + ください te kudasai

予約してください。	Yoyakushite kudasai.	*Please make an appointment/ a reservation.*

POLITE EXPRESSIONS

POLITE FORM	STANDARD FORM	
Xでございます。 X de gozaimasu.	Xです。 X desu.	*(It) is X.*
お待ちください。 Omachi kudasai.	待ってください。 Matte kudasai.	*Please wait.*
お待たせいたしました。 Omatase itashimashita. *(humble)*	待たせました。 Matasemashita.	*I kept you waiting.*

POLITE FORM	STANDARD FORM	
お待ちしております。 Omachishite orimasu. (humble)	待っています。 Matte imasu.	*I'm waiting for you.*
お話ししたいです。 Ohanashishitai desu. (humble)	話したいです。 Hanashitai desu.	*I want to talk.*
いらっしゃいます。 irasshaimasu (honorific)	います/行きます/ 来ます imasu/ikimasu/kimasu	*exist/come/go*
失礼いたします。 Shitsuree itashimasu. (humble)	失礼します。 Shitsureeshimasu.	*Goodbye.*
申し訳ございません/ ありません。 Mooshiwake gozaimasen/arimasen. (humble)	ごめんなさい。/ すみません。 Gomennasai./ Sumimasen.	*I am sorry.*
よろしいですか。 Yoroshii desu ka.	いいですか。 Ii desu ka.	*Is it okay?*

EXPRESSING WANTS AND DESIRES

Conjunctive form of verbs (ます masu-form minus ます masu) + たいです tai desu

すしが食べたいです。	Sushi ga tabetai desu.	*I want to eat sushi.*
イタリアへ行きたいです。	Itaria e ikitai desu.	*I want to go to Italy.*

THE 時 TOKI-CLAUSES

Plain form of verbs + 時 toki, …

Noun + の no + 時 toki, …

Plain/Non-past form of い i-adjectives + 時 toki, …

Stem of な na-adjectives + な na + 時 toki, …

家に来る時、電話して ください。	Uchi ni kuru toki, denwashite kudasai.	*Please call me when you come to my house.*
学生の時、たくさん 勉強しました。	Gakusee no toki, takusan benkyooshimashita.	*When I was a student, I studied a lot.*
暑い時、ビーチに行き ます。	Atsui toki, biichi ni ikimasu.	*I go to the beach when it's hot.*
暇な時、よく映画を 見ます。	Hima na toki, yoku eega o mimasu.	*When I am free, I often see a movie.*
日本へ行く時、ニュー ヨークのデパートで カメラを買いました。	Nihon e iku toki, nyuuyooku no depaato de kamera o kaimashita.	*I bought a camera at a department store in New York when I was going to Japan.*
日本へ行った時、東京 のデパートでカメラを 買いました。	Nihon e itta toki, tookyoo no depaato de kamera o kaimashita.	*I bought a camera at a department store in Tokyo when I went to Japan.*

Unit 4 Quiz

A. Tell the following times in Japanese.

1. *11:11 a.m.* _____

2. *5:05 p.m.* _____

B. Give the following dates in Japanese.

1. *January 20* _____

2. *July 15* _____

C. Complete the following sentences by inserting the particle に ni. If inserting the particle is not possible, write "X" instead.

1. 七時半_{しちじはん}_____起_おきます。

   Shichiji han _____ okimasu.

   I wake up/get up at 7:30.

2. 八月_{はちがつ} _____日本_{にほん}へ行_いきます。

   Hachigatsu _____ nihon e ikimasu.

   I will go to Japan in August.

3. 去年_{きょねん} _____大学_{だいがく}を卒業_{そつぎょう}しました。

   Kyonen _____ daigaku o sotsugyooshimashita.

   I graduated from the university last year.

D. Based on the English translation provided, change the verb 行きます
   ikimasu into the appropriate form to fill in each of the blanks.

1. テイラーさんはへ来年日本へ _____ でしょう。

   Teiraa san wa rainen nihon e _____ deshoo.

   Mr./Ms. Taylor will probably go to Japan next year.

2. テイラーさんはへ来年日本へ _____ でしょう。

   Teiraa san wa rainen nihon e _____ deshoo.

   Mr./Ms. Taylor will probably not go to Japan next year.

3. テイラーさんはへ去年日本へ_____ でしょう。

   Teiraa san wa kyonen nihon e _____ deshoo.

   Mr./Ms. Taylor probably went to Japan last year.

E. Based on the English translation provided, change the phrase 先生です
   sensee desu into the appropriate form to fill in each of the blanks.

1. 山田さんは _____ でしょう。

   Yamada san wa _____

   _____ deshoo.

   Mr. Yamada was probably not a teacher.

2. 山田さんは _____ かもしれません。

   Yamada san wa _____ kamoshiremasen.

   Mr./Ms. Yamada may have been a teacher.

F. Make a request using the verbs in parentheses.

1. _____ ください。(予約する)

   _____ kudasai. (yoyakusuru)

2. _____ ください。(来る)

_____ kudasai. (kuru)

G. Give the standard forms of the following polite expressions.

1. 失礼いたします。Shitsuree itashimasu.

_____

2. 申し訳ございません/ありません。Mooshiwake gozaimasen/arimasen.

_____

H. Change the following sentences using たいです tai desu.

1. すしを食べます。Sushi o tabemasu.

_____

2. コーヒーを飲みます。Koohii o nomimasu.

_____

I. Change the form of the expressions in parentheses to fill in the blanks.

1. _____ 時、電話してください。(家に来ます)

_____ toki, denwashite kudasai. (uchi ni kimasu)

Please call me when you come to my house.

2. _____ 時は、聞いてください。(分かりません)

_____ toki wa, kiite kudasai. (wakarimasen)

Please ask me when you don't understand.

ANSWER KEY
A. 1. 午前十一時十一分 gozen juuichiji juuippun; 2. 午後五時五分 gogo goji gofun
B. 1. 一月二十日 ichigatsu hatsuka; 2. 七月十五日 shichigatsu juugonichi
C. 1. に ni; 2. に ni; 3. X
D. 1. 行く iku; 2. 行かない ikanai; 3. 行った itta

E. 1. 先生(じゃ/では)なかった sensee (ja/de wa) nakatta; 2. 先生だった sensee datta
F. 1. 予約して yoyakushite; 2. 来て kite
G. 1. 失礼します。Shitsureeshimasu. 2. ごめんなさい。Gomennasai. or すみません。 Sumimasen.
H. 1. すしが食べたいです。Sushi ga tabetai desu. 2. コーヒーが飲みたいです。Koohii ga nomitai desu.
I. 1. 家に来る Uchi ni kuru; 2. 分からない Wakaranai

How Did You Do?

Give yourself a point for every correct answer, then use the following key to tell whether you're ready to move on:

0-7 points: It's probably a good idea to go back through the lesson again. You may be moving too quickly, or there may be too much "down time" between your contact with Japanese. Remember that it's better to spend 30 minutes with Japanese three or four times a week than it is to spend two or three hours just once a week. Find a pace that's comfortable for you, and spread your contact hours out as much as you can.

8-12 points: You would benefit from a review before moving on. Go back and spend a little more time on the specific points that gave you trouble. Re-read the Grammar Builder sections that were difficult, and do the work out one more time. Don't forget about the online supplemental practice material, either. Go to **www.livinglanguage.com/languagelab** for games and quizzes that will reinforce the material from this unit.

13-17 points: Good job! There are just a few points that could consider reviewing before moving on. If you haven't worked with the games and quizzes on **www.livinglanguage.com/languagelab**, please give them a try.

18-20 points: Great! You're ready to move on to the next unit.

[ ][ ] **points**

Unit 5:
Asking Directions

In Unit 5 you will learn how to ask and give directions. By the end of the unit, you'll be able to:

- ☐ use key vocabulary for getting around town
- ☐ use adjectives in the prenominal position
- ☐ use words indicating location
- ☐ use demonstratives
- ☐ use the verb become
- ☐ use the たら tara-conditional
- ☐ use the と to-conditional

Lesson 17: Words

By the end of Lesson 17, you'll be able to:

- ☐ use key vocabulary for getting around town
- ☐ use adjectives in the prenominal position
- ☐ use words indicating location

Word Builder 1

▶ 17A Word Builder 1 (CD 6, Track 11)

タクシー	takushii	*taxi*
町	machi	*town*
所	tokoro	*place*
道	michi	*street, road*
角	kado	*corner*
右	migi	*right*
左	hidari	*left*
ビル	biru	*high-rise building*
一つ目	hitotsume	*first*
二つ目	futatsume	*second*
三つ目	mittsume	*third*
ゆっくり	yukkuri	*slowly*
まっすぐ	massugu	*straight*
しばらく	shibaraku	*for a while*
曲がります、曲がる	magarimasu, magaru	to turn
歩きます、歩く	arukimasu, aruku	to walk
走ります、走る	hashirimasu, hashiru	to run

* The word, 所 tokoro (*place*), is always accompanied by a modifier, such as an adjective.

Adjectives in the
prenominal position

Demonstratives

Words indicating location

"Become" nouns and
な na-adjectives

Take It Further

Reading Japanese names (of people or places) can be difficult because sometimes very special readings are assigned. Furthermore, uncommon characters (i.e. ones that are not listed in the 常用漢字 Jooyoo Kanji *Kanji Characters in Common Use* announced by the Japanese Ministry of Education) can be used in names. Even adult native speakers of Japanese sometimes have trouble reading names of people and places. In order to prevent mispronouncing names, it is normally required to put furigana over your name and address when filling out documents such as application forms. Do not hesitate to ask how to read a name in kanji when there is no furigana, because mispronouncing names can be insulting to some people.

Word Practice 1

Translate the following words into Japanese.

1. *taxi* _____

2. *town* _____

3. *place* _____

4. *corner* _____

5. *first* _____

6. *second* _____

7. *third* _____

8. *slowly* _____

9. *straight* _____

10. *for a while* _____

ANSWER KEY

1. タクシー takushii; 2. 町 machi; 3. 所 tokoro; 4. 角 kado; 5. 一つ目 hitotsume; 6. 二つ目 futatsume; 7. 三つ目 mittsume; 8. ゆっくり yukkuri; 9. まっすぐ massugu; 10. しばらく shibaraku

Grammar Builder 1
ADJECTIVES IN THE PRENOMINAL POSITION

▶ 17B Grammar Builder 1 (CD 6, Track 12)

There are two different types of adjectives in Japanese: い i-adjectives and な na-adjectives. You already learned い i-adjectives in *Essential Japanese*; い i-adjectives end in い i like 大きい ookii (*big*) and 新しい atarashii (*new*). Adjectives that do not end with い i are な na-adjectives. Let's look at examples of each adjective type.

い I-ADJECTIVES			
大きい ookii	*big*	小さい chiisai	*small*
新しい atarashii	*new*	古い furui	*old*
高い takai	*high, tall, expensive*	低い hikui	*low*
面白い omoshiroi	*interesting*	つまらない tsumaranai	*boring*
おいしい oishii	*delicious*	まずい mazui	*bad (taste)*

Unit 5 Lesson 17: Words　　　335

い I-ADJECTIVES

近い chikai	near	遠い tooi	far
易しい yasashii	easy	難しい muzukashii	difficult
優しい yasashii	kind, gentle		

な NA-ADJECTIVES

きれい kiree	beautiful, pretty, clean	有名 yuumee	famous
便利 benri	convenient	不便 fuben	inconvenient
親切 shinsetsu	kind, generous	簡単 kantan	easy, simple
賑やか nigiyaka	lively	静か shizuka	quiet
暇 hima	have a lot of free time	大切 taisetsu	important

These adjectives appear before nouns in Japanese, just like in English. It is very important to remember that in the case of な na-adjectives, the ending な na is added to adjectives, e.g., 親切な人 shinsetsuna hito (kind person).

大きい大学

ookii daigaku

big university

新しい電車

atarashii densha

new train

高いビル

takai biru

tall building

面白い本

omoshiroi hon

interesting book

古い映画

furui eega

old movie

便利なコンピューター

benrina konpyuutaa

convenient computer

賑やかな町

nigiyakana machi

lively town

簡単な宿題

kantanna shukudai

easy homework

Adjectives in the
prenominal position

Demonstratives

Words indicating location

"Become" nouns and
な na-adjectives

しんせつ ひと
親切な人

shinsetsuna hito

kind person

ゆうめい かいしゃ
有名な会社

yuumeena kaisha

famous company

Now, let's look at the sentences containing adjectives. Note that some of the sentences contain multiple adjectives.

にぎ　　　　　まち
ニューヨークは賑やかな町です。

Nyuuyooku wa nigiyakana machi desu.

New York is a lively town.

きのうあたら　　　　　　　　　　　か
昨日新しいコンピューターを買いました。

Kinoo atarashii konpyuutaa o kaimashita.

I bought a new computer yesterday.

た なか　　　　 しんせつ　 ひと
田中さんは親切な人です。

Tanaka san wa shinsetsuna hito desu.

Mr./Ms. Tanaka is a kind person.

あね ちい　　 あか くるま か
姉は小さい赤い車を買いました。

Ane wa chiisai akai kuruma o kaimashita.

My older sister bought a small red car.

ふる　 おもしろ えい が　 み
古い面白い映画が見たいです。

Furui omoshiroi eega ga mitai desu.

I want to see an interesting old movie.

Note that な na is added to な na-adjectives even if they don't immediately precede a noun, being separated from it by another adjective, e.g., 有名^{ゆうめい}ないいレストラン yuumeena ii resutoran (*famous good restaurant*).

✎ Work Out 1

A. Choose the appropriate adjectives from the list below to complete the sentences. English equivalents are given in parentheses.

新^{あたら}しい atarashii, 親切^{しんせつ}な shinsetsuna, 簡単^{かんたん}な kantanna, おいしい oishii, 面白^{おもしろ}い omoshiroi, 有名^{ゆうめい}な yuumeena

1. _____ すしが食^たべたいです。(*delicious*)

   _____ sushi ga tabetai desu.

2. 兄^{あに}は _____ 大学^{だいがく}で勉強^{べんきょう}でしています。(*famous*)

   Ani wa _____ daigaku de benkyooshite imasu.

3. _____ 映画^{えいが}が見^みたいです。(*interesting*)

   _____ eega ga mitai desu.

4. 父^{ちち}は _____ 車^{くるま}を買^かいました。(*new*)

   Chichi wa _____ kuruma o kaimashita.

5. 森^{もり}さんは _____ 人^{ひと}です。(*kind*)

   Mori san wa _____ hito desu.

6. _____ 仕事^{しごと}ですが、三時間^{さんじかん}かかりました。(*easy*)

   _____ shigoto desu ga, sanjikan kakarimashita.

Adjectives in the
prenominal position

Demonstratives

Words indicating location

"Become" nouns and
な na-adjectives

B. Fill in the blanks with Japanese equivalents of the English adjectives in parentheses.

1. _____ 部屋ですね。 *(clean)*

   _____ heya desu ne.

2. 週末映画を見ましたが、_____ 映画でした。 *(boring)*

   Shuumatsu eega o mimashita ga, _____ eega deshita.

3. 鈴木さんは _____ 会社で働いています。 *(famous)*

   Suzuki san wa _____ kaisha de hataraite imasu.

4. 新宿や渋谷は _____ 所です。 *(lively)*

   Shinjuku ya shibuya wa _____ tokoro desu.

5. _____ コーヒーが飲みたいです。 *(delicious)*

   _____ koohii ga nomitai desu.

ANSWER KEY

A: 1. おいしい Oishii; 2. 有名な yuumeena; 3. 面白い Omoshiroi; 4. 新しい atarashii; 5. 親切な shinsetsuna; 6. 簡単な Kantanna

B: 1. きれいな Kireena; 2. つまらない tsumaranai; 3. 有名な yuumeena; 4. 賑やかな nigiyakana; 5. おいしい Oishii

Word Builder 2

▶ 17C Word Builder 2 (CD 6, Track 13)

郵便局	yuubinkyoku	*post office*
銀行	ginkoo	*bank*
喫茶店	kissaten	*coffee shop*

映画館 (えいがかん)	eegakan	movie theater
建物 (たてもの)	tatemono	building
交差点 (こうさてん)	koosaten	intersection
信号 (しんごう)	shingoo	traffic light
メートル	meetoru	meter
かばん	kaban	bag
手前 (てまえ)	temae	before, this side
渡ります (わた)、渡る (わた)	watarimasu, wataru	to cross
見えます (み)、見える (み)	miemasu, mieru	to be able to be seen, to be visible
なります、なる	narimasu, naru	to become

✎ Word Practice 2

Translate the following words into Japanese.

1. *post office* _____

2. *bank* _____

3. *coffee shop* _____

4. *movie theater* _____

5. *building* _____

6. *intersection* _____

7. *traffic light* _____

8. *meter* _____

Adjectives in the prenominal position — Demonstratives

Words indicating location — "Become" nouns and な na-adjectives

9. *bag* _____

10. *before, this side* _____

ANSWER KEY
1. 郵便局 yuubinkyoku; 2. 銀行 ginkoo; 3. 喫茶店 kissaten; 4. 映画館 eegakan; 5. 建物 tatemono;
6. 交差点 koosaten; 7. 信号 shingoo; 8. メートル meetoru; 9. かばん kaban; 10. 手前 temae

Grammar Builder 2
WORDS INDICATING LOCATION

▶ 17D Grammar Builder 2 (CD 6, Track 14)

Let's learn some words indicating location in Japanese.

X の前	X no mae	*in front of X*
X の上	X no ue	*on/above X*
X の横	X no yoko	*the side of X*
X の中	X no naka	*inside X*
X と Y の間	X to Y no aida	*between X and Y*
X の後ろ	X no ushiro	*behind X*
X の下	X no shita	*under X*
X の隣	X no tonari	*next to X*
X の向かい(側)	X no mukai(gawa)	*across from X*
X のまわり	X no mawari	*around X*

Now, let's look at words indicating location used in sentences.

Intermediate Japanese

A: 銀行はどこですか。

Ginkoo wa doko desu ka.

Where is the bank?

B: 銀行は郵便局の前ですよ。

Ginkoo wa yuubinkyoku no mae desu yo.

The bank is in front of the post office.

A: 映画館の前に何がありますか。

Eegakan no mae ni nani ga arimasu ka.

What's in front of the movie theater?

B: 映画館の前にレストランがあります。

Eegakan no mae ni resutoran ga arimasu.

There's a restaurant in front of the movie theater.

A: かばんの中に何がありますか。

Kaban no naka ni nani ga arimasu ka.

What's in the bag?

B: かばんの中に本とノートがあります。

Kaban no naka ni hon to nooto ga arimasu.

There are (a) book(s) and (a) notebook(s) in the bag.

A: 辞書はどこですか。

Jisho wa doko desu ka.

Where is the dictionary?

Adjectives in the
prenominal position

Demonstratives

Words indicating location

"Become" nouns and
な na-adjectives

B: 辞書は机の上にありますよ。

Jisho wa tsukue no ue ni arimasu yo.

The dictionary is on the desk.

A: デパートと映画館の間に何がありますか。

Depaato to eegakan no aida ni nani ga arimasu ka.

What's between the department store and the movie theater?

B: デパートと映画館の間にレストランがあります。

Depaato to eegakan no aida ni resutoran ga arimasu.

There's a restaurant between the department store and the movie theater.

✎ Work Out 2

Choose the appropriate words indicating location to complete the sentences.
You will also need to insert the appropriate particles in the spaces indicated by
parentheses.

前 mae, 後ろ ushiro, 上 ue, 下 shita, 隣 tonari, 向かい(側) mukai (gawa),
間 aida, 中 naka

1. *The post office is in front of the bank.*

   郵便局は銀行(_____) _____ (_____)あります。

   Yuubinkyoku wa ginkoo (_____) _____ (_____) arimasu.

2. *There's a movie theater next to the station.*

   駅 (_____) _____ (_____) 映画館があります。

   Eki (_____) _____ (_____) eegakan ga arimasu.

3. *There are books and pens on the desk.*

机 (＿＿＿＿) ＿＿＿＿ (＿＿＿) 本とペンがあります。

Tsukue (＿＿＿＿) ＿＿＿＿ (＿＿＿) hon to pen ga arimasu.

4. *The restaurant is behind the department store.*

レストランはデパート (＿＿＿＿) ＿＿＿＿＿＿＿ です。

Resutoran wa depaato (＿＿＿＿) ＿＿＿＿＿＿＿ desu.

5. *Ms.Yamada is between Ms. Watanabe and Ms. Koyama*

山田さんは渡辺さん (＿＿＿＿) 小山さん (＿＿＿＿) ＿＿＿＿＿

(＿＿＿＿)います。

Yamada san wa Watanabe san (＿＿＿＿) Koyama san (＿＿＿＿)

＿＿＿＿＿ (＿＿＿＿) imasu.

ANSWER KEY

1. の no, 前mae, に ni; 2. の no, 隣tonari, に ni; 3. の no, 上ue, に ni; 4. の no, 後ろushiro; 5. と to, の no, 間aida, に ni

✎ Drive It Home

A. Fill in the blanks with adjectives based on the English translation.

1. ＿＿＿＿＿＿＿ 建物

＿＿＿＿＿＿＿＿＿ tatemono

new building

2. ＿＿＿＿＿＿＿ 建物

＿＿＿＿＿＿＿ tatemono

old building

Words indicating location

"Become" nouns and
な na-adjectives

3. _____ 建物
たてもの

_____ tatemono

tall building

4. _____ 建物
たてもの

_____ tatemono

pretty building

5. _____ 建物
たてもの

_____ tatemono

famous building

B. Fill in the blanks with expressions indicating location.

1. 建物 _____
たてもの

tatemono _____

in front of the building

2. 建物 _____
たてもの

tatemono _____

around the building

3. 建物 _____
たてもの

tatemono _____

across the building

4. 建物 _____
たてもの

tatemono _____

next to the building

5. 公園と建物 _____
   <ruby>公園<rt>こうえん</rt></ruby> <ruby>建物<rt>たてもの</rt></ruby>

kooen to tatemono _____

between the park and the building

ANSWER KEY
A: 1. 新しい atarashii; 2. 古い furui; 3. 高い takai; 4. きれいな kireena; 5. 有名な yuumeena
B: 1. の前 no mae; 2. のまわり no mawari; 3. の向かい(側) no mukai(gawa); 4. の隣 no tonari;
5. の間 no aida

🌐 Culture Note

In the United States every street has a name. In Japan, on the other hand, only
major roads have names, while most smaller streets don't. Of course, this can
make getting around a Japanese town or a city a bit of a challenge. The best thing
to do if you're lost is to ask a passerby or a policeman for help with finding the
place you're looking for. You'll find a policeman at a police box, which is a small
building where policemen are located. In big cities like Tokyo, there are many
such police boxes, and people often refer to them to ask for directions and report
lost or found items.

How Did You Do?

Let's see how you did! By now, you should be able to:

☐ use key vocabulary for getting around town (Still unsure? Jump back to page 333)

☐ use adjectives in the prenominal position (Still unsure? Jump back to page 335)

☐ use words indicating location (Still unsure? Jump back to page 342)

✎ Word Recall

1. 電話する denwasuru

2. 探す sagasu

3. 使う tsukau

4. 予約する yoyakusuru

5. 待つ matsu

6. かかる kakaru

7. 貸す kasu

8. 待たせる mataseru

9. 遅れる okureru

10. 働く hataraku

a. *to make a reservation, to make an appointment*

b. *to make a phone call*

c. *to work*

d. *to keep someone waiting*

e. *to be late*

f. *to lend*

g. *to use*

h. *to look for*

i. *to take (time)*

j. *to wait*

ANSWER KEY

1. b; 2. h; 3. g; 4. a; 5. j; 6. i; 7. f; 8. d; 9. e; 10. c

Lesson 18: Phrases

By the end of Lesson 18, you'll be able to:

☐ use demonstratives

☐ use the verb *become*

Phrase Builder 1

▶ 18A Phrase Builder 1 (CD 6, Track 15)

地下鉄の駅	chikatetsu no eki	subway station
この道	kono michi	this street
一つ目の角	hitotsume no kado	the first corner
左に曲がります	hidari ni magarimasu	turn left
もう少しゆっくり	moo sukoshi yukkuri	a little more slowly
そうか。	Sooka.	I see. (casual)
まっすぐ行くと	massugu iku to	if you go straight
白い大きいビル	shiroi ookii biru	big white building (lit., white big building)
そのビル	sono biru	that building (closer to the addressee)
そのビルの前	sono biru no mae	in front of that building
歩いて五分ぐらい	aruite gofun gurai	about a five minute walk
日本に着きます	nihon ni tsukimasu	arrive in Japan

✎ Phrase Practice 1

Fill in the missing words below.

1. _____駅

_____eki

subway station

2. _____ 道
       みち

   _____michi

   this street

3. _____ 角
       かど

   _____ kado

   the first corner

4. 左に _____
   ひだり

   hidari ni _____

   turn left

5. _____ ゆっくり

   _____ yukkuri

   a little more slowly

6. _____ と

   _____ to

   if you go straight

7. _____ 五分ぐらい
       ごふん

   _____ gofun gurai

   about a five minute walk

8. 日本に _____
   にほん

   nihon ni _____

   arrive in Japan

ANSWER KEY

1. 地下鉄の chikatetsu no; 2. この kono; 3. 一つ目の hitotsume no; 4. 曲がります magarimasu; 5. もう少し moo sukoshi; 6. まっすぐ行く massugu iku; 7. 歩いて aruite; 8. 着きます tsukimasu

Grammar Builder 1
DEMONSTRATIVES

▶ 18B Grammar Builder 1 (CD 6, Track 16)

Let's review Japanese demonstratives—words like *this* and *that*. We'll also review the question word equivalent *which*.

これ	kore	*this (closer to the speaker)*
それ	sore	*that (closer to the addressee)*
あれ	are	*that (far from both the speaker and the addressee)*
どれ	dore	*which one*

Note that there are two Japanese words—それ sore and あれ are—meaning *that*. それ Sore refers to something closer to the addressee, while あれ are refers to something far from both the speaker and the addressee.

A: これは何ですか。

Kore wa nan desu ka.

What's this?

B: それは日本語の辞書ですよ。

Sore wa nihongo no jisho desu yo.

That's a Japanese dictionary.

A: あれは何ですか。

Are wa nan desu ka.

What's that?

B: あれは郵便局です。

Are wa yuubinkyoku desu.

That's a post office.

A: どれを買いますか。

Dore o kaimasu ka.

Which one will you buy?

B: これとそれを買います。

Kore to sore o kaimasu.

I will buy this (one) and that (one).

Remember that when demonstratives appear before nouns, they become この kono, その sono, and あの ano; どれ dore becomes どの dono.

この本	kono hon	*this book*
その本	sono hon	*that book (closer to the addressee)*
あの本	ano hon	*that book (far from both the speaker and the addressee)*
どの本	dono hon	*which book*

この本は面白いですが、その本はつまらないです。

Kono hon wa omoshiroi desu ga, sono hon wa tsumaranai desu.

This book is interesting, but that book is boring.

A: あのきれいな建物は何ですか。

Ano kireena tatemono wa nan desu ka.

What's that beautiful building?

B: あれは新しいデパートです。

Are wa atarashii depaato desu.

That's a new department store.

A: どの映画が見たいですか。

Dono eega ga mitai desu ka.

Which movie do you want to see?

B: この映画が見たいです。

Kono eega ga mitai desu.

I want to see this movie.

It is important to know that the demonstratives これ kore, それ sore, and あれ are cannot be used when referring to people. For instance, when introducing 鈴木さん Suzuki san (*Mr./Ms. Suzuki*), it would be very rude to say, これは鈴木さんです Kore wa Suzuki san desu (*This is Mr./Ms. Suzuki*). In this situation, you have to use demonstrative words こちら kochira, あちら achira and そちら sochira. These words mean *this way, that way (closer to the addressee)* and *that way (far from both the speaker and the addressee)* and are used when pointing the direction. They can also be used when making introductions.

Adjectives in the prenominal position

Demonstratives

Words indicating location

"Become" nouns and な na-adjectives

こちらへどうぞ。

Kochira e doozo.

Please come this way.

こちらは鈴木さんです。

Kochira wa Suzuki san desu.

This is Mr./Ms. Suzuki.

On the other hand, これ kore (*this*) and この人 kono hito (*this person*) can be used when referring to a person in a picture. Next, let's look at Japanese expressions corresponding to English *here* and *there*.

ここ	koko	*here*
そこ	soko	*there (closer to the addressee)*
あそこ	asoko	*there (far from both the speaker and the addressee)*
どこ	doko	*where*

A: 高橋さんのノートはどこですか。

Takahashi san no nooto wa doko desu ka.

Where's Mr./Ms. Takahashi's notebook?

B: 高橋さんのノートはここにありますよ。

Takahashi san no nooto wa koko ni arimasu yo.

Mr./Ms. Takahashi's notebook is here.

A: そこに何_{なに}がありますか。

Soko ni nani ga arimasu ka.

What's there?

B: 新聞_{しんぶん}があります。

Shinbun ga arimasu.

There's newspaper.

A: 駅_{えき}はどこですか。

Eki wa doko desu ka.

Where is a station?

B: あそこです。

Asoko desu.

It's over there.

✎ Work Out 1

Fill in the blanks with the appropriate demonstratives.

1. _____ はテイラーさんの車_{くるま}です。

   _____ wa Teiraa san no kuruma desu.

   This is Taylor's car.

2. A:どれがいいですか。

   Dore ga ii desu ka.

   Which (one) is good?

B: _____ がいいです。

_____ **ga ii desu.**

That one (over there) is good.

3. _____建物は郵便局です。
<small>たてもの　ゆうびんきょく</small>

_____ **tatemono wa yuubinkyoku desu.**

That building (closer to you) is a post office.

4. *A:* 病院はどこですか。
<small>びょういん</small>

Byooin wa doko desu ka.

Where is a hospital?

B: _____ です。

_____ **desu.**

It's over there.

5. _____映画は面白いです。
<small>えいが　おもしろ</small>

_____ **eega wa omoshiroi desu.**

This movie is interesting.

6. _____に来てください。
<small>き</small>

_____ **ni kite kudasai.**

Please come here.

ANSWER KEY

1. これ Kore; **2.** あれ Are; **3.** その Sono; **4.** あそこ Asoko; **5.** この Kono; **6.** ここ Koko

Phrase Builder 2

▶ 18C Phrase Builder 2 (CD 6, Track 17)

この辺に	kono hen ni	in this area
ここから	koko kara	from here
どうやって	doo yatte	how
二つ目の交差点	futatsume no koosaten	the second intersection
50メートルぐらい	gojuu meetoru gurai	about fifty meters
スペイン料理の レストラン	supein ryoori no resutoran	Spanish restaurant
新しいきれいな建物	atarashii kireena tatemono	nice new building (lit., new nice building)
信号の手前	shingoo no temae	before the traffic light
(メール/イーメール) で聞く	(meeru/iimeeru) de kiku	inquire by e-mail
四月になります	shigatsu ni narimasu	April has come (lit., become April)

Take It Further

The phrase, どうやって doo yatte, is a combination of どう doo (how) and the て te-form of やります yarimasu (do); it can be translated as how. This may be a little confusing because どう doo by itself also means how: どうですか Doo desu ka. (How is it?). The difference is that どうやって doo yatte is used only when asking about how to do something or how to get to a certain destination.

Adjectives in the
prenominal position

Demonstratives

Words indicating location

"Become" nouns and
な na-adjectives

✎ Phrase Practice 2

Translate the expressions below.

1. *in this area* _____

2. *from here* _____

3. *how* _____

4. *the second intersection* _____

5. *about fifty meters* _____

6. *nice new building* _____

7. *before the traffic light* _____

8. *April has come* _____

ANSWER KEY

1. この辺に kono hen ni; 2. ここから koko kara; 3. どうやって doo yatte; 4. 二つ目の交差点 futatsume no koosaten; 5. 50メートルぐらい gojuu meetoru gurai; 6. 新しいきれいな建物 atarashii kireena tatemono; 7. 信号の手前 shingoo no temae; 8. 四月になります shigatsu ni narimasu

Grammar Builder 2
"BECOME" NOUNS AND な NA-ADJECTIVES

▶ 18D Grammar Builder 2 (CD 6, Track 18)

It is possible to express the concept of becoming, e.g., *to become a teacher* or *to become famous*, in Japanese using the structure with になります/になる ni narimasu/ni naru.

noun + になります/なる	*noun* + ni narimasu/naru
stem of な-*adjective* + になります/なる	*stem of* na-*adjective* + ni narimasu/naru

大学生になる

daigakusee ni naru

become a college student

会社員になる

kaishain ni naru

become a company employee

春になる

haru ni naru

become spring (i.e., it's spring/spring arrived)

有名になる

yuumee ni naru

become famous

〜が上手になる

… ga joozu ni naru

become good at …

便利になる

benri ni naru

become convenient

Now, let's look at some sentences containing these structures.

Adjectives in the
prenominal position

Demonstratives

Words indicating location

"Become" nouns and
な na-adjectives

伊藤さんは来年大学生になります。

Itoo san wa rainen daigakusee ni narimasu.

Mr./Ms. Ito will become a college student next year.

A: 将来何になりたいですか。

Shoorai nani ni naritai desu ka.

What do you want to be (lit., become) in the future?

B: 英語の先生になりたいです。

Eego no sensee ni naritai desu.

I want to be (lit., become) an English teacher.

車を買いましたから、便利になりました。

Kuruma o kaimashita kara, benri ni narimashita.

I bought a car, so it became convenient.

この辺は週末とても賑やかになります。

Kono hen wa shuumatsu totemo nigiyaka ni narimasu.

This area becomes very lively on a weekend.

毎日練習していますから、テニスが上手になりました。

Mainichi renshuushite imasu kara, tenisu ga joozu ni narimashita.

Since I'm practicing every day, I became good at tennis.

✎ Work Out 2

A. Translate the following Japanese sentences into English.

1. 将来何になりたいですか。
   ^{しょうらいなに}

   Shoorai nani ni naritai desu ka.

   _____

2. 医者になりたいです。
   ^{いしゃ}

   Isha ni naritai desu.

   _____

3. その会社は最近有名になりました。
   ^{かいしゃ　さいきんゆうめい}

   Sono kaisha wa saikin (_recently_) yuumee ni narimashita.

   _____

4. この辺は夜とても静かになります。
   ^{へん　よる　　　しず}

   Kono hen wa yoru totemo shizuka ni narimasu.

   _____

5. 十二時半になりましたから、昼ご飯を食べに行きませんか。
   ^{じゅうにじはん　　　　　　　　　ひる　はん　た　い}

   Juuniji han ni narimashita kara, hirugohan o tabe ni ikimasen ka.

   _____

B. Fill in the blanks with the appropriate expressions from the list below.

その角 sono kado, この辺 kono hen, あの建物 ano tatemono, この道 kono michi, ここから koko kara

1. _____ をまっすぐ行ってください。

_____ o massugu itte kudasai.

Please go straight along this street.

2. _____ に銀行はありますか。

_____ ni ginkoo wa arimasu ka.

Is there a bank in this area?

3. 地下鉄の駅は _____ の手前にあります。

Chikatetsu no eki wa _____ no temae ni

arimasu.

The subway station is before that building over there.

4. _____ 大学まで歩いて二十分ぐらいかかります。

_____ daigaku made aruite nijuppun gurai kakarimasu.

It's about a twenty minute walk from here to the university.

5. _____ を左に曲がって、まっすぐ行きます。

_____ o hidari ni magatte, massugu ikimasu.

Turn left at that corner (closer to you), and go straight ahead.

ANSWER KEY

A: 1. *What do you want to be in the future?* 2. *I want to be a doctor.* 3. *That company has recently become famous.* 4. *This area becomes very quiet (in the evening/at night).* 5. *It turned twelve thirty, so why don't we go to have lunch?*

B: 1. この道 Kono michi; 2. この辺 Kono hen; 3. あの建物 ano tatemono; 4. ここから Koko kara; 5. その角 Sono kado

✎ Drive It Home

A. Fill in the blanks with the appropriate demonstratives.

1. _____ は何ですか。

    _____ wa nan desu ka.

    What's this?

2. _____ は何ですか。

    _____ wa nan desu ka.

    What's that? (closer to the addressee)

3. _____ は何ですか。

    _____ wa nan desu ka.

    What's that? (far from both the speaker and the addressee)

4. _____ がいいですか。

    _____ ga ii desu ka.

    Which (one) is good?

B. Fill in each of the blanks with an appropriate particle.

1. 大学生_____ なりました。

    Daigakusee _____ narimashita.

2. 医者_____なりたいです。

    Isha _____ naritai desu.

3. 山田さんは有名_____なりました。

    Yamada san wa yuumee _____ narimashita.

4. 十二時半<ruby>じゅうにじはん</ruby>＿＿＿＿＿なりました。

Juuniji han ＿＿＿＿＿ narimashita.

ANSWER KEY

A: 1. これ Kore; 2. それ Sore; 3. あれ Are; 4. どれ Dore

B: 1.-4. all に ni

💡 Tip!

The best way to practice demonstratives is to practice them in real situations by pointing to objects around you and referring to the objects using appropriate demonstratives. For instance, if you are in the living room, you can point to a sofa, a table, a television, and whatever other objects you see, and form sentences using demonstratives. You can say これはソファーです Kore wa sofaa (*sofa*) desu or このソファーはいいです Kono sofaa wa ii desu. Then, you can change your location in the living room and try referring to the same objects from a new perspective.

How Did You Do?

Let's see how you did! By now, you should be able to:

☐ use demonstratives (Still unsure? Jump back to page 351)

☐ use the verb *become* (Still unsure? Jump back to page 358)

✎ Word Recall

1. グループ発表<ruby>はっぴょう</ruby> gruupu happyoo   a. *this year*

2. 休み<ruby>やす</ruby> yasumi   b. *group presentation*

3. 晩<ruby>ばん</ruby> ban   c. *spring*

4. 今年 kotoshi   d. *evening, night*

5. 経済 keezai   e. *fall, autumn*

6. 春 haru   f. *economy*

7. 万年筆 mannenhitsu   g. *day off, holiday, vacation*

8. 少々 shooshoo   h. *fountain pen*

9. 昼食 chuushoku   i. *lunch*

10. 秋 aki   j. *a little*

ANSWER KEY

1. b; 2. g; 3. d; 4. a; 5. f; 6. c; 7. h; 8. j; 9. i; 10. e

Lesson 19: Sentences

By the end of this lesson, you'll be able to:

☐ use the たら tara-conditional

Sentence Builder 1

▶ 19A Sentence Builder 1 (CD 6, Track 19)

地下鉄の駅へ行きたいんですけど。

Chikatetsu no eki e ikitai n desu kedo.

I want to go to the subway station, but ...

Adjectives in the
prenominal position

Demonstratives

Words indicating location

"Become" nouns and
な na-adjectives

地下鉄の駅だったら、この道をまっすぐ行きます。

Chikatetsu no eki dattara, kono michi o massugu ikimasu.

If it's a subway station, go straight on this street.

一つ目の角を左に曲がります。

Hitotsume no kado o hidari ni magarimasu.

Turn left at the first corner.

もう少しゆっくりお願いします。

Moo sukoshi yukkuri onegaishimasu.

A little more slowly, please.

まっすぐ行くと、右側に大きいビルがあります。

Massugu iku to, migigawa ni ookii biru ga arimasu.

If you go straight, there's a big building on your right.

ビルの前に地下鉄の駅があります。

Biru no mae ni chikatetsu no eki ga arimasu.

There's a subway station in front of the building.

歩いて五分ぐらいでしょう。

Aruite gofun gurai deshoo.

It will probably be about a five minute walk.

✎ Sentence Practice 1

Fill in the missing words in each of the following sentences.

1. _____ へ行^いきたいんですけど。

_____ e ikitai n desu kedo.

I want to go to the subway station, but …

2. 地下鉄^{ちかてつ}の駅^{えき}だったら、この道^{みち}を _____ 。

Chikatetsu no eki dattara, kono michi o _____

_____ .

If it's a subway station, go straight on this street.

3. _____ を左^{ひだり}に曲^まがります。

_____ o hidari ni magarimasu.

Turn left at the first corner.

4. もう少^{すこ}し _____ 。

Moo sukoshi _____ .

A little more slowly, please.

5. _____ 、右側^{みぎがわ}に大^{おお}きいビルがあります。

_____ , migigawa ni ookii biru ga arimasu.

If you go straight, there's a big building on your right.

6. _____ 地下鉄^{ちかてつ}の駅^{えき}があります。

_____ chikatetsu no eki ga arimasu.

There's a subway station in front of the building.

7. _____ 五分ぐらいでしょう。
<ruby>五分<rt>ご ふん</rt></ruby>

_____ gofun gurai deshoo.

It will probably be about a five minute walk.

ANSWER KEY
1. 地下鉄の駅 Chikatetsu no eki; 2. まっすぐ行きます massugu ikimasu; 3. 一つ目の角 Hitotsume no kado; 4. ゆっくりお願いします yukkuri onegaishimasu; 5. まっすぐ行くと Massugu iku to; 6. ビルの前に Biru no mae ni; 7. 歩いて Aruite

Grammar Builder 1
THE たら TARA-CONDITIONAL

▶ 19B Grammar Builder 1 (CD 6, Track 20)

Conditional sentences express a condition and a possible outcome, such as the English conditional sentence *If I buy a car, it will be easier to get to work*. Japanese has two different types of conditional sentences: the たら tara-conditional and the と to-conditional. Let's first discuss the たら tara-conditional, which corresponds to English clauses starting in *if* or *when*. In English we talk about clauses: the *if/when*-clause and the main clause. The same structure applies to Japanese.

> *Plain past tense form of verbs/adjectives/copula +* ら ra, ...

The clause that expresses the condition (corresponding to the English *if/when*-clause) ends in ら ra. Since the plain past tense form of verbs, adjectives, or copula precede ら ra and all end with た ta, e.g., 来た kita (*came, arrived*), 学生だった gakusee datta (*was a student*) and 高かった takakatta (*was expensive*), the *if*-clause always ends with た+ら ta + ra, which explains the name of this construction.

日本に着いたら、電話してください。

Nihon ni tsuitara, denwashite kudasai.

If/When you arrive in Japan, please call me.

車を買ったら、車で会社に行きます。

Kuruma o kattara, kuruma de kaisha ni ikimasu.

If/When I buy a car, I will go to work (lit., the company) by car.

大学に電車で行ったら、三十分かかります。

Daigaku ni densha de ittara, sanjuppun gurai kakarimasu.

If I go to the university by train, it will take about thirty minutes.

学生だったら、もっと勉強してください。

Gakusee dattara, motto benkyooshite kudasai.

If you are a student, please study more.

Note that the main clauses following the たら tara-clauses above are all in the non-past tense; they can also be in the past tense as shown in the following examples.

家に帰ったら、家の前に友達がいました。

Uchi ni kaettara, ie no mae ni tomodachi ga imashita.

When I went home, my friend was in front of the house.

会社に歩いて行ったら、一時間かかりました。

Kaisha ni aruite ittara, ichijikan kakarimashita.

When I went to the company on foot (lit., by walking), it took one hour.

クラスに行ったら、先生も学生もいませんでした。

Kurasu ni ittara, sensee mo gakusee mo imasen deshita.

When I went to the class, neither a teacher nor students were there.

When the main clause of the たら tara-conditional in the past tense, the event or the action described is something the speaker was not expecting, and therefore, beyond the speaker's control.

日本人だったら、もっとたくさん漢字を知っているんですが・・・。

Nihonjin dattara, motto takusan kanji o shitte iru n desu ga …

If I were Japanese, I would know more kanji, but …

お金があったら、新しい車を買うでしょう。

Okane ga attara, atarashii kuruma o kau deshoo.

If I had money, I would probably buy a new car.

✎ Work Out 1

Match the Japanese sentences to their English translations.

1. 日本へ行ったら、相撲が見たいです。
   Nihon e ittara, sumoo ga mitai desu.

2. 時間があったら、映画が見たいです。
   Jikan ga attara, eega ga mitai desu.

3. 分からなかったら、聞いてください。
   Wakaranakattara, kiite kudasai.

4. 山田さんが来たら、教えてください。
   Yamada san ga kitara, oshiete kudasai.

a. *If I had money, I would buy a new computer, but …*

b. *If I had siblings, it would be nice, but …*

c. *If I go to Japan, I want to see sumo.*

d. *When I went to the new Italian restaurant, Mr./Ms. Kawamura and Mr./Ms. Mori were there.*

5. 駅_{えき}に歩_{ある}いて行_いったら、二十分_{にじゅっぷん}かかりました。**Eki ni aruite ittara, nijuppun kakarimashita.**

e. Please tell me when Mr./ Ms.Yamada comes.

6. タイムズスクエアへ行_いったら、人_{ひと}がたくさんいました。 **Taimuzu sukuea e ittara, hito ga takusan imashita.**

f. If you don't understand, please ask me.

7. お金_{かね}があったら、新_{あたら}しいコンピューターを買_かうんですが・・・。**Okane ga attara, atarashii konpyuutaa o kau n desu ga …**

g. When I walked to the station, it took twenty minutes.

8. 兄弟_{きょうだい}がいたら、いいんですけど・・・。**Kyoodai ga itara, ii n desu kedo …**

h. I don't have time today, but if it's tomorrow, it will be ok.

9. 新_{あたら}しいイタリア料理_{りょうり}のレストランへ行_いったら、川村_{かわむら}さんと森_{もり}さんがいました。**Atarashii itaria ryoori no resutoran e ittara, Kawamura san to Mori san ga imashita.**

i. When I went to Times Square, there were many people.

10. 今日_{きょう}は時間_{じかん}がありませんが、明日_{あした}だったら大丈夫_{だいじょうぶ}です。**Kyoo wa jikan ga arimasen ga, ashita dattara daijoobu desu.**

j. If I have time, I want to see a movie.

ANSWER KEY

1. c; 2. j; 3. f; 4. e; 5.g; 6. i; 7. a; 8. b; 9. d; 10. h

Adjectives in the
prenominal position

Demonstratives

Words indicating location

"Become" nouns and
な na-adjectives

Sentence Builder 2

▶ 19C Sentence Builder 2 (CD 6, Track 21)

この辺に郵便局はありますか。

Kono hen ni yuubinkyoku wa arimasu ka.

Is there a post office in this area?

ここから歩いて十五分ぐらいかかります。

Koko kara aruite juugofun gurai kakarimasu.

It's about a fifteen minute walk from here.

どうやって行ったらいいでしょうか。

Doo yatte ittara ii deshoo ka.

How should I go/get there?

二つ目の交差点を渡って、50メートルぐらいきます。

Futatsume no koosaten o watatte, gojuu meetoru gurai ikimasu.

Cross the second intersection, and go for about fifty meters.

50メートルぐらい行くと、左側にレストランがあります。

Gojuu meetoru gurai iku to, hidarigawa ni resutoran ga arimasu.

If you go for about fifty meters, there will be a restaurant on your left.

新しいきれいな建物です。

Atarashii kireena tatemono desu.

It's a nice new building.

そのレストランの角を右に曲がって、しばらくまっすぐ行きます。

Sono resutoran no kado o migi ni magatte, shibaraku massugu ikimasu.

Turn right at the corner of that restaurant, and go straight for a while.

しばらくまっすぐ<ruby>行<rt>い</rt></ruby>くと、<ruby>左側<rt>ひだりがわ</rt></ruby>に<ruby>郵便局<rt>ゆうびんきょく</rt></ruby>が<ruby>見<rt>み</rt></ruby>えます。

Shibaraku massugu iku to, hidarigawa ni yuubinkyoku ga miemasu.

If you go straight for a while, you will see a post office on your left.

<ruby>信号<rt>しんごう</rt></ruby>の<ruby>手前<rt>てまえ</rt></ruby>です。

Shingoo no temae desu.

It's before the traffic light.

✎ Sentence Practice 2

Fill in the missing words in each of the following sentences.

1. ここから<ruby>歩<rt>ある</rt></ruby>いて<ruby>十五分<rt>じゅうごふん</rt></ruby>ぐらい ＿＿＿＿＿＿＿＿＿ 。

   Koko kara aruite juugofun gurai ＿＿＿＿＿＿＿＿＿＿＿.

   It's about a fifteen minute walk from here.

2. どうやってつったら<ruby>行<rt>い</rt></ruby>ったら ＿＿＿＿＿＿＿＿＿＿＿ 。

   Doo yatte ittara ＿＿＿＿＿＿＿＿＿＿.

   How should I go/get there?

3. <ruby>二<rt>ふた</rt></ruby>つ<ruby>目<rt>め</rt></ruby>の ＿＿＿＿＿＿＿＿＿＿、50メートルぐらい<ruby>行<rt>い</rt></ruby>きます。

   Futatsume no ＿＿＿＿＿＿＿＿＿＿＿＿, gojuu meetoru gurai ikimasu.

   Cross the second intersection, and go for about fifty meters.

4. ＿＿＿＿＿＿＿＿＿＿＿ と、<ruby>左側<rt>ひだりがわ</rt></ruby>ににレストランがあります。

   ＿＿＿＿＿＿＿＿＿＿＿＿＿ to, hidarigawa ni resutoran ga arimasu.

   If you go for about fifty meters, there will be a restaurant on your left.

5. _____ 建物^{たてもの}です。

_____ tatemono desu.

It's a nice new building.

6. そのレストランの角^{かど}を _____ 、しばらくまっすぐ行^いきます。

Sono resutoran no kado o _____ ,

shibaraku massugu ikimasu.

Turn right at the corner of that restaurant, and go straight for a while.

7. しばらく _____ と、左側^{ひだりがわ}に郵便局^{ゆうびんきょく}が見^みええます。

Shibaraku _____ to, hidarigawa ni yuubinkyoku

ga miemasu.

If you go straight for a while, you will see a post office on your left.

8. _____ です。

_____ desu.

It's before the traffic light.

ANSWER KEY

1. かかります kakarimasu; 2. いいでしょうか ii deshoo ka; 3. 交差点^{こうさてん}を渡^{わた}って koosaten o watatte; 4. 50メートルぐらい行^いく Gojuu meetoru gurai iku; 5. 新^{あたら}しいきれいな Atarashii kireena; 6. 右^{みぎ}に曲^まがって migi ni magatte; 7. まっすぐ行^いく massugu iku; 8. 信号^{しんごう}の手前^{てまえ} Shingoo no temae

Grammar Builder 2
MORE USES OF THE たら TARA-CONDITIONAL

▶ 19D Grammar Builder 2 (CD 6, Track 22)

The たら tara-conditional is also used when asking for or giving advice.

A: 日本語を勉強したいんですけど、どうしたらいいですか。

Nihongo o benkyooshitai n desu kedo, doo (how) shitara ii desu ka.

I want to study Japanese; what shall I do?

B: 日本に留学したらいいですよ。

Nihon ni ryuugakushitara ii desu yo.

It would be good if you went to Japan to study.

A: 東京駅に行きたいんですけど、どうやって行ったらいいですか。

Tookyoo eki ni ikitai n desu kedo, doo yatte ittara ii desu ka.

I want to go to the Tokyo Station; how should I get there?

B: 電車で行ったらいいでしょう。

Densha de ittara ii deshoo.

It would probably be good if you go by train.

✎ Work Out 2

Match the appropriate suggestions on the right with the questions on the left.

1. この漢字が分からないんですが、どう
したらいいですか。

   **Kono kanji ga wakaranai n desu ga,
doo shitara ii desu ka.**

a. 会社に電話したらどうですか。

   **Kaisha ni denwashitara doo
desu ka.**

2. 渋谷へ行きたいんですけど、どうやっ
て行ったらいいでしょうか。

   **Shibuya e ikitai n desu kedo, doo
yatte ittara ii deshoo ka.**

b. 辞書を見たらどうですか。

   Jisho o mitara doo desu ka.

Adjectives in the
prenominal position

Demonstratives

Words indicating location

"Become" nouns and
な na-adjectives

3.森さんと話したいんですけど、どうし
たらいいですか。

Mori san to hanashitai n desu
kedo, doo shitara ii desu ka.

4.日本語が上手になりたいんですが、
どうしたらいいでしょうか。

Nihongo ga joozu ni naritai n desu
ga, doo shitara ii deshoo ka.

5.おいしいスペイン料理が食べたいんで
すけど、どこへ行ったらいいですか。

Oishii supein ryoori ga tabetai n
desu kedo, doko e ittara ii desu ka.

c.映画館の前のレストランに行ったら
どうですか。

Eegakan no mae no resutoran ni
ittara doo desu ka.

d.地下鉄で行ったらいいですよ。

Chikatetsu de ittara ii desu yo.

e.毎日二時間ぐらい勉強したらいい
ですよ。

Mainichi nijikan gurai
benkyooshitara ii desu yo.

ANSWER KEY

1. b; 2. d; 3. a; 4. e; 5. c

✎ Drive It Home

Fill in the blanks by choosing appropriate words from the word bank.

聞いたら kiitara, 行ったら ittara, 着いたら tsuitara, だったら dattara, あったら
attara

1.日本に _____、電話してください。

Nihon ni _____, denwashite kudasai.

If/When you arrive in Japan, please call me.

2.学生 _____、もっと勉強してください。

Gakusee _____, motto benkyooshite kudasai.

If you are a student, please study more.

3. 会社に歩いて _____ 、一時間かかりました。

かいしゃ ある / いち じ かん

Kaisha ni aruite _____ , **ichijikan kakarimashita.**

When I went to the company on foot (lit., by walking), it took one hour.

4. お金が _____ 、新しい車を買うでしょう。

かね / あたら くるま か

Okane ga _____ , **atarashii kuruma o kau deshoo.**

If I had money, I would probably buy a new car.

5. メールで _____ どうですか。

Meeru de _____ **doo desu ka.**

How about if you inquire by e-mail?

ANSWER KEY

1. 着いたら tsuitara; 2. だったら dattara; 3. 行ったら ittara; 4. あったら attara; 5. 聞いたら kiitara

How Did You Do?

Let's see how you did! By now, you should be able to:

☐ use the たら tara-conditional (Still unsure? Jump back to pages 368 and 374)

🖉 Word Recall

1. 大変 taihen   a. *next year*
たいへん

2. 受付係 uketsukegakari   b. *summer*
うけつけがかり

3. 来年 rainen   c. *other*
らいねん

4. 夏 natsu   d. *receptionist*
なつ

5. 五年間 gonenkan   e. *for five years*
ご ねんかん

6. 他 hoka   f. *winter*
ほか

Adjectives in the
prenominal position

Demonstratives

Words indicating location

"Become" nouns and
な na-adjectives

7. ミーティング miitingu

g. *older sister (someone else's)*

8. お姉<ruby>姉<rt>ねえ</rt></ruby>さん oneesan

h. *breakfast*

9. <ruby>冬<rt>ふゆ</rt></ruby> fuyu

i. *hard, very*

10. <ruby>朝食<rt>ちょうしょく</rt></ruby> chooshoku

j. *meeting*

ANSWER KEY

1. i; 2. d; 3. a; 4. b; 5. e; 6. c; 7. j; 8. g; 9. f; 10. h

Lesson 20: Conversations

Welcome to your last lesson of *Intermediate Japanese* ! By the end of your final lesson, you'll be able to:

☐ use the と to-conditional

Conversation 1

▷ 20A Conversation 1 (Japanese: CD 6, Track 23; Japanese and English: CD 6, Track 24)

Mr. White is in Tokyo trying to find the way to the subway station.

ホワイト/Howaito:	すみません。<ruby>地下鉄<rt>ちかてつ</rt></ruby>の<ruby>駅<rt>えき</rt></ruby>へ<ruby>行<rt>い</rt></ruby>きたいんですけど。
	Sumimasen. Chikatetsu no eki e ikitai n desu kedo.
<ruby>通行人<rt>つうこうにん</rt></ruby>/Tsuukoonin:	<ruby>地下鉄<rt>ちかてつ</rt></ruby>の<ruby>駅<rt>えき</rt></ruby>ですか。<ruby>地下鉄<rt>ちかてつ</rt></ruby>の<ruby>駅<rt>えき</rt></ruby>だったら、この<ruby>道<rt>みち</rt></ruby>をまっすぐ<ruby>行<rt>い</rt></ruby>って、<ruby>一<rt>ひと</rt></ruby>つ<ruby>目<rt>め</rt></ruby>の<ruby>角<rt>かど</rt></ruby>を<ruby>左<rt>ひだり</rt></ruby>に<ruby>曲<rt>ま</rt></ruby>がって···
	Chikatetsu no eki desu ka. Chikatetsu no eki dattara, kono michi o massugu itte, hitotsume no kado o hidari ni magatte...

ホワイト/Howaito:	あのう、すみませんが、もう少しゆっくりお願いします。
	Anoo, sumimasen ga, moo sukoshi yukkuri onegaishimasu.
通行人/Tsuukoonin:	ああそうか。えっと、この道をまっすぐ行って、一つ目の角を左に曲がります
	Aa soo ka. Etto, kono michi o massugu itte, hitotsume no kado o hidari ni magarimasu.
ホワイト/Howaito:	まっすぐ行って、左ですね。
	Massugu itte, hidari desu ne.
通行人/Tsuukoonin:	ええ。それから、しばらくまっすぐ行くと、右側に白い大きいビルがあります。
	Ee. Sorekara, shibaraku massugu iku to, migigawa ni shiroi ookii biru ga arimasu.
ホワイト/Howaito:	白い大きいビルですね。
	Shiroi ookii biru desu ne.
通行人/Tsuukoonin:	ええ。そのビルの前に地下鉄の駅がありますよ。
	Ee. Sono biru no mae ni chikatetsu no eki ga arimasu yo.
ホワイト/Howaito:	ビルの前ですね。
	Biru no mae desu ne.
通行人/Tsuukoonin:	たぶん歩いて十五分ぐらいでしょう。
	Tabun aruite juugofun gurai deshoo.
ホワイト/Howaito:	どうもありがとうございます。
	Doomo arigatoo gozaimasu.

White:	*Excuse me, I want to go to the subway station, but ...*
Passerby:	*Subway station? If it's the subway station, go straight along this street, and turn left at the first corner, and ...*
White:	*Oh, I'm sorry, but a little more slowly, please.*
Passerby:	*Oh, I see. Well, go straight on this street, and turn left at the first corner.*

White:	Go straight and left, right?
Passerby:	Yes. After that, if you go straight for a while, there will be a big white building on your right.
White:	Big white building, right?
White:	Yes. There will be a subway station in front of that building.
Passerby:	In front of the building, right?
Passerby:	Perhaps, it will be about a fifteen minute walk.
White:	Thank you very much.

Take It Further

People often confirm the information they heard by repeating the sentence. For instance, when listening to street directions, you'll probably want to make sure you understood the directions correctly. One way to check your understanding is to repeat the whole sentence, as in この道をまっすぐ行って、左に曲がるんですね? **Kono michi o massugu itte, hidari ni magaru n desu ne?** If the sentence ends with a verb, んです **n desu** is used and the sentential particle ね **ne** is added, as in 左に曲がるんですね? **Hidari ni magaru n desu ne?** Alternatively, you can repeat the key part of the sentence or expression, as in 左ですね? **Hidari desu ne?** In all cases, the final particle ね **ne** is used when confirming information.

✎ Conversation Practice 1

Let's repeat the directions for how to get to the subway station based on the conversation. Fill in the blanks with the missing words. If you're unsure of the answer, listen to the conversation one more time.

1. 道を ＿＿＿＿＿＿＿＿＿＿＿ 行きます。

   Michi o ＿＿＿＿＿＿＿＿＿＿＿ ikimasu.

2. _____ を左に曲がります。

ひだり ま

_____ o hidari ni magarimasu.

3. しばらくまっすぐ行くと、_____に白い大きいビルがあります。

い   しろ おお

Shibaraku massugu iku to, _____ ni shiroi ookii biru ga

arimasu.

4. そのビルの _____ に地下鉄の駅があります

ち か てつ えき

Sono biru no _____ ni chikatetsu no eki ga arimasu.

ANSWER KEY

1. まっすぐ massugu; 2. 一つ目の角 Hitotsume no kado; 3. 右側 migigawa; 4. 前 mae

ひと め かど   みぎがわ   まえ

Grammar Builder 1
と TO-CONDITIONAL

▶ 20B Grammar Builder 1 (CD 6, Track 25)

Now, let's learn another conditional form, the と to-conditional. Unlike the たら tara-conditional, the と to-conditional uses the plain non-past form of verbs, adjectives and the copula です desu.

> *Plain non-past form of verbs/adjectives/copula +* と *to, …*

The と to-conditional is often used when describing a natural consequence of an act or action. For instance, sentences like *When spring comes, it becomes warm* and *If you press this button, the door opens* describe a natural sequence of event, and therefore would use the と to-conditional. The と to-conditional often also expresses the meaning of the English *whenever*. Look at the following sentences.

Unit 5 Lesson 20: Conversations

Adjectives in the
prenominal position

Demonstratives

Words indicating location

"Become" nouns and
な na-adjectives

九月になると台風が来ます。

Kugatsu ni naru to taifuu ga kimasu.

When September comes, typhoons come.

日本へ行くと、いつも歌舞伎を見ます。

Nihon e iku to, itsumo kabuki o mimasu.

When I go to Japan, I always see kabuki.

Note that the above sentences can also be translated using *whenever*. Just as with the たら tara-conditional, when the main clause is in the past tense, it describes an unexpected event.

郵便局へ行くと、斉藤さんがいました。

Yuubinkyoku e iku to, Saitoo san ga imashita.

When I went to the post office, Mr./Ms. Saito was there.

In this sentence the speaker did not expect that Mr./Ms. Saitoo would be at the post office. Since the と to-conditional describes a natural sequence of events, it is often used when giving street directions.

まっすぐ行くと、銀行があります。

Massugu iku to, ginkoo ga arimasu.

If you go straight, there's a bank.

交差点を渡ると、映画館があります。

Koosaten o wataru to, eegakan ga arimasu.

If you cross the intersection, there's a movie theater.

It is important to remember that in directions, the と to-conditional can be used only once.

この道をまっすぐ行って、一つ目の角を左に曲がって、しばらく行くと、右側に銀
行があります。

Kono michi o massugu itte, hitotsume no kado o hidari ni magatte, shibaraku iku to, migigawa ni ginkoo ga arimasu.

Go straight on this street, turn left at the first corner, and if you go for a while, there will be a bank on your right.

Also, since the と to-conditional describes a natural sequence of events, the main clause cannot contain expressions describing a speaker's will and wish, invitation, making a request, asking for and giving a permission, obligation, and command. In this sense, we can say that the と to-conditional is more restricted in its usage than the たら tara-conditional.

✎ Work Out 1

Translate the following Japanese sentences into English.

1. その道をまっすぐ行くと、銀行があります。

   Sono michi o massugu iku to, ginkoo ga arimasu.

   _____

2. あのビルに入ると、フランス料理のレストランがあります。

   Ano biru ni hairu to, furansu ryoori no resutoran ga arimasu.

   _____

3. 居間に行くと、父が寝ていました。

   Ima ni iku to, chichi ga nete imashita.

   _____

Adjectives in the
prenominal position

Demonstratives

Words indicating location

"Become" nouns and
な na-adjectives

4. 交差点を渡って左に曲がると、映画館あります。

   Koosaten o watatte hidari ni magaru to, eegakan ga arimasu.

5. 電車で行くと、四十分ぐらいかかるでしょう。

   Densha de iku to, yonjuppun gurai kakaru deshoo.

ANSWER KEY

1. *If you go straight on that street, there's a bank.* 2. *If you enter that building, there's a French restaurant.* 3. *When I went to the living room, my father was sleeping.* 4. *If you cross the intersection and turn left, there's a movie theater.* 5. *It will probably take about forty minutes if you go by train.*

🔊 Conversation 2

▶ 20C Conversation 2 (Japanese: CD 6, Track 26; Japanese and English: CD 6, Track 27)

Ms. Watanabe, who is in Kyoto, is trying to find a post office.

渡辺/Watanabe:	すみません。この辺に郵便局はありますか。
	Sumimasen. Kono hen ni yuubinkyoku wa arimasu ka.
通行人/Tsuukoonin:	ええ。でも、ここから歩いて十五分ぐらいかかりますよ。
	Ee. Demo, koko kara aruite juugofun gurai kakarimasu yo.
渡辺/Watanabe:	どうやって行ったらいいでしょうか。
	Doo yatte ittara ii deshoo ka.

通行人/Tsuukoonin: えっと、この道をまっすぐ行って、二つ目の交差点を渡って、50メートルぐらい行くと、左側にスペイン料理のレストランがあります。名前はカーサです。

Etto, kono michi o massugu itte, futatsume no koosaten o watatte, gojuu meetoru gurai iku to, hidarigawa ni supein ryoori no resutoran ga arimasu. Namae wa Kaasa desu.

渡辺/Watanabe: カーサですね。

Kaasa desu ne.

通行人/Tsuukoonin: ええ。新しいきれいな建物です。そのレストランの角を右に曲がって、しばらくまっすぐ行くと、左側に郵便局が見えますよ

Ee. Atarashii kireena tatemono desu. Sono resutoran no kado o migi ni magatte, shibaraku massugu iku to, hidarigawa ni yuubinkyoku ga miemasu yo.

渡辺/Watanabe: レストランの角を右に曲がって、まっすぐ行くと、左側ですね。

Resutoran no kado o migi ni magatte, massugu iku to, hidarigawa desu ne.

通行人/Tsuukoonin: ええ。信号の手前です。

Ee. Shingoo no temae desu.

渡辺/Watanabe: 分かりました。どうもありがとうございます。

Wakarimashita. Doomo arigatoo gozaimasu.

Watanabe:	Excuse me. Is there a post office in this area?
Passerby:	Yes. But, it will be about a fifteen minute walk from here.
Watanabe:	How should I get there?
Passerby:	Well, go straight on this street, cross the second intersection, and if you go straight for about fifty meters, there will be a Spanish restaurant on your left. Its name is Casa.
Watanabe:	Casa, right?

Passerby:	Yes. It's a nice new building. Turn right at the corner of that restaurant, and if you go straight for a while, you will see a post office on your left.
Watanabe:	Turn right at the corner of the restaurant, and if I go straight, on my left, right?
Passerby:	Yes. It's before the traffic light.
Watanabe:	I got it. Thank you very much.

✎ Conversation Practice 2

Let's review the directions on how to get to the post office based on the conversation. Fill in the blanks with the missing words. If you're unsure of the answer, listen to the conversation one more time.

1. この道を _____ 行きます。

   Kono michi o _____ ikimasu.

2. _____の交差点を渡ります。

   _____ no koosaten o watarimasu.

3. 50メートルぐらい行くと、___ にスペイン料理のレストランがあります。

   Gojuu meetoru gurai iku to, _____ ni supein ryoori no resutoran ga arimasu.

4. そのレストランの角を _____ に曲がります。

   Sono resutoran no kado o _____ ni magarimasu.

5. しばらくまっすぐ行くと、_____ に郵便局が見えます。

   Shibaraku massugu iku to, _____ ni yuubinkyoku ga miemasu.

ANSWER KEY

1. まっすぐ massugu; 2. 二つ目 Futatsume; 3. 左側 hidarigawa; 4. 右 migi; 5. 左側 hidarigawa

Grammar Builder 2
BACK CHANNEL EXPRESSIONS

▶ 20D Grammar Builder 2 (CD 6, Track 28)

A listener can use different expressions, the so-called あいづち aizuchi (*back-channel expressions*), to show the speaker that he/she is listening to what the speaker is saying. Expressions like そうですか Soo desu ka (*I see*) and そうですね Soo desu ne (*That's right*), as well as ええ Ee (*Yes*) and はい Hai (*Yes*), are used in such a way.

Of course, a listener can also show that he/she is participating in a conversation nonverbally, just by nodding.

✎ Work Out 2

Choose the right expression from the options given in parentheses to fill in the blanks.

1. その角を右に、_____(曲がる / 曲がると) 大学があります。

   Sono kado o migi ni _____ (magaru / magaru to), daigaku ga arimasu.

2. 駅に _____(着いたら / 着くと)、電話してください。

   Eki ni _____(tsuitara / tsuku to), denwashite kudasai.

Adjectives in the
prenominal position

Demonstratives

Words indicating location

"Become" nouns and
な na-adjectives

3. 家に _____ (帰ったら / 帰る時)、母の友達がいました。

Uchi ni _____ (kaettara / kaeru toki), haha no
tomodachi ga imashita.

4. デパートへ _____ (行くと / 行った時)、このかばんを買いました。

Depaato e _____ (iku to / itta toki), kono kaban o
kaimashita.

5. A: この漢字が分からないんですが・・・。

Kono kanji ga wakaranai n desu ga …

B: 先生に _____ (聞いたら / 聞くと) どうですか。

Sensee ni _____ (kiitara / kiku to) doo desu ka.

ANSWER KEY
1. 曲がると magaru to; 2. 着いたら tsuitara; 3. 帰ったら kaettara; 4. 行った時 itta toki; 5. 聞いたら
kiitara.

✎ Drive It Home

Fill in the blanks by choosing appropriate words from the word bank.
渡ると wataru to, 入ると hairu to, 行くと iku to, なると naru to, 曲がると
magaru to

1. 九月に _____ 、台風が来ます。

Kugatsu ni _____, taifuu ga kimasu.

When September comes, typhoons come.

2. 交差点を _____ 、映画館があります。

Koosaten o _____, eegakan ga arimasu.

If you cross the intersection, there's a movie theater.

3. 左に _____ 、デパートがあります。

Hidari ni _____, depaato ga arimasu.

If you turn left, there's a department store.

4. あのビルに _____ 、フランス料理のレストランがあります。

Ano biru ni _____, furansu ryoori no resutoran ga arimasu.

If you enter that building, there's a French restaurant.

5. 郵便局へ _____ 、斉藤さんがいました。

Yuubinkyoku e _____, Saito san ga imashita.

When I went to the post office, Mr./Ms. Saito was there.

ANSWER KEY

1. なると naru to; 2. 渡ると wataru to; 3. 曲がると magaru to; 4. 入ると hairu to; 5. 行くと iku to

How Did You Do?

Let's see how you did! By now, you should be able to:

☐ use the と to-conditional (Still unsure? Jump back to page 381)

✎ Word Recall

1. 有名 yuumee
ゆうめい

2. 高い takai
たか

3. 静か shizuka
しず

4. 面白い omoshiroi
おもしろ

5. おいしい oishii

6. 遠い tooi
とお

7. 難しい muzukashii
むずか

8. 大切 taisetsu
たいせつ

9. つまらない tsumaranai

10. 易しい yasashii
やさ

a. *important*

b. *delicious*

c. *famous*

d. *easy*

e. *interesting*

f. *difficult*

g. *high, tall, expensive*

h. *far*

i. *quiet*

j. *boring*

ANSWER KEY

1. c; 2. g; 3. i; 4. e; 5. b; 6. h; 7. f; 8. a; 9. j; 10. d

Don't forget to practice and reinforce what you've learned by visiting **www.livinglanguage.com/ languagelab** for flashcards, games, and quizzes for Unit 5!

Unit 5 Essentials

Vocabulary Essentials

Test your knowledge of the key material in this unit by filling in the blanks in the following charts. Once you've completed these pages, you'll have tested your retention, and you'll have your own reference for the most essential vocabulary.

GETTING AROUND TOWN

	taxi
	town
	place
	street, road
	corner
	right
	left
	high-rise building
	first
	second
	third
	slowly
	straight
	for a while
	about a five minute walk
	how
	post office

	bank
	coffee shop
	movie theater
	building
	intersection
	traffic light
	meter
	bag
	before, this side

VERBS

	to turn
	to walk
	to run
	to arrive
	to inquire
	to cross
	to be able to be seen, to be visible
	to become

い I-ADJECTIVES

	big
	small
	new

	old
	high, tall, expensive
	low
	interesting
	boring
	delicious
	bad (taste)
	near
	far
	easy
	difficult
	kind, gentle

な NA-ADJECTIVES

	beautiful, pretty, clean
	famous
	convenient
	inconvenient
	kind, generous
	easy, simple
	lively
	quiet
	have a lot of free time
	important

LOCATIONS

	in front of X
	on /above X
	the side of X
	inside X
	between X and Y
	behind X
	under X
	next to X
	across from X
	around X

DEMONSTRATIVES

	this (closer to the speaker)
	that (closer to the addressee)
	that (far from both the speaker and the addressee)
	which one
	this book
	that book (closer to the addressee)
	that book (far from both the speaker and the addressee)
	which book
	this (closer to the speaker, referring to a person)

	that (closer to the addressee, referring to a person)
	that (far from both the speaker and the addressee)
	here
	there (closer to the addressee)
	there (far from both the speaker and the addressee)
	where

Grammar Essentials

Here is a reference of the key grammar that was covered in Unit 5. Make sure you understand the summary and can use all of the grammar it covers.

な NA-ADJECTIVES IN THE PRENOMINAL POSITION

便利なコンピューター	benrina konpyuutaa	*convenient computer*
賑やかな町	nigiyakana machi	*lively town*

"BECOME" NOUNS AND な NA-ADJECTIVES

noun + になります/なる noun + ni narimasu/naru

stem of な-adjective + になります/なる

stem of na-adjective + ni narimasu/naru

将来何になりたいですか。	Shoorai nani ni naritai desu ka.	*What do you want to be (lit., become) in the future?*
英語の先生になりたいです。	Eego no sensee ni naritai desu.	*I want to be (lit., become) an English teacher.*

くるまか 車を買いましたから、便 り 利になりました。	Kuruma o kaimashita kara, benri ni narimashita.	I bought a car, so it became convenient.

THE たら TARA-CONDITIONAL

Plain past tense form of verbs/adjectives/copula + ら ra, …

にほん つ でんわ 日本に着いたら、電話 してください。	Nihon ni tsuitara, denwashite kudasai.	If/When you arrive in Japan, please call me.
かいしゃ ある い 会社に歩いて行ったら、 いちじかん 一時間かかりました。	Kaisha ni aruite ittara, ichijikan kakarimashita.	When I went to the company on foot (lit., by walking), it took one hour.
かね お金があったら、新しい くるまか 車を買うでしょう。	Okane ga attara, atarashii kuruma o kau deshoo.	If I had money, I would probably buy a new car.
とうきょうえき い 東京駅に行きたいんで すけど、どうやって行っ い たらいいですか。	Tookyoo eki ni ikitai n desu kedo, doo yatte ittara ii desu ka.	I want to go to the Tokyo Station; how should I get there?
でんしゃ い 電車で行ったらいいで しょう。	Densha de ittara ii deshoo.	It would probably be good if you go by train.

と TO-CONDITIONAL

Plain non-past form of verbs/adjectives/copula + と to, …

日本へ行くと、いつも歌舞伎を見ます。	Nihon e iku to, itsumo kabuki o mimasu.	*When I go to Japan, I always see kabuki.*
郵便局へ行くと、斉藤さんがいました。	Yuubinkyoku e iku to, Saito san ga imashita.	*When I went to the post office, Mr./Ms. Saito was there.*
まっすぐ行くと、銀行があります。	Massugu iku to, ginkoo ga arimasu.	*If you go straight, there's a bank.*

Unit 5 Quiz

A. Fill in the blanks with adjectives based on the English translation.

1. _____ 台所
   <ruby>台所<rt>だいどころ</rt></ruby>

   _____ daidokoro

   clean kitchen

2. _____ 問題
   <ruby>問題<rt>もんだい</rt></ruby>

   _____ mondai

   difficult problem

3. _____ コーヒー

   _____ koohii

   bad (tasting) coffee

B. Fill in the blanks with expressions indicating location.

1. <ruby>公園<rt>こうえん</rt></ruby>_____

   kooen _____

   in front of the park

2. <ruby>公園<rt>こうえん</rt></ruby>_____

   kooen _____

   around the park

3. 公園^{こうえん}_____

   kooen _____

   across the park

C. Fill in the blanks with the appropriate demonstratives.

1. _____ は何^{なん}ですか。

   _____ wa nan desu ka.

   What's this?

2. _____ 映画^{えいが}が見^みたいですか。

   _____ eega ga mitai desu ka.

   Which movie do you want to see?

3. _____ は鈴木^{すずき}さんです。

   _____ wa Suzuki san desu.

   This is Mr./Ms. Suzuki.

4. _____ です。

   _____ desu.

   It's over there.

D. Fill in each of the blanks with an appropriate particle.

1. 将来何^{しょうらいなに}_____ なりたいですか。

   Shoorai nani _____ naritai desu ka.

2. 医者^{いしゃ}_____ なりたいです。

   Isha _____ naritai desu.

3. その会社は最近有名^{かいしゃ さいきんゆうめい} _____ なりました。

   Sono kaisha wa saikin *(recently)* yuumee _____ narimashita.

4. この辺は夜とても静か＿＿＿＿＿＿なります。

Kono hen wa yoru totemo shizuka ＿＿＿＿＿＿ narimasu.

E. Complete the following sentences by inserting "verb + ら ra" in the blanks.

1. 日本に ＿＿＿＿＿＿＿＿＿＿＿＿＿＿、電話してください。

Nihon ni ＿＿＿＿＿＿＿＿＿＿＿＿＿, denwashite kudasai.

If/When you arrive in Japan, please call me.

2. 学生 ＿＿＿＿＿＿＿＿＿＿＿＿＿＿、もっと勉強してください。

Gakusee ＿＿＿＿＿＿＿＿＿＿＿＿＿, motto benkyooshite kudasai.

If you are a student, please study more.

3. 会社に歩いて ＿＿＿＿＿＿＿＿＿＿、一時間かかりました。

Kaisha ni aruite ＿＿＿＿＿＿＿＿＿＿, ichijikan kakarimashita.

When I went to the company on foot (lit., by walking), it took one hour.

F. Complete the following sentences by inserting "verb + と to" in the blanks.

1. 交差点を ＿＿＿＿＿＿＿＿＿＿＿＿＿＿＿＿、映画館があります。

Koosaten o ＿＿＿＿＿＿＿＿＿＿＿＿＿＿＿, eegakan ga arimasu.

If you cross the intersection, there's a movie theater.

2. まっすぐ ＿＿＿＿＿＿＿＿＿＿、銀行があります。

Massugu ＿＿＿＿＿＿＿＿＿＿, ginkoo ga arimasu.

If you go straight, there's a bank.

3. あのビルに ＿＿＿＿＿＿＿＿、フランス料理[りょうり]のレストランがあります。

Ano biru ni ＿＿＿＿＿＿＿＿＿＿＿, furansu ryoori no resutoran ga arimasu.

If you enter that building, there's a French restaurant.

ANSWER KEY

A. 1. きれいな kireena; 2. 難[むずか]しい muzukashii; 3. まずい mazui
B. 1. の前[まえ] no mae; 2. のまわり no mawari; 3. の向[む]かい(側[がわ]) no mukai(gawa)
C. 1. これ Kore; 2. どの Dono; 3. こちら Kochira; 4. あそこ Asoko
D. 1. に ni; 2. に ni; 3. に ni; 4. に ni
E. 1. 着[つ]いたら tsuitara; 2. だったら dattara; 3. 行[い]ったら ittara
F. 1. 渡[わた]ると wataru to; 2. 行[い]くと iku to; 3. 入[はい]ると hairu to

How Did You Do?

Congratulations! You've successfully completed *Living Language Intermediate Japanese.*

Give yourself a point for every correct answer, then use the following key to tell whether you're ready to move on:

0-7 points: It's probably a good idea to go back through the lesson again. You may be moving too quickly, or there may be too much "down time" between your contact with Japanese. Remember that it's better to spend 30 minutes with Japanese three or four times a week than it is to spend two or three hours just once a week. Find a pace that's comfortable for you, and spread your contact hours out as much as you can.

8-12 points: You would benefit from a review before moving on. Go back and spend a little more time on the specific points that gave you trouble. Re-read the Grammar Builder sections that were difficult, and do the work out one more time. Don't forget about the online supplemental practice material, either. Go to www.livinglanguage.com/ languagelab for games and quizzes that will reinforce the material from this unit.

13-17 points: Good job! There are just a few points that you could consider reviewing before moving on. If you haven't worked with the games and quizzes on www.livinglanguage.com/languagelab, please give them a try.

18-20 points: Great! You're ready to move on to *Living Language Advanced Japanese.*

points

Glossary

Note that the following abbreviations will be used in this glossary: (m.) = masculine, (f.) = feminine, (sg.) = singular, (pl.) = plural, (fml.) = formal/polite, (infml.) = informal/familiar. If a word has two grammatical genders, (m./f.) or (f./m.) is used.

Japanese-English

A

aa ああ *ah, oh*

achira あちら *that, that way (far from both the speaker and the listener) (polite)*

ageru, agemasu あげる、あげます *to give*
... te ageru, ... te agemasu ～てあげる、～てあげます *to give a favor of ... ing*

(... to ... no) aida (～と～の)間 *between (... and ...)*

aisukuriimu アイスクリーム *ice cream*

aka 赤 *red (noun)*

aka wain 赤ワイン *red wine*

akai 赤い *red (adjective)*

akarui 明るい *bright*

akeru, akemasu 開ける、開けます *to open (transitive verb)*

aki 秋 *fall, autumn*

amai 甘い *sweet*

ame 雨 *rain*
Ame desu. 雨です。 *It's raining.*
Ame ga futte imasu. 雨が降っています。 *It's raining.*

amerika アメリカ *the United States*

amerikajin アメリカ人 *American (person)*

anata あなた *you (sg.) (subject pronoun)*
anatagata あなた方 *you (pl.) (subject pronoun)*
anata no あなたの *your (sg.)*
anatatachi あなた達 *you (pl.) (subject pronoun)*

ane 姉 *older sister (one's own)*

ani 兄 *older brother (one's own)*

a(n)mari (+ negative) あ（ん）まり *not so often, not so much*

ano あの *that (far from both the speaker and the listener)*
ano pen あのペン *that pen*

anoo あのう *Well ...*

ao 青 *blue (noun)*

aoi 青い *blue (adjective)*

apaato アパート *apartment*

arau, araimasu 洗う、洗います *to wash*

are あれ *that (far from both the speaker and the listener)*

arerugii アレルギー *allergy*

Arigatoo gozaimashita. ありがとうございました。 *Thank you.*
Arigatoo gozaimasu. ありがとうございます。 *Thank you.*
Doomo arigatoo gozaimashita. どうもありがとうございました。 *Thank you very much.*
Doomo arigatoo gozaimasu. どうもありがとうございます。 *Thank you very much.*

aru, arimasu ある、あります *there is ... / to have ... (inanimate)*

aruku, arukimasu 歩く、歩きます *to walk*
aruite gofun 歩いて五分 *five minute walk*

asa 朝 *morning*

asagohan 朝ご飯 *breakfast (infml.)*

asatte あさって *the day after tomorrow*

ashi 足 *foot*

ashi 脚 *leg*

ashisutanto アシスタント *assistant*

ashita 明日 *tomorrow*

asobu, asobimasu 遊ぶ、遊びます *to play (a game)*

asoko あそこ *there (far from both the speaker and the listener)*

asu 明日 *tomorrow*

atama 頭 *head*
atama ga itai, atama ga itai desu 頭が痛い、頭が痛いです *to have a headache*

atarashii 新しい *new*

atatakai 暖かい *warm*

atesaki 宛先 *(sent) to*

ato de 後で *later, after*

resutoran o deta ato de レストランを出た後で
  after leaving a restaurant
atsui 暑い *hot (weather, room temperature)*
atsui 熱い *hot (to the touch)*
au, aimasu 会う、会います *to meet*
au, aimasu 合う、合います *to match*
  jiinzu ni au ジーンズに合う *to match with jeans*
azukaru, azukarimasu 預かる、預かります
  to keep
baa バー *bar*
baggu バッグ *bag*
baiorin バイオリン *violin*
ban バン *van*
ban 晩 *evening, night*
  konban 今晩 *tonight*
  maiban 毎晩 *every night*
bareebooru バレーボール *volleyball*
basu バス *bus*
basukettobooru バスケットボール *basketball*
basutee バス停 *bus stop*
bataa バター *butter*
batto バット *bat*
beddo ベッド *bed*
bengoshi 弁護士 *lawyer*
benkyoosuru, benkyooshimasu 勉強する、
  勉強します *to study*
benri 便利 *convenient*
besuto ベスト *vest, best*
biichi ビーチ *beach*
biiru ビール *beer*
  biiru ken ビール券 *beer gift coupon*
bikkurisuru, bikkurishimasu びっくりする、
  びっくりします *to be surprised, to be scared*
bin 瓶 *bottle*
biru ビル *high-rise building*
bitaminzai ビタミン剤 *vitamin supplement*
biyooin 美容院 *beauty salon*
biyooshi 美容師 *hair dresser*
bojoreenuuboo ボジョレーヌーボー *Beaujolais
  nouveau*
boku (used only by male speakers) 僕 *I*
booeki 貿易 *trade, export and import business*
booekigaisha 貿易会社 *trading company*
booru ボール *ball*
boorupen ボールペン *ballpoint pen*
bu 部 *set, copy (counter for written materials)*
buchoo 部長 *division manager*
bukka 物価 *prices (of commodities)*

bungaku 文学 *literature*
buranchi ブランチ *brunch*
burausu ブラウス *blouse*
buta 豚 *pig*
butaniku 豚肉 *pork*
byakuya 白夜 *white night*
byooin 病院 *hospital*
byooki 病気 *illness*
canada カナダ *Canada*
chairo 茶色 *brown (noun)*
chairoi 茶色い *brown (adjective)*
… chaku 〜着 *arriving…*
  Naha chaku 那覇着 *arriving in Naha*
chansu チャンス *chance*
chanto ちゃんと *properly, exactly, accurately
  (infml.)*
cheen チェーン *chain*
chero チェロ *cello*
chichi 父 *father (one's own)*
chichi no hi 父の日 *father's day*
chiisai 小さい *small*
chiizu チーズ *cheese*
chikai 近い *close*
chikaku 近く *nearby*
chikatetsu 地下鉄 *subway*
chikin sarada チキンサラダ *chicken salad*
chokoreeto チョコレート *chocolate*
choo 腸 *intestine*
choomiryoo 調味料 *seasoning*
chooshoku 朝食 *breakfast (fml.)*
chotto ちょっと *a little*
chuugakkoo 中学校 *junior high school*
chuugoku 中国 *China*
chuugokugo 中国語 *Chinese (language)*
chuugokujin 中国人 *Chinese (person)*
chuumon 注文 *order*
chuumonsuru, chuumonshimasu 注文する、
  注文します *to order*
chuusha 注射 *injection, shot*
chuushasuru, chuushashimasu 注射する、
  注射します *to give an injection*
chuushoku 昼食 *lunch (fml.)*
da, desu だ、です *to be*
daasu ダース *dozen*
dai 台 *counter for mechanical items*
daidokoro 台所 *kitchen*
daigaku 大学 *college, university*
daigakuin 大学院 *graduate school*

daigakuinsee 大学院生 *graduate school student*

daigakusee 大学生 *college student*

daijoobu 大丈夫 *all right*

daisuki da, daisuki desu 大好きだ、大好きです *to like very much, to like a lot*

dake だけ *only*

dansu ダンス *dance, dancing*

dare 誰 *who*

dare ka 誰か *someone*

dare mo (+ negative) 誰も *no one, nobody*

daroo, deshoo だろう、でしょう *will probably*

… te (mo) ii deshoo ka. 〜て(も)いいでしょうか。 *May I … ? (polite)*

… te (mo) yoroshii deshoo ka. 〜て(も)よろしいでしょうか。 *May I … ? (polite)*

de で *particle (marks a place where some action takes place; marks means and instruments)*

dekakeru, dekakemasu 出掛ける、出掛けます *to go out*

kamera o motte dekakemasu カメラを持って出掛けます *to go out with a camera*

dekiru, dekimasu できる、できます *can do*

demo でも *however, but*

… demo 〜でも *… or something like that*

koohii demo コーヒーでも *coffee or something like that*

denki gishi 電気技師 *electrical engineer*

densha 電車 *train*

denshirenji 電子レンジ *microwave oven*

(o)denwa (お)電話 *telephone (polite with o)*

(o)denwabangoo (お)電話番号 *telephone number (polite with o)*

denwasuru, denwashimasu 電話する、電話します *to make a phone call*

depaato デパート *department store*

deru, demasu 出る、出ます *to leave, to attend*

dete iru, dete imasu 出ている、出ています *to have left*

… ni deru 〜に出る *to attend …*

… o deru 〜を出る *to leave …*

deshi 弟子 *disciple*

dewa では *then*

dezaato デザート *dessert*

dezain デザイン *design*

diizeru ディーゼル *diesel*

disupurei ディスプレイ *display*

do 度 *degree*

sanjuuhachi do 三十八度 *38 degrees*

dochira どちら *where, which one, which way (polite)*

dochira no hoo どちらの方 *which one*

doitsu ドイツ *Germany*

doitsugo ドイツ語 *German (language)*

doitsujin ドイツ人 *German (person)*

doko どこ *where*

doko ka どこか *somewhere*

doko mo (+ negative) どこも *nowhere*

doku 毒 *poison*

dokusho 読書 *reading books*

donata どなた *who (polite)*

donna どんな *what kind of*

dono どの *which (one)*

dono pen どのペン *which pen*

dono gurai どのぐらい *how long, how much*

doo どう *how*

Doo deshita ka. どうでしたか。 *How was it?*

Doo desu ka. どうですか。 *How is it?/What about … ?/How about … ?*

Doo nasaimashita ka. どうなさいましたか。 *What's the matter? (polite)*

Doo shimashita ka. どうしましたか。 *What's the matter?*

doo yatte どうやって *how*

dooitsu 同一 *identical*

dookoo 同行 *accompaniment*

dooshite どうして *why*

Doozo. どうぞ。 *Here you go./Please.*

Doozo yoroshiku. どうぞよろしく。 *Nice to meet you.*

dore どれ *which one*

doresshingu ドレッシング *dressing*

doyoobi 土曜日 *Saturday*

e 絵 *drawing, painting*

e へ *particle (marks the goal of movement)*

ebi えび *shrimp*

ee ええ *yes (infml.)*

eega 映画 *movie*

eega kanshoo 映画鑑賞 *seeing movies (lit., movie appreciation)*

eegakan 映画館 *movie theater*

eego 英語 *English (language)*

eegyoo hookokusho 営業報告書 *business report*

eki 駅 *station*

en 円 *yen*

ichiman en 一万円 *10,000 yen*

sen en 千円 *1,000 yen*

enjin エンジン *engine*

enjinia エンジニア *engineer*

enpitsu 鉛筆 *pencil*

ensoosuru, ensooshimasu 演奏する、演奏します *to perform (music)*

etto えっと *Well...*

fakkusu ファックス *fax*

fensu フェンス *fence*

finrando フィンランド *Finland*

fonto フォント *font*

fooku フォーク *fork*

fuben 不便 *inconvenient*

fujisan 富士山 *Mt. Fuji*

fukee 父兄 *fathers and eldest sons (fml.)*

fuku, fukimasu 吹く、吹きます *to play (a wind instruments)*

fukumu, fukumimasu 含む、含みます *to be included*

fukutsuu 腹痛 *stomachache*

fuminshoo 不眠症 *insomnia*

fuminshoo da, fuminshoo desu 不眠症だ、不眠症です *to suffer from insomnia*

fumon 不問 *passing over a matter*

furansu フランス *France*

furansu ryoori フランス料理 *French cuisine*

furansugo フランス語 *French (language)*

furansujin フランス人 *French (person)*

furu, furimasu 降る、降ります *to fall, to come down*

Ame ga futte imasu. 雨が降っています。 *It's raining.*

Yuki ga futte imasu. 雪が降っています。 *It's snowing.*

furui 古い *old*

furuuto フルート *flute*

futa 蓋 *lid*

futari 二人 *two people*

futatsu 二つ *two (native Japanese number)*

futsuka 二日 *second (day of the month)*

futtobooru フットボール *football*

(go)fuufu (ご)夫婦 *married couple (polite with go)*

fuyu 冬 *winter*

ga が *particle (marks a subject)*

ga が *but*

ga 蛾 *moth*

gaarufurendo ガールフレンド *girlfriend*

gakki 楽器 *musical instrument*

gakkoo 学校 *school*

gakusee 学生 *student*

gan 癌 *cancer*

geemu ゲーム *game*

genkan 玄関 *entrance hall*

genki 元気 *vigorous*

Genki desu. 元気です。 *I'm fine.*

Ogenki desu ka. お元気ですか。 *How are you?*

genkin 現金 *cash*

geri 下痢 *diarrhea*

geri o suru, geri o shimasu 下痢をする、下痢をします *to have diarrhea*

getsuyoobi 月曜日 *Monday*

ginkoo 銀行 *bank*

ginkooin 銀行員 *bank clerk*

gishi 技師 *engineer*

go 五 *five*

go 後 *later, after*

sanjuppun go 三十分後 *30 minutes later*

gobyuu 誤びゅう *error (fml.)*

gofun 五分 *five minutes*

gogatsu 五月 *May*

gogo 午後 *afternoon, p.m.*

gohan ご飯 *cooked rice, meal*

goji 五時 *five o'clock*

gojitsu 後日 *later, some other day*

gojuu 五十 *fifty*

gokai 五階 *fifth floor*

gokyoodai ご兄弟 *siblings (someone else's)*

Gomennasai. ごめんなさい。 *I'm sorry.*

goran ni naru, goran ni narimasu ご覧になる、ご覧になります *to see, to look, to watch (honorific)*

goro 頃 *about, approximately*

gorufu ゴルフ *golf*

goshujin ご主人 *husband (someone else's)*

gozaimasu ございます *to exist, there is, to have (polite)*

... de gozaimasu. ～でございます。 *to be ... (polite)*

gozen 午前 *morning, a.m.*

gruupu happyoo グループ発表 *group presentation*

gurai ぐらい *about, approximately*

guree グレー *grey (noun)*

guriin sarada グリーンサラダ *green salad*

guuzen 偶然 *coincidence*

gyaku 逆 *opposite*

gyuuniku 牛肉 *beef*

ha 歯 *tooth*

haadowea ハードウエア *hardware*

haato ハート *heart*

hachi 八 *eight*

hachifun 八分 *eight minutes*

hachigatsu 八月 *August*

hachiji 八時 *eight o'clock*

hachijuu 八十 *eighty*

hade 派手 *showy, loud*

haha 母 *mother (one's own)*

hai はい *yes*

hai 杯 *counter for liquid in cups/glasses/bowls*

hai 肺 *lung*

haikensuru, haikenshimasu 拝見する、
  拝見します *to see, to look, to watch (humble)*

hairu, hairimasu 入る、入ります *to enter, to join*
  haitte iru, haitte imasu 入っている、
    入っています *to have entered, to belong*
  ofuro ni hairu, ofuro ni hairimasu お風呂に入
    る、お風呂に入ります *to take a bath*

Hajimemashite. はじめまして。 *How do you do?*

hajimete 初めて *first time, for the first time*

hakaru, hakarimasu 測る、測ります *to measure*
  netsu o hakaru, netsu o hakarimasu 熱を測
    る、熱を測ります *to check one's temperature*

hakike 吐き気 *nausea*
  hakike ga suru, hakike ga shimasu 吐き気がす
    る、吐き気がします *to feel like vomiting*

hakka 発火 *ignition*

haku 泊 *staying over night*
  nihaku 二泊 *two nights*
  nihaku mikka 二泊三日 *two nights three days*

hamu ハム *ham*

han 半 *half, half past the hour*
  goji han 五時半 *five thirty*

hana 花 *flower*

hana 鼻 *nose*

hanasu, hanashimasu 話す、話します *to speak*

hanbun 半分 *half*

hankachi ハンカチ *handkerchief*

hantoshi 半年 *half a year*
  hantoshikan 半年間 *for half a year*

happun 八分 *eight minutes*

happyoo 発表 *presentation*

hara 腹 *belly, abdomen*

harau, haraimasu 払う、払います *to pay*

hare 晴れ *sunny*

Hare desu. 晴れです。 *It's sunny.*

Harete imasu. 晴れています。 *It's sunny.*

haru 春 *spring*

hashi 箸 *chopsticks*

hashiru, hashirimasu 走る、走ります *to run*

hataraku, hatarakimasu 働く、働きます
  to work

… hasu ～発 *leaving …*
  Haneda hatsu 羽田発 *leaving Haneda*

hatsuka 二十日 *twentieth (day of the month)*

hayabaya 早々 *promptly*

hayai 早い *early*

hayaku 早く *early, quickly*

hayashi 林 *woods*

Hee. へえ。 *Well … /Wow./I see.*

heejitsu 平日 *weekday*

heta 下手 *unskillful, poor at*

heya 部屋 *room*

hi 日 *day*

hidari 左 *left*

hidarigawa 左側 *left side*

hidoi ひどい *terrible, severe*

higashigawa 東側 *east side*

hiki 匹 *counter for animal*

hikkosu, hikkoshimasu 引っ越す、引っ越します
  to move (to a new location)

hikooki 飛行機 *airplane*

hiku, hikimasu 弾く、弾きます *to play (piano)*

hikui 低い *low*

hima 暇 *be free (having a lot of free time)*

hin 品 *dignity*

hinketsu 貧血 *anemia*

hippuhoppu ヒップホップ *hip-hop*

hiragana 平仮名 *hiragana characters*

hiroi 広い *spacious*

hiroo 疲労 *exhaustion, fatigue*

hiroshima 広島 *Hiroshima*

(o)hiru (お)昼 *noon (polite with o)*

hirugohan 昼ご飯 *lunch (infml.)*

hisabisa 久々 *long-absence*

Hisashiburi desu ne. 久しぶりですね。
  Long time no see.

hito 人 *person*
  onna no hito 女の人 *woman*
  otoko no hito 男の人 *man*

hitori 一人 *one person*

hitorikko 一人っ子 *only child*

hitotsu 一つ *one (native Japanese number)*

hiyaku 飛躍 *leap*

hiyoo 費用 *cost, expense*
  kootsuuhi 交通費 *transportation costs*

hoka 他 *other*

hoken 保険 *insurance*
  shakaihoken 社会保険 *social insurance*

hokenshoo 保険証 *health insurance card*

hon 本 *book*

hon 本 *counter for long cylindrical objects*

hone 骨 *bone*
  hone o oru, hone o orimasu 骨を折る、骨を折り
  ます *to break a bone*

honkon 香港、ホンコン *Hong Kong*

hontoo 本当 *true*
  Hontoo desu ka. 本当ですか。 *Really?/Is that
  true?*
  hontoo ni 本当に *really*

hon-ya 本屋 *book store*

hoo 方 *direction, side*
  dochira no hoo どちらの方 *which one*
  ~ nai hoo ga ii desu. 〜ない方がいいです。 *You'd
  better not …*
  … (ta/da) hoo ga ii desu. 〜(た/だ)方がいい
  です。 *You'd better …*

hookoo 方向 *direction*

hooritsu 法律 *law*

hooritsu jimusho 法律事務所 *law firm*

hoshii, hoshii desu 欲しい、欲しいです *to want*
  hoshigatte iru, hoshigatte imasu 欲しがってい
  る、欲しがっています *(Someone) wants*

hotate 帆立 *scallop*

hoteru ホテル *hotel*

hyaku 百 *hundred*

hyakupaasento 100パーセント *hundred percent*
  uuru hyakupaasento ウール100パーセント
  100% wool

hyoogen 表現 *expression*

i 胃 *stomach*

ichi 一 *one*
  ichiman 一万 *ten thousand*
  ichiman en 一万円 *ten thousand yen*

ichiban 一番 *number one, the most*
  ichiban ii 一番いい *the best*

ichido 一度 *once*
  ichido mo (+negative) 一度も *never*
  moo ichido もう一度 *once more*

ichigatsu 一月 *January*

ichiji 一時 *one o'clock*

ie 家 *house*

igirisu イギリス *England*

igirisujin イギリス人 *English (person)*

ii いい *good*
  emu de ii エムでいい *medium is okay*
  Junbi wa ii desu ka. 準備はいいですか。
  Are you ready?
  moshi yokattara もし良かったら *if it's okay,
  if you like*
  Sore wa yokatta. それはよかった。 *I'm glad to
  hear that.*
  … te (mo) ii?/… te (mo) ii desu ka./… te
  (mo) ii deshoo ka. 〜て(も)いい?/〜て(も)いい
  ですか。/〜て(も)いいでしょうか。 *May I …?*

iie いいえ *no*

iimeeru イーメール *e-mail*

ijoo 以上 *more than*

ika いか *cuttlefish, squid*

ikaga いかが *how (polite)*
  Ikaga deshita ka. いかがでしたか。 *How was
  it? (polite)*
  Ikaga desu ka. いかがですか。 *How is it?
  (polite)*
  … wa ikaga desu ka. 〜はいかがですか。
  How about …? (polite)

iku, ikimasu 行く、行きます *to go*
  itte iru, itte imasu 行っている、行っています
  to have gone

(o)ikura (polite with o) （お）いくら *how much*

(o)ikutsu (polite with o) （お）いくつ *how many,
  how old*

ima 今 *now*

ima 居間 *living room*

ima made ni 今までに *up to now*

imi 意味 *meaning*

imooto 妹 *younger sister (one's own)*

imootosan 妹さん *younger sister (someone else's)*

inchi インチ *inch*

indo インド *India*

intaanetto インターネット *internet*

inu 犬 *dog*

ippai 一杯 *full*

ipponjooshi 一本調子 *monotonous*

ippun 一分 *one minute*

Irasshaimase. いらっしゃいませ。 *Welcome
  (to our store).*

irassharu, irasshaimasu いらっしゃる、いらっしゃいます *to go, to come, to exist, there is (honorific)*

ireru, iremasu 入れる、入れます *to put into*
　sarada ni ireru, sarada ni iremasu サラダに入れる、サラダに入れます *to put into a salad*

iru, imasu いる、います *to have … /there is … (animate)*
　uchi ni iru, uchi ni imasu 家にいる、家にいます *to stay home*

isha 医者 *medical doctor*

isogashii 忙しい *busy*

issho ni 一緒に *together*

isu 椅子 *chair*

itadaku, itadakimasu いただく、いただきます *to eat, to drink, to receive (humble)*
　… te itadaku, … te itadakimasu 〜ていただく、〜ていただきます *to receive a favor of … ing (humble)*

itai 痛い *painful*
　atama ga itai, atama ga itai desu 頭が痛い、頭が痛いです *to have a headache*
　nodo ga itai, nodo ga itai desu 喉が痛い、喉が痛いです *to have a sore throat*
　onaka ga itai, onaka ga itai desu お腹が痛い、お腹が痛いです *to have a stomachache*

itaria イタリア *Italy*

itaria ryoori イタリア料理 *Italian cuisine*

itariago イタリア語 *Italian (language)*

itasu, itashimasu いたす、いたします *to do (humble)*

itoko 従兄弟 *cousin*

itsu いつ *when*

itsuka 五日 *fifth (day of the month)*

itsumo いつも *always*

itsutsu 五つ *five (native Japanese number)*

iu, iimasu 言う、言います *to say*

izen 以前 *before*

ja(a) じゃ(あ) *then*

jagaimo じゃがいも *potato*

jama 邪魔 *obstruction*
　Ojamashimasu. お邪魔します。 *Pardon the intrusion.*

jazu ジャズ *jazz*

jiinzu ジーンズ *jeans*

jikan 時間 *time, hour(s)*
　nijikan 二時間 *two hours*

jimi 地味 *sober, quiet (color)*

jimu 事務 *office (clerical) work*

jimusho 事務所 *office*

jinja 神社 *shrine*

jinjibu 人事部 *human resources department*

jisho 辞書 *dictionary*

jitsu wa 実は *actually*

jiyuu 自由 *freedom*

jiyuu 自由 *free*
　jiyuujikan 自由時間 *free time*

jogingu ジョギング *jog, jogging*

joozu 上手 *skillful, good at*

jugyoo 授業 *class*

junbi 準備 *preparation*
　Junbi wa ii desu ka. 準備はいいですか。 *Are you ready?*

juppun 十分 *ten minutes*

juu 十 *ten*

juu 銃 *gun*

juudoo 柔道 *judo*

juugatsu 十月 *October*

juugo 十五 *fifteen*

juuhachi 十八 *eighteen*

juuichi 十一 *eleven*

juuichigatsu 十一月 *November*

juuichiji 十一時 *eleven o'clock*

juuji 十時 *ten o'clock*

juuku 十九 *nineteen*

juukyuu 十九 *nineteen*

juunana 十七 *seventeen*

juuni 十二 *twelve*

juunigatsu 十二月 *December*

juuniji 十二時 *twelve o'clock*

juuroku 十六 *sixteen*

juusan 十三 *thirteen*

juushi 十四 *fourteen*

juushichi 十七 *seventeen*

juusu ジュース *juice, soft drink*

juuyon 十四 *fourteen*

ka か *particle (marks a question; used to express surprise)*

ka 蚊 *mosquito*

ka か *or*

kaado カード *card, credit card*

kaato カート *shopping cart*

kaban かばん *bag*

kabushikigaisha 株式会社 *joint-stock cooperation*

kachoo 課長 *section manager*

kado 角 *corner*

kaeru, kaerimasu 帰る、帰ります *to go back, to return, to go home, to come home*

kafeore カフェオレ *café au lait*

kagu 家具 *furniture*

kai 貝 *shellfish*

kaidan 階段 *stairs*

kaigi 会議 *meeting*

kaii moji 会意文字 *compound ideographic characters*

kaimono 買い物 *shopping*

kaisha 会社 *company*

kaishain 会社員 *office worker, company employee*

kakaru, kakarimasu かかる、かかります *to take (time)*

kakijun 書き順 *stroke order*

kaku 画 *stroke (for writing characters)*

kaku, kakimasu 書く、書きます *to write*

kakushu 各種 *various*

kakusuu 画数 *number of strokes*

kamau, kamaimasu 構う、構います *to mind*

... te (mo) kamaimasen ka. 〜て（も）構いませんか。 *Do you mind ... ing?*

kamera カメラ *camera*

kami 紙 *paper*

kami 髪 *hair (on the head)*

kami no ke 髪の毛 *hair (on the head)*

kamoshirenai, kamoshiremasen かもしれない、かもしれません *may (conjecture)*

... kana(a) 〜かな(あ) *I wonder ...*

kanadajin カナダ人 *Canadian (person)*

kanai 家内 *wife (one's own)*

kanbi 完備 *fully furnished*

kangae 考え *idea*

kangoshi 看護師 *nurse*

kanja 患者 *patient*

kanji 漢字 *Chinese characters*

kankoku 韓国 *Korea*

kankoo 観光 *sightseeing*

kannu カンヌ *Cannes*

kanojo 彼女 *she*

kanojo no 彼女の *her*

kanojora 彼女ら *they (people, feminine)*

kanojotachi 彼女達 *they (people, feminine)*

kansuru 関する *concerning, regarding*

kantan 簡単 *easy, simple*

kao 顔 *face*

kaoiro 顔色 *complexion*

kaoiro ga warui, kaoiro ga warui desu 顔色が悪い、顔色が悪いです *to look pale*

kapuchiino カプチーノ *cappuccino*

kara から *from*

... kara ... made 〜から〜まで *from ... to ...*

kara から *because, so*

karaa カラー *hair dye, hair color*

karada 体、身体 *body*

karai 辛い *spicy*

kare 彼 *he*

kare no 彼の *his*

karera 彼ら *they (people)*

karee カレー *curry*

kariru, karimasu 借りる、借ります *to borrow*

karate iru, karate imasu 借りている、借りています *to have borrowed*

karui 軽い *light*

Kashikomarimashita. かしこまりました。 *Certainly. (polite)*

... kashira. 〜かしら。 *I wonder ...*

kashu 歌手 *singer*

kasu, kashimasu 貸す、貸します *to lend*

kashite iru, kashite imasu 貸している、貸しています *to have lent*

kata 方 *person (polite)*

kata 肩 *shoulders*

kata ga kotte iru, kata ga kotte imasu 肩が凝っている、肩が凝っています *to have stiff shoulders*

katakana 片仮名 *katakana characters*

katsu かつ *cutlet*

katsute かつて *formerly*

katte 勝手 *selfish*

katto カット *haircut*

kau, kaimasu 買う、買います *to buy*

kawa 川 *river*

kawaii かわいい *cute*

kawaru, kawarimasu 代わる、代わります *to replace (a person), to transfer (a phone line)*

kawaru, kawarimasu 変わる、変わります *to change*

kayoobi 火曜日 *Tuesday*

kaze 風 *wind*

kaze 風邪 *cold*

kaze o hiku, kaze o hikimasu 風邪をひく、風邪をひきます *to catch a cold*

(go)kazoku (polite with go) （ご）家族 *family*

gonin kazoku 五人家族 *five people in a family*
ke 毛 *hair*
kedo けど *but*
kee-eegaku 経営学 *business management*
keekaku 計画 *plan*
keeken 経験 *experience*
keeki ケーキ *cake*
keeri 経理 *accounting*
keesatsu 警察 *police*
keesatsukan 警察官 *police officer*
keesee moji 形声文字 *phonetic-ideographic characters*
keetai (denwa) 携帯(電話) *cell phone*
keezai 経済 *economy*
keezaigaku 経済学 *economics*
kega 怪我 *injury*
　kega o suru, kega o shimasu 怪我をする、怪我を します *to get injured*
Kekkoo desu. 結構です。 *No, thank you.*
ken 件 *matter, case*
ken 券 *coupon, voucher*
　biiru ken ビール券 *beer gift coupon*
kendoo 剣道 *kendo*
kenmee 件名 *subject (letter, e-mail)*
kensa 検査 *examination*
kensasuru, kensashimasu 検査する、検査します *to examine*
kesa 今朝 *this morning*
ketsuatsu 血圧 *blood pressure*
　ketsuatsu ga takai, ketsuatsu ga takai desu 血圧が高い、血圧が高いです *to have high blood pressure*
　ketsuatsu ga hikui, ketsuatsu ga hikui desu 血圧が低い、血圧が低いです *to have low blood pressure*
ki 木 *tree*
kibun 気分 *feeling*
　kibun ga warui, kibun ga warui desu 気分が 悪い、気分が悪いです *to feel sick*
kichinto きちんと *properly, exactly, accurately*
kiiboodo キーボード *keyboard*
kiiro 黄色 *yellow (noun)*
kiiroi 黄色い *yellow (adjective)*
kikai 機会 *chance*
kiku, kikimasu 聞く、聞きます *to listen, to inquire*
kiku, kikimasu 聴く、聴きます *to listen (with focus, such as listening to music)*

kinmu 勤務 *work (fml.)*
　kinmuchi 勤務地 *place of work*
kinoo 昨日 *yesterday*
kin-yoobi 金曜日 *Friday*
kinyuusuru, kinyuushimasu 記入する、記入しま す *to fill out (a form)*
kirai da, kirai desu 嫌いだ、嫌いです *to dislike*
kiree きれい *beautiful, pretty, clean*
kiru, kirimasu 切る、切ります *to cut*
kissaten 喫茶店 *coffee shop*
kitagawa 北側 *north side*
kitanai 汚い *dirty*
kiyaku 規約 *agreement, rules*
kiyoo 起用 *promotion, appointment*
kochira こちら *this, this way (polite)*
kodomo 子供 *child*
kodomosan 子供さん *child (somebody else's)*
kokage 木陰 *tree shadow*
koko ここ *here*
kokonoka 九日 *ninth (day of the month)*
kokonotsu 九つ *nine (native Japanese number)*
kokoro 心 *heart*
komu, komimasu 混む、混みます *to get crowded*
　konde iru, konde imasu 混んでいる、混んでい ます *to be crowded*
komugi 小麦 *wheat*
konban 今晩 *tonight*
Konban wa. こんばんは。 *Good evening.*
konbini コンビニ *convenience store*
kondo 今度 *next time, this time, shortly*
Konnichi wa. こんにちは。 *Hello./Good afternoon.*
konnyaku こんにゃく *konnyaku potato*
kono この *this*
　kono hen ni この辺に *in this area*
　kono pen このペン *this pen*
konpyuutaa コンピューター *computer*
konsaato コンサート *concert*
konshuu 今週 *this week*
konshuumatsu 今週末 *this weekend*
kooban 交番 *police booth*
koobe 神戸 *Kobe*
koocha 紅茶 *black tea*
kooen 公園 *park*
koohii コーヒー *coffee*
kooka 効果 *effect*
kookoku 広告 *advertisement*
kookoo 高校 *high school*

kookoosee 高校生 *high school student*
koosaten 交差点 *intersection*
kootsuu 交通 *transportation*
 kootsuuhi 交通費 *transportation costs*
kopii コピー *copy*
kopiisuru, kopiishimasu コピーする、コピーします *to copy*
kore これ *this*
kore made ni これまでに *up to now*
korokke コロッケ *croquette*
koru, korimasu 凝る、凝ります *to get stiff*
 kata ga kotte iru, kata ga kotte imasu 肩が凝っている、肩が凝っています *to have stiff shoulders*
koshi 腰 *waist, hip*
koshoo 胡椒 *pepper*
kossetsusuru, kossetsushimasu 骨折する、骨折します *to break a bone*
kotae 答え *answer*
koto こと *thing*
 … koto ga aru, … koto ga arimasu 〜ことがある、〜ことがあります *to have done …, to have an experience of … ing*
 taberu koto to nomu koto 食べることと飲むこと *eating and drinking*
kotoba 言葉 *word, language*
kotoshi 今年 *this year*
ku 九 *nine*
kubaru, kubarimasu 配る、配ります *to distribute*
kuchi 口 *mouth*
kudasaru, kudasaimasu くださる、くださいます *to give (honorific)*
 … naide kudasai 〜ないでください。 *Please don't …*
 … o kudasai. 〜をください。 *Please give me …*
 … te kudasai 〜てください。 *Please …*
 … te kudasaru, … te kudasaimasu 〜てくださる、〜てくださいます *to give a favor of … ing (honorific)*
kugatsu 九月 *September*
kuji 九時 *nine o'clock*
kukkii クッキー *cookie*
kumori 曇り *cloudy*
 Kumori desu. 曇りです。 *It's cloudy.*
kuni 国 *country, nation*
kurabu クラブ *club*
kurai 暗い *dark*

kurarinetto クラリネット *clarinet*
kurashikku クラシック *classical*
kurasu クラス *class*
kurasumeeto クラスメート *classmate*
kurejitto kaado クレジットカード *credit card*
kureru, kuremasu くれる、くれます *to give*
 … te kureru, … te kuremasu 〜てくれる、〜てくれます *to give a favor of … ing*
kurisumasu クリスマス *Christmas*
kuroi 黒い *black*
kuru, kimasu 来る、来ます *to come*
 kite iru, kite imasu 来ている、来ています *to have come, to be here*
kuruma 車 *car*
kuruujingu クルージング *cruise*
kusuri 薬 *medicine*
kutsu 靴 *shoes*
kuuki 空気 *air*
kyabetsu キャベツ *cabbage*
kyaku 客 *customer, guest*
kyappu キャップ *cap*
kyonen 去年 *last year*
kyoo 今日 *today*
kyoodai 兄弟 *siblings (one's own)*
 sannin kyoodai 三人兄弟 *three children in a family*
kyookasho 教科書 *textbook*
kyooshi 教師 *teacher*
kyooto 京都 *Kyoto*
kyuu 九 *nine*
kyuubo 急募 *immediate opening*
kyuufun 九分 *nine minutes*
kyuujin (kookoku) 求人(広告) *job posting*
kyuujuu 九十 *ninety*
kyuuri きゅうり *cucumber*
(o)kyuuryoo (polite with o) (お)給料 *salary*
kyuuyo 給与 *salary*
maa maa まあまあ *so so*
maaketingu マーケティング *marketing*
machi 町 *town*
machiaishitsu 待合室 *waiting room*
mada まだ *still, yet (in negative)*
made まで *until*
 … kara … made 〜から〜まで *from … to …*
mado 窓 *window*
(… no) mae (〜の)前 *in front of …*
 mae ni 前に *before*

paatii e iku mae ni パーティーへ行く前に *before going to the party*

magaru, magarimasu 曲がる、曲がります *to turn*

mai 枚 *counter for thin flat objects*

maiban 毎晩 *every night*

mainichi 毎日 *every day*

mairu, mairimasu 参る、参ります *to go, to come (humble)*

majime 真面目 *earnest*

maku, makimasu 蒔く、蒔きます *to plant (seeds)*

mannenhitsu 万年筆 *fountain pen*

manshon マンション *condominium*

… masen ka. 〜ませんか。 *Why don't we … ?*

… mashoo. 〜ましょう。 *Let's …*

… mashoo ka. 〜ましょうか。 *Shall we … ?*

massugu まっすぐ *straight*

mata また *again*

mataseru, matasemasu 待たせる、待たせます *to keep someone waiting*

　Omatase itashimashita. お待たせいたしました。 *I have kept you waiting. (polite)*

matsu, machimasu 待つ、待ちます *to wait*

　Omachi kudasai. お待ちください。 *Please wait. (polite)*

　Omachishite orimasu. お待ちしております。 *I/We will be waiting for you. (polite)*

matto マット *mat*

mausu マウス *mouse*

(… no) mawari (〜の)まわり *around …*

mazui まずい *bad (taste)*

me 目 *eye*

… me 〜目 *the … th/the … rd*

　futatsume 二つ目 *second*

　hitotsume 一つ目 *first*

　ichinichime 一日目 *the first day*

　mittsume 三つ目 *third*

medium エム *medium (size)*

　emu de ii エムでいい *medium is okay*

mee 名 *counter for customers in restaurants, clubs, bars (polite)*

　nimeesama 二名様 *two people (polite)*

meeru メール *e-mail*

meetoru メートル *meter*

mekishiko メキシコ *Mexico*

mekishiko ryoori メキシコ料理 *Mexican cuisine*

mekishikojin メキシコ人 *Mexican (person)*

memai めまい *dizziness*

memai ga suru, memai ga shimasu めまいがする、めまいがします *to feel dizzy*

men 綿 *cotton*

mensetsu 面接 *interview*

menyuu メニュー *menu*

meotojawan 夫婦茶碗 *"his and hers" rice bowl set*

meshiagaru, meshiagarimasu 召し上がる、召し上がります *to eat, to drink (honorific)*

michi 道 *street, road*

midori 緑 *green (noun)*

mieru, miemasu 見える、見えます *to be able to be seen, to be visible*

migaku, migakimasu 磨く、磨きます *to brush, to polish*

migi 右 *right*

migigawa 右側 *right side*

miitingu ミーティング *meeting*

mijikai 短い *short*

mikka 三日 *third (day of the month)*

mikkusu sarada ミックスサラダ *mixed salad*

mimi 耳 *ear*

minamigawa 南側 *south side*

minasan 皆さん *everyone (polite)*

minna みんな *everyone*

miru, mimasu 見る、見ます *to watch, to look*

miru, mimasu 診る、診ます *to check, to examine*

… te miru, … te mimasu 〜てみる、〜てみます *to try … ing*

miruku ミルク *milk*

mise 店 *store*

miso 味噌 *soy bean paste*

(o)misoshiru (polite with o) (お)味噌汁 *miso soup*

mittsu 三つ *three (native Japanese number)*

(o) mizu (polite with o) (お)水 *water*

mo も *also, too, both … and*

modoru, modorimasu 戻る、戻ります *to return*

　modotte iru, modotte imasu 戻っている、戻っています *to have returned*

mokuyoobi 木曜日 *Thursday*

mondai 問題 *problem*

monitaa モニター *monitor*

mono 者 *person (humble)*

　tantoo no mono 担当の者 *a person in charge*

moo もう *already*

　moo ichido もう一度 *once more*

　moo sukoshi もう少し *a little more*

Mooshiwake arimasen. 申し訳ありません。
  I'm very sorry. (polite)
Mooshiwake gozaimasen. 申し訳ございません。
  I'm very sorry. (polite)
moosu, mooshimasu 申す、申します *to say*
  (humble)
morau, moraimasu もらう、もらいます *to receive*
  … te morau, … te moraimasu 〜てもらう、〜て
  もらいます *to receive a favor of … ing*
mori 森 *forest*
moshi もし *if, in case*
  moshi yokattara もし良かったら *if it's okay, if*
  you like
moshi moshi もしもし *hello (on the phone)*
motsu, mochimasu 持つ、持ちます *to hold,*
  to own
  kamera o motte dekakeru, kamera o motte
  dekakemasu カメラを持って出掛ける、カメラを
  持って出掛けます *to go out with a camera*
  motte iru, motte imasu 持っている、持ってい
  ます *to have*
  omochi desu ka. お持ちですか。 *Do you have …*
  ? (polite)
motte iku, motte ikimasu 持って行く、持って行き
  ます *to take something (inanimate object)*
motte kuru, motte kimasu 持って来る、持って来
  ます *to bring something (inanimate object)*
motto もっと *more*
muika 六日 *sixth (day of the month)*
muji 無地 *solid (color)*
(… no) mukai (gawa) (〜の)向かい(側) *across*
  from …
mukashimukashi 昔々 *once upon a time*
mune 胸 *chest*
musuko 息子 *son (one's own)*
musukosan 息子さん *son (someone else's)*
musume 娘 *daughter (one's own)*
musumesan 娘さん *daughter (someone else's)*
muttsu 六つ *six (native Japanese number)*
muurugai ムール貝 *mussel*
muzukashii 難しい *difficult*
myaku 脈 *pulse*
myoo 妙 *strange*
nagai 長い *long*
naifu ナイフ *knife*
(… no) naka (〜の)中 *inside … , among …*
nakanaka なかなか *not easily, not readily (in*
  negative); quite (in affirmative)

nakanaka ii なかなかいい *quite good*
nakanaka konai, nakanaka kimasen なかなか来
  ない、なかなか来ません *to not come readily*
… nakereba ikenai, … nakereba ikemasen 〜
  なければいけない、〜なければいけません
  to have to …
… nakereba naranai, … nakereba narimasen
  〜なければならない、〜なければなりません *to*
  have to …
… nakute wa ikenai, … nakute wa ikemasen
  〜なくてはいけない、〜なくてはいけません *to have*
  to …
… nakute wa naranai, … nakute wa
  narimasen 〜なくてはならない、〜なくてはなりま
  せん *to have to …*
(o)namae (polite with o) (お)名前 *name*
  Onamae wa? お名前は？ *What's your name?*
nan(i) 何 *what*
  nani ka 何か *something*
  nani mo (+ negative) 何も *nothing*
nana 七 *seven*
nanafun 七分 *seven minutes*
nanajuu 七十 *seventy*
nanatsu 七つ *seven (native Japanese number)*
nande なんで *why (infml.)*
nando ka 何度か *several times*
nando mo 何度も *many times*
nanji 何時 *what time*
nanoka 七日 *seventh (day of the month)*
narau, naraimasu 習う、習います *to take lessons*
  on
naru, narimasu なる、なります *to become*
  natte iru, natte imasu なっている、なってい
  ます *to have become*
  oyasuku natte imasu お安くなっています *has*
  been priced down (polite)
nasaru, nasaimasu なさる、なさいます *to do*
  (honorific)
nasu なす *eggplant*
natsu 夏 *summer*
natsu yasumi 夏休み *summer vacation*
naze なぜ *why*
ne ね *particle (used to seek agreement; express*
  agreement; confirm information)
nedan 値段 *price*
nekki 熱気 *hot air*
neko 猫 *cat*
nekutai ネクタイ *necktie*

nen 年 *year*
  ichinenkan 一年間 *for a year*
nenree 年齢 *age*
nenzasuru, nenzashimasu 捻挫する、捻挫します *to have a sprain*
neru, nemasu 寝る、寝ます *to go to sleep, to sleep*
netsu 熱 *fever*
  netsu ga aru, netsu ga arimasu 熱がある、熱があります *to have a fever*
  netsu o hakaru, netsu o hakarimasu 熱を測る、熱を測ります *to check one's temperature*
netsuki 寝つき *wake-to-sleep transition*
ni 二 *two*
ni に *particle (marks a location; marks time, day, month; marks a purpose, goal)*
nichiyoobi 日曜日 *Sunday*
nifun 二分 *two minutes*
nigai 苦い *bitter*
nigate 苦手 *poor at*
nigatsu 二月 *February*
nigiyaka 賑やか *lively*
nihon 日本 *Japan*
nihongo 日本語 *Japanese (language)*
nihonjin 日本人 *Japanese (person)*
nihonshu 日本酒 *sake*
niji 二時 *two o'clock*
nijuu 二十 *twenty*
niku 肉 *meat*
nin 人 *counter for people*
ninki 人気 *popularity*
  ninki ga aru, ninki ga arimasu 人気がある、人気があります *to be popular*
nishigawa 西側 *west side*
niwa 庭 *garden, yard*
nizakana 煮魚 *boiled fish*
no の *particle (connects nouns)*
no の *one (indefinite pronoun)*
  amerika no アメリカの *the American one*
  muji no 無地の *the one in solid color*
node ので *because, since*
nodo 喉 *throat*
  nodo ga itai, nodo ga itai desu 喉が痛い、喉が痛いです *to have a sore throat*
nomimono 飲み物 *drink*
noo 脳 *brain*
nooto ノート *notebook*
noru, norimasu 乗る、乗ります *to ride, to get on*

noru, norimasu 載る、載ります *to get into, to be put on*
  notte iru, notte imasu 載っている、載っています *to have been put on*
  nugu, nugimasu 脱ぐ、脱ぎます *to take off (shoes, clothes)*
nyoo 尿 *urine*
nyuugakusuru, nyuugakushimasu 入学する、入学します *to enter school*
nyuuinsuru, nyuuinshimasu 入院する、入院します *to be hospitalized*
nyuuyooku ニューヨーク *New York*
o を *particle (marks a direct object)*
obaasan おばあさん *grandmother (someone else's)*
ocha お茶 *Japanese tea*
odoru, odorimasu 踊る、踊ります *to dance*
ofisu オフィス *office*
ofuro お風呂 *bath*
  ofuro ni hairu, ofuro ni hairimasu お風呂に入る、お風呂に入ります *to take a bath*
ogawa 小川 *stream*
Ohayoo gozaimasu. おはようございます。 *Good morning.*
oishii おいしい *delicious*
ojiisan おじいさん *grandfather (someone else's)*
ojoosan お嬢さん *daughter (someone else's)*
okaasan お母さん *mother (someone else's)*
okaeshi お返し *return, change (polite)*
Okagesama de. おかげさまで。 *I'm fine. (polite)*
okaikee お会計 *check*
okane お金 *money*
okazu おかず *dish eaten with cooked rice*
okinawa 沖縄 *Okinawa*
okiru, okimasu 起きる、起きます *to get up*
okosan お子さん *child (someone else's)*
oku, okimasu 置く、置きます *to put*
  … te oku, … te okimasu 〜ておく、〜ておきます *to do … beforehand*
okureru, okuremasu 遅れる、遅れます *to be late*
okusan 奥さん *wife (someone else's)*
okyakusan, okyakusama お客さん、お客さま *customer, guest (polite)*
ome ni kakaru, ome ni kakarimasu お目にかかる、お目にかかります *to see, to meet (humble)*
Omedetoo gozaimasu. おめでとうございます。 *Congratulations.*
omoi 重い *heavy*

omoshiroi 面白い *interesting*
omou, omoimasu 思う、思います *to think*
onaji 同じ *same*
onaka お腹 *belly, abdomen*
  onaka ga itai, onaka ga itai desu お腹が痛い、お腹が痛いです *to have a stomachache*
oneesan お姉さん *older sister (someone else's)*
onegaisuru, onegaishimasu お願いする、お願いします *to ask for*
  Onegaishimasu. お願いします。 *Please. (asking for a favor)*
  … o onegaishimasu. 〜をお願いします。 *I'd like to have …*
  ongaku 音楽 *music*
oniisan お兄さん *older brother (someone else's)*
onna 女 *female*
  onna no hito 女の人 *woman*
oobo 応募 *application*
ooi 多い *many, much, a lot*
ookii 大きい *big*
oosaka 大阪 *Osaka*
oosama 王様 *king*
opushonaru tsuaa オプショナルツアー *optional tour*
orenji オレンジ *orange*
oriru, orimasu 降りる、降ります *to get off*
  orite iru, orite imasu 降りている、降りています *to have gotten off, to be off*
oru, orimasu おる、おります *to exit, there is (humble)*
oshieru, oshiemasu 教える、教えます *to teach, to tell*
osoi 遅い *late*
ossharu, osshaimasu おっしゃる、おっしゃいます *to say (honorific)*
otearai お手洗い *restroom*
otoko 男 *male*
  otoko no hito 男の人 *man*
otoosan お父さん *father (someone else's)*
otooto 弟 *younger brother (one's own)*
otootosan 弟さん *younger brother (someone else's)*
ototoi おととい *the day before yesterday*
otsuri お釣り *change*
otto 夫 *husband (one's own)*
Oyasuminasai. おやすみなさい。 *Good night.*
oyogu, oyogimasu 泳ぐ、泳ぎます *to swim*
paama パーマ *perm*

paatii パーティー *party*
pan パン *bread*
panda パンダ *panda*
pantsu パンツ *pants*
pasokon パソコン *personal computer*
pen ペン *pen*
piano ピアノ *piano*
pin ピン *pin*
pinku ピンク *pink (noun)*
piza ピザ *pizza*
poppusu ポップス *pop*
porutogarugo ポルトガル語 *Portuguese (language)*
puuru プール *pool*
rainen 来年 *next year*
raishuu 来週 *next week*
raito ライト *light*
rajio ラジオ *radio*
ree 零 *zero*
reezooko 冷蔵庫 *refrigerator*
renrakusuru, renrakushimasu 連絡する、連絡します *to contact*
renshuusuru, renshuushimasu 練習する、練習します *to practice*
repooto レポート *report*
resutoran レストラン *restaurant*
retasu レタス *lettuce*
ringo りんご *apple*
rinku リンク *link, rink*
rirakkusususu, rirakkusushimasu リラックスする、リラックスします *to relax*
rirekisho 履歴書 *curriculum vitae, resume*
riyuu 理由 *reason*
rokku ロック *rock*
roku 六 *six*
rokugatsu 六月 *June*
rokuji 六時 *six o'clock*
rokujuu 六十 *sixty*
rooka 廊下 *hallway*
rooma ローマ *Rome*
roosoku 蝋燭 *candle*
roppun 六分 *six minutes*
ryakugo 略語 *abbreviation*
ryokoo 旅行 *travel*
ryokoosha 旅行社 *travel company*
ryoo 量 *amount*
ryoori 料理 *cooking, cuisine*

ryoori o suru, ryoori o shimasu 料理をする、料理をします *to cook*
(go)ryooshin (polite with go) (ご)両親 *parents*
ryuu 竜 *dragon*
ryuugakusuru, ryuugakushimasu 留学する、留学します *to study abroad*
sagasu, sagashimasu 探す、探します *to look for*
saikin 最近 *recently*
saizu サイズ *size*
sakana 魚 *fish*
(o)sake (polite with o) (お)酒 *alcoholic beverage*
sakkaa サッカー *soccer*
sama 様 *Mr., Ms. (polite)*
samui 寒い *cold (weather, room temperature)*
samuke 寒気 *chill*
　samuke ga suru, samuke ga shimasu 寒気がする、寒気がします *to have chills*
san さん *Mr., Ms.*
san 三 *three*
sangatsu 三月 *March*
sanji 三時 *three o'clock*
sanjuppun 三十分 *thirty minutes*
sanjuu 三十 *thirty*
sanpun 三分 *three minutes*
sarada サラダ *salad*
sashiageru, sashiagemasu さしあげる、さしあげます *to give (humble)*
　… te sashiageru, … te sashiagemasu 〜てさしあげる、〜てさしあげます *to give a favor of … ing (humble)*
sashimi 刺身 *sliced raw fish*
satoo 砂糖 *sugar*
satsu 冊 *counter for bound objects*
Sayoonara. さようなら。 *Goodbye.*
seekatsu 生活 *everyday life*
seetaa セーター *sweater*
seeyakugaisha 製薬会社 *pharmaceutical company*
semai 狭い *narrow*
seminaa セミナー *seminar*
sen 千 *thousand*
　sen en 千円 *thousand yen*
senjitsu 先日 *the other day*
senmenjo 洗面所 *area with a wash stand*
sensee 先生 *teacher*
　Tanaka sensee 田中先生 *Prof./Dr. Tanaka*
senshuu 先週 *last week*
sentakuki 洗濯機 *washing machine*

setsumee 説明 *description*
shaabetto シャーベット *sherbet*
shachoo 社長 *president of a company*
shain 社員 *company employee*
shakai 社会 *society*
　shakaihoken 社会保険 *social insurance*
shakoo dansu 社交ダンス *ballroom daincing*
shashin 写真 *photograph, photography*
shatsu シャツ *shirt*
shawaa シャワー *shower*
　shawaa o abiru, shawaa o abimasu シャワーを浴びる、シャワーを浴びます *to take a shower*
sheedo シェード *shade*
shepaado シェパード *Shepherd*
shi 四 *four*
shiai 試合 *game (of sport)*
shibaraku しばらく *for a while*
shichi 七 *seven*
shichigatsu 七月 *July*
shichiji 七時 *seven o'clock*
shigatsu 四月 *April*
(o)shigoto (polite with o) (お)仕事 *job, work*
(o)shiharai (polite with o) (お)支払い *payment*
shiifuudo sarada シーフードサラダ *seafood salad*
shiji moji 指示文字 *indicative characters*
shika (+ negative) しか *only*
shikago シカゴ *Chicago*
shikaku 資格 *qualification*
shiken 試験 *exam*
shikyuusuru, shikyuushimasu 支給する、支給します *to provide, to cover*
shima 縞 *stripes*
… te shimau, … te shimaimasu 〜てしまう、〜てしまいます *to finish … ing, to have done …*
shimeru, shimemasu 閉める、閉めます *to close (transitive verb)*
shinbun 新聞 *newspaper*
shingoo 信号 *traffic light*
　shingoo no temae 信号の手前 *before the traffic light*
shinkansen 新幹線 *Japanese bullet train*
shinrigaku 心理学 *psychology*
shinryoojo 診療所 *clinic*
shinsatsu 診察 *medical consultation*
shinsatsushitsu 診察室 *medical consulting room*
(go)shinseki (polite with go) (ご)親戚 *relatives*
shinsetsu 親切 *kind, generous*
shinshitsu 寝室 *bedroom*

shinu, shinimasu 死ぬ、死にます *to die*
　shinde iru, shinde imasu 死んでいる、死んでい
　　ます *to be dead*
shinzoo 心臓 *heart*
shio 塩 *salt*
shiokarai 塩辛い *salty*
shiro wain 白ワイン *white wine*
shiroi 白い *white*
shiru, shirimasu 知る、知ります *to know*
　shitteimasu 知っています *I know*
　shirimasen 知りません *I don't know*
(… no) shita (〜の)下 *under …*
shitee 師弟 *teacher and student*
shitee 子弟 *children (fml.)*
shitsumon 質問 *question*
shitsuree 失礼 *impoliteness, rudeness*
　Shitsuree itashimasu 失礼いたします。 *Good-
　　bye. (polite)*
　Shitsureeshimasu. 失礼します。 *Good-bye.
　　(polite)*
shizuka 静か *quiet*
shokugyoo 職業 *occupation*
shokuji 食事 *meal*
shokuyoku 食欲 *appetite*
　shokuyoku ga aru, shokuyoku ga arimasu
　　食欲がある、食欲があります *to have an appetite*
shoobooshi 消防士 *firefighter*
shoogakkoo 小学校 *elementary school*
shookee moji 象形文字 *pictorial characters*
shookyuu 昇給 *salary increase*
shoorai 将来 *future*
shoosetsu 小説 *novel*
shooshoo 少々 *a few, a little*
shooto keeki ショートケーキ *shortcake*
shooyo 賞与 *bonus, reward*
shooyu 醤油 *soy sauce*
shoshin 初診 *the first medical consultation*
shucchoo 出張 *business trip*
shufu 主婦 *housewife*
shujin 主人 *husband (one's own)*
shujutsu 手術 *operation, surgery*
shujutsusuru, shujutsushimasu 手術する、手術
　します *to operate*
shukudai 宿題 *homework*
shumi 趣味 *hobby*
(go)shusshin (polite with go) (ご)出身 *place of
　origin, hometown*
shuu 週 *week*

isshuukan 一週間 *a week*
shuumatsu 週末 *weekend*
sobo 祖母 *grandmother (one's own)*
sochira そちら *that, that way (far from the
　speaker but close to the listener) (polite)*
sofaa ソファー *sofa*
sofu 祖父 *grandfather (one's own)*
sofuto ソフト *software*
sofutowea ソフトウエア *software*
soko そこ *there (far from the speaker but close to
　the listener)*
sono その *that (far from the speaker but close to
　the listener); its*
　sono pen そのペン *that pen*
soo そう *so*
　Soo da naa. そうだなあ。 *Let me see.*
　Soo desu. そうです。 *That's right.*
　Soo desu ka. そうですか。 *Is that so?/Really?
　　(rising intonation)/I see. (falling intonation)*
　Soo desu ne. そうですね。 *Yes, it is./Let me
　　see./That's right. (falling intonation)/Right?
　　(rising intonation)*
　Soo desu yo. そうですよ。 *That's right.*
　Soo ka. そうか。 *I see.*
　Soo shimashoo! そうしましょう! *Let's do that!*
　soo suru, soo shimasu そうする、そうします
　　to do so
soojisuru, soojishimasu 掃除する、掃除します
　to clean
sooshinsha 送信者 *(sent) from*
soosoo 早々 *promptly*
sora 空 *sky*
sore それ *that (far from the speaker but close to
　the listener); it (subject pronoun)*
　sorera それら *they (inanimate)*
sorede それで *so, for that reason*
sorede wa それでは *then*
　Sorede wa mata. それではまた。 *See you then./
　　See you later.*
　sore ja(a) それじゃ(あ) *then (infml.)*
　Sore ja(a) mata. それじゃ(あ)また。 *See you
　　then./See you later. (infml.)*
sorekara それから *and then*
soshite そして *and, and then*
sotsugyoo 卒業 *graduation*
sotsugyoosuru, sotsugyooshimasu 卒業する、卒
　業します *to graduate*
sugiru, sugimasu すぎる、すぎます *too, too much*

sugoi すごい *amazing*
suiee 水泳 *swimming*
suimin 睡眠 *sleep*
  suimin o toru, suimin o torimasu 睡眠をとる、
  睡眠をとります *to get some sleep*
suiyoobi 水曜日 *Wednesday*
sukaafu スカーフ *scarf*
sukaato スカート *skirt*
sukejuuru スケジュール *schedule*
suki da, suki desu 好きだ、好きです *to like*
sukii スキー *ski, skiing*
sukoshi 少し *a little*
  moo sukoshi もう少し *a little more*
Sumimasen. すみません。 *Excuse me./I'm sorry./*
  Sorry for the trouble.
sumoo 相撲 *sumo wrestling*
supagetti スパゲッティ *spaghetti*
supein スペイン *Spain*
supein ryoori スペイン料理 *Spanish cuisine*
supeingo スペイン語 *Spanish (language)*
supeinjin スペイン人 *Spanish (person)*
supootsu スポーツ *sport*
  suppootsu o suru, supootsu o shimasu スポー
  ツをする、スポーツをします *to play sports*
suppai すっぱい *sour*
supuun スプーン *spoon*
suru, shimasu する、します *to do*
  … ni suru, … ni shimasu ～にする、～にし
  ます *to decide on …*
sushi 寿司 *sushi*
sutoresu ストレス *stress*
  sutoresu ga tamatte iru, sutoresu ga tamatte
  imasu ストレスが溜まっている、ストレスが溜ま
  っています *to be under a lot of stress*
suu, suimasu 吸う、吸います *to inhale*
  tabako o suu, tabako o suimasu 煙草を吸う、
  煙草を吸います *to smoke a cigarette*
suugaku 数学 *mathematics*
suupaa スーパー *supermarket*
suutsukeesu スーツケース *suitcase*
suwaru, suwarimasu 座る、座ります *to sit down*
suzushii 涼しい *cool*
tabako 煙草 *tobacco, cigarette*
  tabako o suu, tabako o suimasu 煙草を吸う、
  煙草を吸います *to smoke a cigarette*
tabemono 食べ物 *food*
taberu, tabemasu 食べる、食べます *to eat*
tabun 多分 *perhaps, probably*

tai, tai desu たい、たいです *to want to*
taiboku 大木 *big tree*
taifuu 台風 *typhoon*
taiguu 待遇 *treatment, labor conditions*
taihen 大変 *hard, very*
taiinsuru, taiinshimasu 退院する、退院します
  to leave the hospital, to be released from hospital
taimuzu sukuea タイムズスクエア *Times Square*
taisetsu 大切 *important*
takai 高い *high, tall, expensive*
tako たこ *octopus*
takusan たくさん *a lot, many, much*
takushii タクシー *taxi*
tamago 卵 *egg*
tamanegi たまねぎ *onion*
tamani たまに *once in a while*
tamaru, tamarimasu 溜まる、溜まります *to*
  accumulate
  sutoresu ga tamatte iru, sutoresu ga tamatte
  imasu ストレスが溜まっている、ストレスが溜ま
  っています *to be under a lot of stress*
tane 種 *seed*
tanjoobi 誕生日 *birthday*
tanoshii 楽しい *enjoyable, fun*
tanoshimi ni suru, tanoshimi ni shimasu 楽し
  みにする、楽しみにします *to look forward*
tansu たんす *chest of drawers*
tantoo 担当 *being in charge*
  tantoo no mono 担当の者 *a person in charge*
tara たら *if, when (conjunction)*
tarinai, tarimasen 足りない、足りません *to be*
  insufficient, to be short
tataku, tatakimasu たたく、たたきます *to play*
  (a percussion instrument)
tatemono 建物 *building*
tatsu, tachimasu 立つ、立ちます *to stand up*
tazuneru, tazunemasu 訪ねる、訪ねます *to visit*
te 手 *hand*
teeburu テーブル *table*
teeshoku 定食 *prefix meal*
tegami 手紙 *letter*
temae 手前 *before, this side*
  shingoo no temae 信号の手前 *before the*
  traffic light
ten-in 店員 *store clerk*
tenisu テニス *tennis*
tenisu kooto テニスコート *tennis court*
tenjoo 天井 *ceiling*

tenjooin 添乗員 *tour guide*

tenpura 天ぷら *tempura*

tenpusuru, tenpushimasu 添付する、添付します *to attach (a document)*

(o)tera (polie with o) (お)寺 *temple*

terebi テレビ *television*

tiishatsu ティーシャツ（Tシャツ）*T-shirt*

to と *and, with; when, if; that (conjunction)*

tochi 土地 *land*

(o)toiawase (polite wih o) (お)問い合わせ *inquiry*

toire トイレ *toilet*

tokee 時計 *watch, clock*

toki 時 *when (conjunction)*

tokidoki 時々 *sometimes*

tokoro 所 *place*

toku 徳 *virtue*

toku ni 特に *especially*

tokugi 特技 *special ability, special skill*

tokui 得意 *good at*

tomato トマト *tomato*

tomodachi 友達 *friend*

(... no) tonari (～の)隣 *next to ...*

tonneru トンネル *tunnel*

too 十 *ten (native Japanese number)*

tooi 遠い *far*

tooka 十日 *tenth (day of the month)*

tookushoo トークショー *talk show*

Tookyoo 東京 *Tokyo*

toonyuu 豆乳 *soy milk*

toriniku 鶏肉 *chicken*

toru, torimasu 撮る、撮ります *to take (photos)*

toshokan 図書館 *library*

totemo とても *very, very much*

tsuaagaido ツアーガイド *tour guide*

tsuchi 土 *soil*

tsuitachi 一日 *first (day of the month)*

(... ni) tsuite (～に) ついて *about ...*

tsukau, tsukaimasu 使う、使います *to use*

tsukeru, tsukemasu 点ける、点けます *to light*

tsuki 月 *moon*

tsuku, tsukimasu 着く、着きます *to arrive*

tsukue 机 *desk*

tsukuru, tsukurimasu 作る、作ります *to make*

tsuma 妻 *wife (one's own)*

tsumaranai つまらない *boring*

tsumetai 冷たい *cold (to the touch)*

tsurete iku, tsurete ikimasu 連れて行く、連れて行きます *to take someone or animal*

tsurete kuru, tsurete kimasu 連れて来る、連れて来ます *to bring someone or animal*

tsuyoi 強い *strong*

uchi 家 *house, one's home, one's family*

uchi ni iru, uchi ni imasu 家にいる、家にいます *to stay home*

ude 腕 *arm*

(... no) ue (～の)上 *on, above ...*

ueru, uemasu 植える、植えます *to plant*

ukeru, ukemasu 受ける、受けます *to take*

shinsatsu o ukeru, shinsatsu o ukemasu 診察を受ける、診察を受けます *to take a medical consultation, to consult a physician*

uketsuke 受付 *reception desk, information desk, front desk*

uketsukegakari 受付係 *receptionist*

umi 海 *ocean*

un うん *yes (infml.)*

unagi うなぎ *eel*

unajuu うな重 *broiled eel on rice*

undoo 運動 *exercise*

undoosuru, undooshimasu 運動する、運動します *to exercise*

urusai うるさい *noisy*

(... no) ushiro (～の)後ろ *behind ...*

uso 嘘 *lie*

uso o tsuku, uso o tsukimasu 嘘をつく、嘘をつきます *to tell a lie*

uun ううん *Well ...*

uuru ウール *wool*

uuru hyakupaasento ウール100パーセント *100% wool*

wa は *particle (marks a topic)*

waapuro ワープロ *word processor*

wafuu 和風 *Japanese style*

wain ワイン *wine*

aka wain 赤ワイン *red wine*

shiro wain 白ワイン *white wine*

wakai 若い *young*

wakaru, wakarimasu 分かる、分かります *to understand*

Wakarimashita. 分かりました。*I got it.*

warui 悪い *bad*

wataru, watarimasu 渡る、渡ります *to cross*

watashi 私 *I*

watashi no 私の *my*

watashitachi 私達 *we*

webudezainaa ウェブデザイナー *web designer*

weeruzu ウェールズ *Wales*

weitoresu ウェイトレス *waitress*

windooshoppingu ウィンドーショッピング *window shopping*

ya や *and*

yakizakana 焼き魚 *broiled fish*

yakyuu 野球 *baseball*

yama 山 *mountain*

yappari やっぱり *after all, as expected*

yaru, yarimasu やる、やります *to give (to a plant, an animal), to do (infml.)*

yasai 野菜 *vegetable*

yasashii 易しい *easy*

yasashii 優しい *kind, gentle*

yasui 安い *cheap*

  oyasuku nattte imasu お安くなっています *has been priced down (polite)*

yasumi 休み *day off, holiday, vacation*

yasumu, yasumimasu 休む、休みます *to take some rest, to be absent, to take a day off*

  kaisha o yasumu, kaisha o yasumimasu 会社を休む、会社を休みます *to take a day off from work*

yattsu 八つ *eight (native Japanese number)*

yo よ *particle (used to make an assertion)*

yobu, yobimasu 呼ぶ、呼びます *to call*

yoji 四時 *four o'clock*

yokka 四日 *fourth (day of the month)*

(… no) yoko (〜の)横 *the side of …*

yoku よく *often, well*

  Yoku dekimashita. よくできました。 *Well done.*

yokushitsu 浴室 *bathroom*

yomu, yomimasu 読む、読みます *to read*

yon 四 *four*

yonfun 四分 *four minutes*

yonjuu 四十 *forty*

yonpun 四分 *four minutes*

yoochien 幼稚園 *kindergarden*

yoofuu 洋風 *Western style*

yooi 用意 *preparation*

yooka 八日 *eighth (day of the month)*

Yookoso. ようこそ。 *Welcome.*

yooshi 用紙 *form (to fill out)*

… yori … 〜より〜 *more … than …*

yorokonde … 喜んで〜 *to be glad to …*

yoroshii よろしい *good (polite)*

… te (mo) yoroshii deshoo ka. 〜て(も)よろしいでしょうか。 *May I … ? (polite)*

… te (mo) yoroshii desu ka. 〜て(も)よろしいですか。 *May I … ? (polite)*

yoroshii desu ka. よろしいですか。 *Is it okay? (polite)*

yoroshikattara よろしかったら *if it's okay, if you like (polite)*

yoru 夜 *evening, night*

yottsu 四つ *four (native Japanese number)*

yoyaku 予約 *appointment, reservation*

yoyakusuru, yoyakushimasu 予約する、予約します *to make an appointment, to make a reservation*

yudetamago ゆで卵 *boiled egg*

yuki 雪 *snow*

  Yuki desu. 雪です。 *It's snowing.*

  Yuki ga futte imasu. 雪が降っています。 *It's snowing.*

yukkuri ゆっくり *slowly*

yuubinkyoku 郵便局 *post office*

yuugata 夕方 *early evening*

yuugohan 夕ご飯 *dinner (infml.)*

yuuhan 夕飯 *dinner*

yuujin 友人 *friend (fml.)*

yuumee 有名 *famous*

yuushoku 夕食 *dinner (fml.)*

yuusoosuru, yuusooshimasu 郵送する、郵送します *to mail*

zangyoosuru, zangyooshimasu 残業する、残業します *to work overtime*

zasshi 雑誌 *magazine*

zehi 是非 *by all means, at any cost*

zen 禅 *zen*

zenbu 全部 *all*

  zenbu de 全部で *all together*

zenzen (+ negative) 全然 *not at all*

zero ゼロ *zero*

zubon ズボン *pants*

zutsu ずつ *each*

zutsuu 頭痛 *headache*

  zutsuu ga suru, zutsuu ga shimasu 頭痛がする、頭痛がします *to have a headache*

English-Japanese

A

a few   *shooshoo* 少々

a little   *chotto, shooshoo, sukoshi* ちょっと、少々、少し

a little more   *moo sukoshi* もう少し

a lot   *ooi, takusan* 多い、たくさん

a.m.   *gozen* 午前

abbreviation   *ryakugo* 略語

abdomen   *hara, onaka* 腹、お腹

able (to be)   *mieru, miemasu* 見える、見えます

about   *goro, gurai* 頃、ぐらい

about ...   *(... ni) tsuite* (〜に)ついて

above ...   *(... no) ue* (〜の)上

absent (to be)   *yasumu, yasumimasu* 休む、休みます

accompaniment   *dookoo* 同行

accounting   *keeri* 経理

accumulate (to)   *tamaru, tamarimasu* 溜まる、溜まります

across from ...   *(... no) mukai (gawa)* (〜の)向かい(側)

actually   *jitsu wa* 実は

advertisement   *kookoku* 広告

after   *ato de, go* 後で、後

after leaving a restaurant   *resutoran o deta ato de* レストランを出た後で

after all   *yappari* やっぱり

afternoon   *gogo* 午後

again   *mata* また

age   *nenree* 年齢

agreement   *kiyaku* 規約

ah   *aa* ああ

air   *kuuki* 空気

hot air   *nekki* 熱気

airplane   *hikooki* 飛行機

alcoholic beverage   *(o)sake (polite with o)* (お)酒

all   *zenbu* 全部

all together   *zenbu de* 全部で

not at all   *zenzen (+ negative)* 全然

all right   *daijoobu* 大丈夫

allergy   *arerugii* アレルギー

already   *moo* もう

also   *mo* も

always   *itsumo* いつも

amazing   *sugoi* すごい

American   *amerikajin (person)* アメリカ人

among ...   *(... no) naka* (〜の)中

amount   *ryoo* 量

and   *soshite, to, ya* そして、と、や

and then   *sorekara, soshite* それから、そして

anemia   *hinketsu* 貧血

answer   *kotae* 答え

apartment   *apaato* アパート

appetite   *shokuyoku* 食欲

have an appetite (to): *shokuyoku ga aru, shokuyoku ga arimasu* 食欲がある、食欲があります

apple   *ringo* りんご

application   *oobo* 応募

appointment   *kiyoo, yoyaku* 起用、予約

make an appointment (to)   *yoyakusuru, yoyakushimasu* 予約する、予約します

approximately   *goro, gurai* 頃、ぐらい

April   *shigatsu* 四月

arm   *ude* 腕

around ...   *(... no) mawari* (〜の)まわり

arrive (to)   *tsuku, tsukimasu* 着く、着きます

arriving ...   *... chaku* 〜着

arriving in Naha   *naha chaku* 那覇着

as expected   *yappari* やっぱり

ask for (to)   *onegaisuru, onegaishimasu* お願いする、お願いします

assistant   *ashisutanto* アシスタント

at any cost   *zehi* 是非

attach (a document) (to)   *tenpusuru, tenpushimasu* 添付する、添付します

attend (to)   *deru, demasu* 出る、出ます

attend ... (to)   *... ni deru* 〜に出る

August   *hachigatsu* 八月

autumn   *aki* 秋

bad   *warui, mazui (taste)* 悪い、まずい

bag   *baggu, kaban* バッグ、かばん

ball   *booru* ボール

ballpoint pen   *boorupen* ボールペン

ballroom dancing   *shakoo dansu* 社交ダンス

bank   *ginkoo* 銀行

bank clerk   *ginkooin* 銀行員

bar   *baa* バー

baseball   *yakyuu* 野球

basketball   *basukettobooru* バスケットボール

bat   *batto* バット

bath   *ofuro* お風呂

take a bath (to) *ofuro ni hairu, ofuro ni hairimasu* お風呂に入る、お風呂に入ります

bathroom *yokushitsu* 浴室

be (to) *da, desu ;... de gozaimasu. (polite)* だ、です;〜でございます。

beach *biichi* ビーチ

Beaujolais nouveau *bojoreenuuboo* ボジョレーヌーボー

beautiful *kiree* きれい

beauty salon *biyooin* 美容院

because *node, kara* ので、から

become (to) *naru, narimasu* なる、なります

have become (to) *natte iru, natte imasu* なっている、なっています

bed *beddo* ベッド

bedroom *shinshitsu* 寝室

beef *gyuuniku* 牛肉

beer *biiru* ビール

beer gift coupon *biiru ken* ビール券

before izen, mae ni, temae 以前、前に、手前

before going the party *paatii e iku mae ni* パーティーへ行く前に

before the traffic light: *shingoo no temae* 信号の手前

behind... (... no) ushiro (〜の)後ろ

being in charge *tantoo* 担当

a person in charge *tantoo no mono* 担当の者

belly *hara, onaka* 腹、お腹

belong (to) *haitte iru, haitte imasu* 入っている、入っています

best *besuto* ベスト

the best *ichiban ii* 一番いい

You'd better... ... *(ta/da) hoo ga ii desu.* 〜(た/だ)方がいいです。

You'd better not... ... *nai hoo ga ii desu.* 〜ない方がいいです。

between (... and...) (... to... no) aida (〜と〜の)間

big *ookii* 大きい

big tree *taiboku* 大木

birthday *tanjoobi* 誕生日

bitter *nigai* 苦い

black *kuroi* 黒い

black tea *koocha* 紅茶

blood pressure *ketsuatsu* 血圧

have high blood pressure (to) *ketsuatsu ga takai, ketsuatsu ga takai desu* 血圧が高い、血圧が高いです

have low blood pressure (to) *ketsuatsu ga hikui, ketsuatsu ga hikui desu* 血圧が低い、血圧が低いです

blouse *burausu* ブラウス

blue *aoi (adjective), ao (noun)* 青い、青

body *karada* 体、身体

boiled egg *yudetamago* ゆで卵

boiled fish *nizakana* 煮魚

bone *hone* 骨

break a bone (to) *hone o oru, hone o orimasu* 骨を折る、骨を折ります

bonus *shooyo* 賞与

book *hon* 本

book store *hon-ya* 本屋

boring *tsumaranai* つまらない

borrow (to) *kariru, karimasu* 借りる、借ります

have borrowed (to) *karate iru, karate imasu* 借りている、借りています

both... and *mo* も

bottle *bin* 瓶

brain *noo* 脳

bread *pan* パン

break a bone (to) *hone o oru, hone o orimasu; kossetsusuru, kossetsushimasu* 骨を折る、骨を折ります;骨折する、骨折します

breakfast *chooshoku (fml.), asagohan (infml.)* 朝食、朝ご飯

bright *akarui* 明るい

bring (to) *tsurete kuru, tsurete kimasu (animate); motte kuru, motte kimasu (inanimate)* 連れて来る、連れて来ます;持って来る、持って来ます

broiled eel on rice *unajuu* うな重

broiled fish *yakizakana* 焼き魚

brown *chairoi (adjective), chairo (noun)* 茶色い、茶色

brunch *buranchi* ブランチ

brush (to) *migaku, migakimasu* 磨く、磨きます

building *tatemono* 建物

high-rise building *biru* ビル

bullet train *shinkansen* 新幹線

bus *basu* バス

bus stop *basutee* バス停

business management *kee-eegaku* 経営学

business report *eegyoo hookokusho* 営業報告書

business trip *shucchoo* 出張

busy *isogashii* 忙しい

but *demo, ga, kedo* でも、が、けど

butter *bataa* バター
buy (to) *kau, kaimasu* 買う、買います
by all means *zehi* 是非
cabbage *kyabetsu* キャベツ
café au lait *kafeore* カフェオレ
cake *keeki* ケーキ
call (to) *yobu, yobimasu* 呼ぶ、呼びます
camera *kamera* カメラ
can do *dekiru, dekimasu* できる、できます
Canada *canada* カナダ
Canadian *kanadajin (person)* カナダ人
cancer *gan* 癌
candle *roosoku* 蝋燭
Cannes *kannu* カンヌ
cap *kyappu* キャップ
cappuccino *kapuchiino* カプチーノ
car *kuruma* 車
card *kaado* カード
  health insurance card *hokenshoo* 保険証
case *ken* 件
cash *genkin* 現金
cat *neko* 猫
catch a cold (to) *kaze o hiku, kaze o hikimasu* 風邪をひく、風邪をひきます
ceiling *tenjoo* 天井
cell phone *keetai (denwa)* 携帯(電話)
cello *chero* チェロ
Certainly. *Kashikomarimashita. (polite)* かしこまりました。
chain *cheen* チェーン
chair *isu* 椅子
chance *chansu, kikai* チャンス、機会
change *otsuri, okaeshi (polite)* お釣り、お返し
change (to) *kawaru, kawarimasu* 変わる、変わります
cheap *yasui* 安い
check *okaikee* お会計
check (to) *miru, mimasu* 診る、診ます
  check one's temperature (to) *netsu o hakaru, netsu o hakarimasu* 熱を測る、熱を測ります
cheese *chiizu* チーズ
chest *mune* 胸
chest of drawers *tansu* たんす
Chicago *shikago* シカゴ
chicken *toriniku* 鶏肉
chicken salad *chikin sarada* チキンサラダ

child *kodomo, kodomosan (somebody else's), okosan (somebody else's)* 子供, 子供さん、お子さん
  children *shitee (fml.)* 子弟
  three children in a family *sannin kyoodai* 三人兄弟
chill *samuke* 寒気
  have chills (to) *samuke ga suru, samuke ga shimasu* 寒気がする、寒気がします
China *chuugoku* 中国
Chinese *chuugokugo (language), chuugokujin (person)* 中国語、中国人
Chinese characters *kanji* 漢字
chocolate *chokoreeto* チョコレート
chopsticks *hashi* 箸
Christmas *kurisumasu* クリスマス
cigarette *tabako* 煙草
  smoke a cigarette (to) *tabako o suu, tabako o suimasu* 煙草を吸う、煙草を吸います
clarinet *kurarinetto* クラリネット
class *jugyoo, kurasu* 授業、クラス
classical *kurashikku* クラシック
classmate *kurasumeeto* クラスメート
clean *kiree* きれい
clean (to) *soojisuru, soojishimasu* 掃除する、掃除します
clinic *shinryoojo* 診療所
clock *tokee* 時計
close *chikai* 近い
close (to) *shimeru, shimemasu (transitive verb)* 閉める、閉めます
cloudy *kumori* 曇り
  It's cloudy. *Kumori desu.* 曇りです。
club *kurabu* クラブ
coffee *koohii* コーヒー
coffee shop *kissaten* 喫茶店
coincidence *guuzen* 偶然
cold *kaze* 風邪
  catch a cold (to) *kaze o hiku, kaze o hikimasu* 風邪をひく、風邪をひきます
cold *tsumetai (to the touch), samui (weather, room temperature)* 冷たい、寒い
college *daigaku* 大学
college student *daigakusee* 大学生
come (to) *kuru, kimasu; irassharu, irasshaimasu (honorific); mairu, mairimasu (humble)* 来る、来ます; いらっしゃる、いらっしゃいます; 参る、参ります

have come (to) *kite iru, kite imasu* 来ている、来ています

not come readily (to) *nakanaka konai, nakanaka kimasen* なかなか来ない、なかなか来ません

come down (to) *furu, furimasu* 降る、降ります

come home (to) *kaeru, kaerimasu* 帰る、帰ります

company *kaisha* 会社

company employee *kaishain, shain* 会社員、社員

complexion *kaoiro* 顔色

compound ideographic characters *kaii moji* 会意文字

computer *konpyuutaa* コンピューター

concerning *kansuru* 関する

concert *konsaato* コンサート

condominium *manshon* マンション

Congratulations. *Omedetoo gozaimasu.* おめでとうございます。

consult a physician (to) *shinsatsu o ukeru, shinsatsu o ukemasu* 診察を受ける、診察を受けます

contact (to) *renrakusuru, renrakushimasu* 連絡する、連絡します

convenience store *konbini* コンビニ

convenient *benri* 便利

cook (to) *ryoori o suru, ryoori o shimasu* 料理をする、料理をします

cooked rice *gohan* ご飯

cookie *kukkii* クッキー

cooking *ryoori* 料理

cool *suzushii* 涼しい

copy *kopii* コピー

copy (counter for written materials) *bu* 部

copy (to) *kopiisuru, kopiishimasu* コピーする、コピーします

corner *kado* 角

cost *hiyoo* 費用

at any cost *zehi* 是非

transportation costs *kootsuuhi* 交通費

cotton *men* 綿

country *kuni* 国

coupon *ken* 券

beer gift coupon *biiru ken* ビール券

cousin *itoko* 従兄弟

cover (to) *shikyuusuru, shikyuushimasu* 支給する、支給します

credit card *kaado, kurejitto kaado* カード、クレジットカード

croquette *korokke* コロッケ

cross (to) *wataru, watarimasu* 渡る、渡ります

crowded (to be) *konde iru, konde imasu* 混んでいる、混んでいます

get crowded (to) *komu, komimasu* 混む、混みます

cruise *kuruujingu* クルージング

cucumber *kyuuri* きゅうり

cuisine *ryoori* 料理

curriculum vitae *rirekisho* 履歴書

curry *karee* カレー

customer *kyaku, okyakusan (polite), okyakusama (polite)* 客、お客さん、お客さま

cut (to) *kiru, kirimasu* 切る、切ります

cute *kawaii* かわいい

cutlet *katsu* かつ

cuttlefish *ika* いか

dance, dancing *dansu* ダンス

dance (to) *odoru, odorimasu* 踊る、踊ります

dark *kurai* 暗い

daughter *musume (one's own), musumesan (someone else's), ojoosan (someone else's)* 娘、娘さん、お嬢さん

day *hi* 日

some other day *gojitsu* 後日

the day after tomorrow *asatte* あさって

the day before yesterday *ototoi* おととい

the first day *ichinichime* 一日目

the other day *senjitsu* 先日

day off *yasumi* 休み

take a day off (to) *yasumu, yasumimasu* 休む、休みます

take a day off from work (to) *kaisha o yasumu, kaisha o yasumimasu* 会社を休む、会社を休みます

dead (to be) *shinde iru, shinde imasu* 死んでいる、死んでいます

December *juunigatsu* 十二月

decide on … (to) *… ni suru, … ni shimasu* ～にする、～にします

degree *do* 度

38 degrees *sanjuuhachi do* 三十八度

delicious *oishii* おいしい

department store *depaato* デパート

description *setsumee* 説明

design *dezain* デザイン

desk *tsukue* 机

dessert *dezaato* デザート

diarrhea *geri* 下痢
  have a diarrhea (to) *geri o suru, geri o shimasu* 下痢をする、下痢をします
dictionary *jisho* 辞書
die (to) *shinu, shinimasu* 死ぬ、死にます
diesel *diizeru* ディーゼル
difficult *muzukashii* 難しい
dignity *hin* 品
dinner *yuuhan, yuushoku (fml.), yuugohan (infml.)* 夕飯、夕食、夕ご飯
direction *hoo, hookoo* 方、方向
dirty *kitanai* 汚い
disciple *deshi* 弟子
dish eaten with cooked rice *okazu* おかず
dislike (to) *kirai da, kirai desu* 嫌いだ、嫌いです
display *disupurei* ディスプレイ
distribute (to) *kubaru, kubarimasu* 配る、配ります
division manager *buchoo* 部長
dizziness *memai* めまい
do (to) *suru, shimasu; yaru, yarimasu (infml.); itasu, itashimasu (humble); nasaru, nasaimasu (honorific)* する、します；やる、やります；いたす、いたします；なさる、なさいます
  do so *soo suru, soo shimasu* そうする、そうします
  do ... beforehand (to) *... te oku, ... te okimasu* 〜ておく、〜ておきます
  have done ... (to) *... te shimau, ... te shimaimasu; ... koto ga aru, ... koto ga arimasu* 〜てしまう、〜てしまいます；〜ことがある、〜ことがあります
  Please don't ... *... naide kudasai* 〜ないでください。
dog *inu* 犬
dozen *daasu* ダース
dragon *ryuu* 竜
drawing *e* 絵
dressing *doresshingu* ドレッシング
drink *nomimono* 飲み物
drink (to) *meshiagaru, meshiagarimasu (honorific); itadaku, itadakimasu (humble)* 召し上がる、召し上がります；いただく、いただきます
each *zutsu* ずつ
ear *mimi* 耳
early *hayai, hayaku* 早い、早く
early evening *yuugata* 夕方
earnest *majime* 真面目
(not) easily *nakanaka (+ negative)* なかなか

east side *higashigawa* 東側
easy *kantan, yasashii* 簡単、易しい
eat (to) *taberu, tabemasu; meshiagaru, meshiagarimasu (honorific); itadaku, itadakimasu (humble)* 食べる、食べます；召し上がる、召し上がります；いただく、いただきます
economics *keezaigaku* 経済学
economy *keezai* 経済
eel *unagi* うなぎ
effect *kooka* 効果
egg *tamago* 卵
eggplant *nasu* なす
eight *hachi, yattsu (native Japanese number)* 八、八つ
eight minutes *hachifun, happun* 八分
eight o'clock *hachiji* 八時
eighteen *juuhachi* 十八
eighth (day of the month) *yooka* 八日
eighty *hachijuu* 八十
electrical engineer *denki gishi* 電気技師
elementary school *shoogakkoo* 小学校
eleven *juuichi* 十一
eleven o'clock *juuichiji* 十一時
e-mail *iimeeru, meeru* イーメール、メール
engine *enjin* エンジン
engineer *enjinia* エンジニア
engineer *gishi* 技師
England *igirisu* イギリス
English *eego (language), igirisujin (person)* 英語、イギリス人
enjoyable *tanoshii* 楽しい
enter (to) *hairu, hairimasu* 入る、入ります
  have entered (to) *haitte iru, haitte imasu* 入っている、入っています
enter school (to) *nyuugakusuru, nyuugakushimasu* 入学する、入学します
entrance hall *genkan* 玄関
error *gobyuu (fml.)* 誤びゅう
especially *toku ni* 特に
evening *ban, yoru* 晩、夜
  early evening *yuugata* 夕方
every day *mainichi* 毎日
every night *maiban* 毎晩
everyday life *seekatsu* 生活
everyone *minna, minasan (polite)* みんな、皆さん
exactly *kichinto, chanto (infml.)* きちんと、ちゃんと
exam *shiken* 試験

examination *kensa* 検査

examine (to) *kensasuru, kensashimasu; miru, mimasu* 検査する、検査します; 診る、診ます

Excuse me. *Sumimasen.* すみません。

exercise *undoo* 運動

exercise (to) *undoosuru, undooshimasu* 運動する、運動します

exhaustion *hiroo* 疲労

exist (to) *irassharu, irasshaimasu (honorific); gozaimasu (polite); oru, orimasu (humble)* いらっしゃる、いらっしゃいます; ございます; おる、おります

expense *hiyoo* 費用

expensive *takai* 高い

experience *keeken* 経験

have an experience of ... ing (to) *... koto ga aru, ... koto ga arimasu* ～ことがある、～ことがあります

export and import business *booeki* 貿易

expression *hyoogen* 表現

eye *me* 目

face *kao* 顔

fall *aki* 秋

fall (to) *furu, furimasu* 降る、降ります

family *(go)kazoku (polite with go)* （ご）家族

five people in a family *gonin kazoku* 五人家族

one's family *uchi* 家

famous *yuumee* 有名

far *tooi* 遠い

father *chichi (one's own), otoosan (someone else's)* 父、お父さん

father's day *chichi no hi* 父の日

fathers and eldest sons *fukee (fml.)* 父兄

fatigue *hiroo* 疲労

fax *fakkusu* ファックス

February *nigatsu* 二月

feel dizzy (to) *memai ga suru, memai ga shimasu* めまいがする、めまいがします

feel like vomiting (to) *hakike ga suru, hakike ga shimasu* 吐き気がする、吐き気がします

feel sick (to) *kibun ga warui, kibun ga warui desu* 気分が悪い、気分が悪いです

feeling *kibun* 気分

female *onna* 女

fence *fensu* フェンス

fever *netsu* 熱

have a fever (to) *netsu ga aru, netsu ga arimasu* 熱がある、熱があります

fifteen *juugo* 十五

fifth (day of the month) *itsuka* 五日

fifth floor *gokai* 五階

fifty *gojuu* 五十

fill out (a form) (to) *kinyuusuru, kinyuushimasu* 記入する、記入します

I'm fine. *Genki desu./Okagesama de. (polite)* 元気です。/おかげさまで。

finish ... ing (to) *... te shimau, ... te shimaimasu* ～てしまう、～てしまいます

Finland *finrando* フィンランド

firefighter *shoobooshi* 消防士

first *hitotsume* 一つ目

first (day of the month) *tsuitachi* 一日

first time, for the first time *hajimete* 初めて

the first day *ichinichime* 一日目

the first medical consultation *shoshin* 初診

fish *sakana* 魚

sliced raw fish *sashimi* 刺身

five *go, itsutsu (native Japanese number)* 五、五つ

five minutes *gofun* 五分

five o'clock *goji* 五時

flower *hana* 花

flute *furuuto* フルート

font *fonto* フォント

food *tabemono* 食べ物

foot *ashi* 足

football *futtobooru* フットボール

for a while *shibaraku* しばらく

forest *mori* 森

fork *fooku* フォーク

form (to fill out) *yooshi* 用紙

formerly *katsute* かつて

forty *yonjuu* 四十

fountain pen *mannenhitsu* 万年筆

four *shi, yon, yottsu (native Japanese number)* 四、四、四つ

four minutes *yonfun, yonpun* 四分

four o'clock *yoji* 四時

fourteen *juushi, juuyon* 十四

fourth (day of the month) *yokka* 四日

France *furansu* フランス

free *jiyuu* 自由

free time *jiyuujikan* 自由時間

free (to be) (having a lot of free time) *hima* 暇

freedom *jiyuu* 自由

French *furansugo (language), furansujin (person)* フランス語、フランス人
French cuisine *furansu ryoori* フランス料理
Friday *kin-yoobi* 金曜日
friend *tomodachi, yuujin (fml.)* 友達、友人
from *kara* から
 (sent) from *sooshinsha* 送信者
 from ... to... *... kara ... made* ～から～まで
front desk *uketsuke* 受付
full *ippai* 一杯
fully furnished *kanbi* 完備
fun *tanoshii* 楽しい
furniture *kagu* 家具
future *shoorai* 将来
game *geemu, shiai (of sport)* ゲーム、試合
garden *niwa* 庭
generous *shinsetsu* 親切
gentle *yasashii* 優しい
German *doitsugo (language), doitsujin (person)* ドイツ語、ドイツ人
Germany *doitsu* ドイツ
get off (to) *oriru, orimasu* 降りる、降ります
 have gotten off (to) *orite iru, orite imasu* 降りている、降りています
get on (to) *noru, norimasu* 乗る、乗ります
get up (to) *okiru, okimasu* 起きる、起きます
girlfriend *gaarufurendo* ガールフレンド
give (to) *ageru, agemasu; kureru, kuremasu; yaru, yarimasu (to a plant, an animal); kudasaru, kudasaimasu (honorific); sashiageru, sashiagemasu (humble)* あげる、あげます；くれる、くれます；やる、やります；くださる、くださいます；さしあげる、さしあげます
 give a favor of ... ing (to) *... te ageru, ... te agemasu; ... te kureru, ... te kuremasu; ... te kudasaru, ... te kudasaimasu (honorific); ... te sashiageru, ... te sashiagemasu (humble)* ～てあげる、～てあげます；～てくれる、～てくれます；～てくださる、～てくださいます；～てさしあげる、～てさしあげます
 give an injection (to) *chuushasuru, chuushashimasu* 注射する、注射します
glad to ... (to be) *yorokonde ...* 喜んで～
 I'm glad to hear that. *Sore wa yokatta.* それはよかった。
go (to) *iku, ikimasu; irassharu, irasshaimasu (honorific); mairu, mairimasu (humble)* 行く、行きます；いらっしゃる、いらっしゃいます；参る、参ります
 have gone (to) *itte iru, itte imasu* 行っている、行っています
go back (to) *kaeru, kaerimasu* 帰る、帰ります
go home (to) *kaeru, kaerimasu* 帰る、帰ります
go out (to) *dekakeru, dekakemasu* 出掛ける、出掛けます
 go out with a camera (to) *kamera o motte dekakemasu* カメラを持って出掛けます
go to sleep (to) *neru, nemasu* 寝る、寝ます
golf *gorufu* ゴルフ
good *ii, yoroshii (polite)* いい、よろしい
 good at *joozu, tokui* 上手、得意
 quite good *nakanaka ii* なかなかいい
Good afternoon. *Konnichi wa.* こんにちは。
Good evening. *Konban wa.* こんばんは。
Good morning. *Ohayoo gozaimasu.* おはようございます。
Good night. *Oyasuminasai.* おやすみなさい。
Goodbye. *Sayoonara./Shitsuree itashimasu. (polite)/Shitsureeshimasu. (polite)* さようなら。/失礼いたします。/失礼します。
(I) got it. *Wakarimashita.* 分かりました。
graduate (to) *sotsugyoosuru, sotsugyooshimasu* 卒業する、卒業します
graduate school *daigakuin* 大学院
graduate school student *daigakuinsee* 大学院生
graduation *sotsugyoo* 卒業
grandfather *sofu (one's own), ojiisan (someone else's)* 祖父、おじいさん
grandmother *sobo (one's own), obaasan (someone else's)* 祖母、おばあさん
green *midori (noun)* 緑
green salad *guriin sarada* グリーンサラダ
grey *guree (noun)* グレー
group presentation *gruupu happyoo* グループ発表
guest *kyaku, okyakusan (polite), okyakusama (polite)* 客、お客さん、お客さま
gun *juu* 銃
hair *ke, kami (on the head), kami no ke (on the head)* 毛、髪、髪の毛
hair dresser *biyooshi* 美容師
hair dye *karaa* カラー
haircut *katto* カット
half *han, hanbun* 半、半分
 for half a year *hantoshikan* 半年間

half a year *hantoshi* 半年
half past the hour *han* 半
hallway *rooka* 廊下
ham *hamu* ハム
hand *te* 手
handkerchief *hankachi* ハンカチ
hard *taihen* 大変
hardware *haadowea* ハードウェア
have (to) *motte iru, motte imasu* 持っている、
　持っています
　Do you have … ? *aru, arimasu (inanimate);*
　　iru, imasu (animate); gozaimasu (polite);
　　omochi desu ka. (polite) ある、あります; いる、い
　　ます; ございます;お持ちですか。
have to … (to) *… nakereba ikenai, … nakereba*
　ikemasen; … nakereba naranai, … nakereba
　narimasen; … nakute wa ikenai, … nakute wa
　ikemasen; … nakute wa naranai, … nakute wa
　narimasen 〜なければいけない、〜なければいけま
　せん; 〜なければならない、〜なければなりません;
　〜なくてはいけない、〜なくてはいけません; 〜なく
　てはならない、〜なくてはなりません
he *kare* 彼
headache *zutsuu* 頭痛
　have a headache (to) *atama ga itai, atama ga*
　　itai desu; zutsuu ga suru, zutsuu ga shimasu
　　頭が痛い、頭が痛いです;頭痛がする、頭痛がし
　　ます
health insurance card *hokenshoo* 保険証
heart *haato, kokoro, shinzoo* ハート、心、心臓
heavy *omoi* 重い
Hello. *Konnichi wa. ; moshi moshi (on the phone)*
　こんにちは。; もしもし
her *kanojo no* 彼女の
here *koko* ここ
　here (to be) *kite iru, kite imasu* 来ている、来て
　　います
　Here you go. *Doozo.* どうぞ。
high *takai* 高い
high school *kookoo* 高校
high school student *kookoosee* 高校生
high-rise building *biru* ビル
hip *koshi* 腰
hip-hop *hippuhoppu* ヒップホップ
hiragana characters *hiragana* 平仮名
Hiroshima *hiroshima* 広島
his *kare no* 彼の

"his and hers" rice bowl set *meotojawan* 夫
　婦茶碗
hobby *shumi* 趣味
hold (to) *motsu, mochimasu* 持つ、持ちます
holiday *yasumi* 休み
home (one's) *uchi* 家
　stay home (to) *uchi ni iru, uchi ni imasu* 家にい
　　る、家にいます
hometown *(go)shusshin (polite with go)* (ご)出身
homework *shukudai* 宿題
Hong Kong *honkon* 香港、ホンコン
hospital *byooin* 病院
hospitalized (to be) *nyuuinsuru,*
　nyuuinshimasu 入院する、入院します
hot *atsui (to the touch), atsui (weather, room*
　temperature) 熱い、暑い
hot air *nekki* 熱気
hotel *hoteru* ホテル
hour(s) *jikan* 時間
　two hours *nijikan* 二時間
house *ie, uchi* 家
housewife *shufu* 主婦
how *doo, doo yatte, ikaga (polite)* どう、どうやっ
　て、いかが
　How about … ? *Doo desu ka.* どうですか。
　How are you? *… wa ikaga desu ka. (polite)*
　　〜はいかがですか。
　How do you do? *Ogenki desu ka.* お元気です
　　か。
　How is it? *Hajimemashite.; Doo desu ka.;*
　　Ikaga desu ka. (polite) はじめまして。; どうです
　　か。; いかがですか。
　How was it? *Doo deshita ka.; Ikaga deshita ka.*
　　(polite) どうでしたか。; いかがでしたか。
how long *dono gurai* どのぐらい
how many *(o)ikutsu (polite with o)* (お)いくつ
how much *(o)ikura (polite with o); dono gurai*
　(お)いくら; どのぐらい
how old *(o)ikutsu (polite with o)* (お)いくつ
however *demo* でも
human resources department *jinjibu* 人事部
hundred *hyaku* 百
　hundred percent *hyakupaasento* 100パーセン
　　ト
　100% wool *uuru hyakupaasento* ウール100
　　パーセント
husband *otto (one's own), shujin (one's own),*
　goshujin (someone else's) 夫、主人、ご主人

I *watashi, boku (used only by male speakers)* 私、
僕
ice cream *aisukuriimu* アイスクリーム
idea *kangae* 考え
identical *dooitsu* 同一
if *moshi, tara, to* もし、たら、と
  if it's okay, if you like *moshi yokattara,
    yoroshikattara (polite)* もし良かったら、よろし
    かったら
ignition *hakka* 発火
illness *byooki* 病気
immediate opening *kyuubo* 急募
impoliteness *shituree* 失礼
important *taisetsu* 大切
in case *moshi* もし
in front of... (... *no) mae* (〜の)前
inch *inchi* インチ
included (to be) *fukumu, fukumimasu* 含む、含
みます
inconvenient *fuben* 不便
India *indo* インド
indicative characters *shiji moji* 指示文字
information desk *uketsuke* 受付
inhale (to) *suu, suimasu* 吸う、吸います
injection *chuusha* 注射
injury *kega* 怪我
  get injured (to) *kega o suru, kega o shimasu* 怪
    我をする、怪我をします
inquire (to) *kiku, kikimasu* 聞く、聞きます
inquiry *(o)toiawase (polite wih o)* (お)問い合わせ
inside... (... *no) naka* (〜の)中
insomnia *fuminshoo* 不眠症
  suffer from insomnia (to) *fuminshoo da,
    fuminshoo desu* 不眠症だ、不眠症です
insufficient (to be) *tarinai, tarimasen* 足りない、
足りません
insurance *hoken* 保険
  social insurance *shakaihoken* 社会保険
interesting *omoshiroi* 面白い
Internet *intaanetto* インターネット
intersection *koosaten* 交差点
interview *mensetsu* 面接
intestine *choo* 腸
it *sore* それ
Italian *itariago (language)* イタリア語
Italian cuisine *itaria ryoori* イタリア料理
Italy *itaria* イタリア
its *sono* その

January *ichigatsu* 一月
Japan *nihon* 日本
Japanese *nihongo (language), nihonjin (person)*
日本語、日本人
Japanese style *wafuu* 和風
jazz *jazu* ジャズ
jeans *jiinzu* ジーンズ
job *o(shigoto) (polite with o)* (お)仕事
job posting *kyuujin (kookoku)* 求人(広告)
jog, jogging *jogingu* ジョギング
join (to) *hairu, hairimasu* 入る、入ります
joint-stock cooperation *kabushikigaisha* 株式
会社
judo *juudoo* 柔道
juice *juusu* ジュース
July *shichigatsu* 七月
June *rokugatsu* 六月
junior high school *chuugakkoo* 中学校
katakana characters *katakana* 片仮名
keep (to) *azukaru, azukarimasu* 預かる、預かり
ます
  keep someone waiting (to) *mataseru,
    matasemasu* 待たせる、待たせます
  I have kept you waiting. *Omatase
    itashimashita. (polite)* お待たせいたしました。
kendo *kendoo* 剣道
keyboard *kiiboodo* キーボード
kind *shinsetsu, yasashii* 親切、優しい
kindergarten *yoochien* 幼稚園
king *oosama* 王様
kitchen *daidokoro* 台所
knife *naifu* ナイフ
know (to) *shiru, shirimasu* 知る、知ります
  I know *shitteimasu* 知っています
  I don't know *shirimasen* 知りません
Kobe *koobe* 神戸
konnyaku potato *konnyaku* こんにゃく
Korea *kankoku* 韓国
Kyoto *kyooto* 京都
labor conditions *taiguu* 待遇
land *tochi* 土地
language *kotoba* 言葉
last week *senshuu* 先週
last year *kyonen* 去年
late *osoi* 遅い
late (to be) *okureru, okuremasu* 遅れる、遅れます
later *ato de, go, gojitsu* 後で、後、後日

See you later. *Sorede wa mata./Sore ja(a) mata. (infml.)* それではまた。/それじゃ(あ)また。

30 minutes later *sanjuppun go* 三十分後

law *hooritsu* 法律

law firm *hooritsu jimusho* 法律事務所

lawyer *bengoshi* 弁護士

leap *hiyaku* 飛躍

leave (to) *deru, demasu* 出る、出ます

have left (to) *dete iru, dete imasu* 出ている、出ています

leave ... (to) *... o deru, ... o demasu* 〜を出る、〜を出ます

leave the hospital (to) *taiinsuru, taiinshimasu* 退院する、退院します

leaving... *... hasu* 〜発

leaving Haneda *Haneda hatsu* 羽田発

left *hidari* 左

left side *hidarigawa* 左側

leg *ashi* 脚

lend (to) *kasu, kashimasu* 貸す、貸します

have lent (to) *kashite iru, kashite imasu* 貸している、貸しています

Let me see. *Soo da naa./Soo desu ne.* そうだなあ。/そうですね。

Let's ... *... mashoo.* 〜ましょう。

Let's do that! *Soo shimashoo!* そうしましょう！

letter *tegami* 手紙

lettuce *retasu* レタス

library *toshokan* 図書館

lid *futa* 蓋

lie *uso* 嘘

tell a lie (to) *uso o tsuku, uso o tsukimasu* 嘘をつく、嘘をつきます

light *karui (adjective), raito (noun)* 軽い、ライト

light (to) *tsukeru, tsukemasu* 点ける、点けます

like (to) *suki da, suki desu* 好きだ、好きです

like very much (to), like a lot (to) *daisuki da, daisuki desu* 大好きだ、大好きです

I'd like to have ... *... o onegaishimasu.* 〜をお願いします。

if you like *moshi yokattara, yoroshikattara (polite)* もし良かったら、よろしかったら

link *rinku* リンク

listen (to) *kiku, kikimasu ; kiku, kikimasu (with focus, such as listening to music)* 聞く、聞きます；聴く、聴きます

literature *bungaku* 文学

lively *nigiyaka* 賑やか

living room *ima* 居間

long *nagai* 長い

Long time no see. *Hisashiburi desu ne.* 久しぶりですね。

long-absence *hisabisa* 久々

look (to) *miru, mimasu* 見る、見ます

look for (to) *goran ni naru, goran ni narimasu (honorific); haikensuru, haikenshimasu (humble)* ご覧になる、ご覧になります；拝見する、拝見します

look forward (to) *sagasu, sagashimasu; tanoshimi ni suru, tanoshimi ni shimasu* 探す、探します；楽しみにする、楽しみにします

look pale (to) *kaoiro ga warui, kaoiro ga warui desu* 顔色が悪い、顔色が悪いです

loud *hade* 派手

low *hikui* 低い

lunch *chuushoku (fml.), hirugohan (infml.)* 昼食、昼ご飯

lung *hai* 肺

magazine *zasshi* 雑誌

mail (to) *yuusoosuru, yuusooshimasu* 郵送する、郵送します

make (to) *tsukuru, tsukurimasu* 作る、作ります

make a phone call (to) *denwasuru, denwashimasu* 電話する、電話します

make a appointment/reservation (to) *yoyakusuru, yoyakushimasu* 予約する、予約します

male *otoko* 男

man *otoko no hito* 男の人

many *ooi, takusan* 多い、たくさん

how many *(o)ikutsu (polite with o)* (お)いくつ

many times *nando mo* 何度も

March *sangatsu* 三月

marketing *maaketingu* マーケティング

married couple *(go)fuufu (polite with go)* (ご)夫婦

mat *matto* マット

match (to) *au, aimasu* 合う、合います

match with jeans (to) *jiinzu ni au* ジーンズに合う

mathematics *suugaku* 数学

matter *ken* 件

May *gogatsu* 五月

may (conjecture) *kamoshirenai, kamoshiremasen* かもしれない、かもしれません

May I … ? … *te (mo) ii?;* … *te (mo) ii desu ka.;* … *te (mo) ii deshoo ka. (polite);* … *te (mo) yoroshii desu ka. (polite);* … *te (mo) yoroshii deshoo ka. (polite)* 〜て(も)いい?；〜て(も)いいですか。；〜て(も)いいでしょうか。；〜て(も)よろしいですか。；〜て(も)よろしいでしょうか。

meal *gohan (infml.), shokuji (fml.)* ご飯、食事

meaning *imi* 意味

measure (to) *hakaru, hakarimasu* 測る、測ります

meat *niku* 肉

medical consultation *shinsatsu* 診察

the first medical consultation *shoshin* 初診

medical consulting room *shinsatsushitsu* 診察室

medical doctor *isha* 医者

medicine *kusuri* 薬

medium (size) *medium* エム

medium is okay *emu de ii* エムでいい

meet (to) *au, aimasu; ome ni kakaru, ome ni kakarimasu (humble)* 会う、会います；お目にかかる、お目にかかります

meeting *kaigi, miitingu* 会議、ミーティング

menu *menyuu* メニュー

meter *meetoru* メートル

Mexican *mekishikojin (person)* メキシコ人

Mexican cuisine *mekishiko ryoori* メキシコ料理

Mexico *mekishiko* メキシコ

microwave oven *denshirenji* 電子レンジ

milk *miruku* ミルク

mind (to) *kamau, kamaimasu* 構う、構います

Do you mind … ing? … *te (mo) kamaimasen ka.* 〜て(も)構いませんか。

miso soup *(o)misoshiru (polite with o)* (お)味噌汁

mixed salad *mikkusu sarada* ミックスサラダ

Monday *getsuyoobi* 月曜日

money *okane* お金

monitor *monitaa* モニター

monotonous *ipponjooshi* 一本調子

moon *tsuki* 月

more *motto* もっと

a little more *moo sukoshi* もう少し

more than *ijoo* 以上

more … than … … *yori* … 〜より〜

once more *moo ichido* もう一度

morning *asa, gozen* 朝、午前

this morning *kesa* 今朝

mosquito *ka* 蚊

(the) most *ichiban* 一番

moth *ga* 蛾

mother (one's own) *haha (one's own), okaasan (someone else's)* 母、お母さん

mountain *yama* 山

mouse *mausu* マウス

mouth *kuchi* 口

move (to a new location) (to) *hikkosu, hikkoshimasu* 引っ越す、引っ越します

movie *eega* 映画

movie theater *eegakan* 映画館

Mr., Ms. *san, sama (polite)* さん、様

Mt. Fuji *fujisan* 富士山

much *ooi, takusan* 多い、たくさん

how much *(o)ikura (polite with o)* (お)いくら

not so much *a(n)mari (+ negative)* あ(ん)まり

music *ongaku* 音楽

musical instrument *gakki* 楽器

mussel *muurugai* ムール貝

my *watashi no* 私の

name *(o)namae (polite with o)* (お)名前

What's your name? *Onamae wa?* お名前は？

narrow *semai* 狭い

nation *kuni* 国

nausea *hakike* 吐き気

nearby *chikaku* 近く

necktie *nekutai* ネクタイ

never *ichido mo (+negative)* 一度も

new *atarashii* 新しい

New York *nyuuyooku* ニューヨーク

newspaper *shinbun* 新聞

next time *kondo* 今度

next to … (… *no) tonari* (〜の)隣

next week *raishuu* 来週

next year *rainen* 来年

Nice to meet you. *Doozo yoroshiku.* どうぞよろしく。

night *ban, yoru* 晩、夜

every night *maiban* 毎晩

two nights *nihaku* 二泊

two nights three days *nihaku mikka* 二泊三日

nine *ku, kyuu, kokonotsu (native Japanese number)* 九、九、九つ

nine minutes *kyuufun* 九分

nine o'clock *kuji* 九時

nineteen *juuku, juukyuu* 十九

ninety *kyuujuu* 九十

ninth (day of the month) *kokonoka* 九日

no *iie* いいえ

no one *dare mo (+ negative)* 誰も
No, thank you. *Kekkoo desu.* 結構です。
nobody *dare mo (+ negative)* 誰も
noisy *urusai* うるさい
noon *(o)hiru (polite with o)* (お)昼
north side *kitagawa* 北側
nose *hana* 鼻
not at all *zenzen (+ negative)* 全然
not so much *a(n)mari (+ negative)* あ(ん)まり
not so often *a(n)mari (+ negative)* あ(ん)まり
notebook *nooto* ノート
nothing *nani mo (+ negative)* 何も
novel *shoosetsu* 小説
November *juuichigatsu* 十一月
now *ima* 今
nowhere *doko mo (+ negative)* どこも
number one *ichiban* 一番
nurse *kangoshi* 看護師
obstruction *jama* 邪魔
occupation *shokugyoo* 職業
ocean *umi* 海
October *juugatsu* 十月
octopus *tako* たこ
off (to be), have gotten off (to) *orite iru, orite imasu* 降りている、降りています
office *jimusho, ofisu* 事務所、オフィス
office (clerical) work *jimu* 事務
office worker *kaishain* 会社員
often *yoku* よく
not so often *a(n)mari (+ negative)* あ(ん)まり
oh *aa* ああ
okay (good) *ii, yoroshii (polite)* いい、よろしい
if it's okay *moshi yokattara, yoroshikattara (polite)* もし良かったら、よろしかったら
Is it okay? *Yoroshii desu ka. (polite)* よろしいですか。
medium is okay *emu de ii* エムでいい
Okinawa *okinawa* 沖縄
old *furui* 古い
how old *(o)ikutsu (polite with o)* (お)いくつ
older brother *ani (one's own), oniisan (someone else's)* 兄、お兄さん
older sister *ane (one's own), oneesan (someone else's)* 姉、お姉さん
on *(... no) ue* (〜の)上
once *ichido* 一度
once in a while *tamani* たまに
once more *moo ichido* もう一度

once upon a time *mukashimukashi* 昔々
one (number) *ichi, hitotsu (native Japanese number)* 一、一つ
one (indefinite pronoun) *no* の
the American one *amerika no* アメリカの
the one in solid color *muji no* 無地の
one minute *ippun* 一分
one o'clock *ichiji* 一時
one person *hitori* 一人
onion *tamanegi* たまねぎ
only *dake, shika (+ negative)* だけ、しか
only child *hitorikko* 一人っ子
open (to) *akeru, akemasu (transitive verb)* 開ける、開けます
operate (to) *shujutsusuru, shujutsushimasu* 手術する、手術します
operation *shujutsu* 手術
opposite *gyaku* 逆
optional tour *opushonaru tsuaa* オプショナルツアー
or *ka* か
... or something like that ... *demo* 〜でも
coffee or something like that *koohii demo* コーヒーでも
orange *orenji* オレンジ
order *chuumon* 注文
order (to) *chuumonsuru, chuumonshimasu* 注文する、注文します
Osaka *oosaka* 大阪
other *hoka* 他
the other day *senjitsu* 先日
own (to) *motsu, mochimasu* 持つ、持ちます
p.m. *gogo* 午後
painful *itai* 痛い
painting *e* 絵
panda *panda* パンダ
pants *pantsu, zubon* パンツ、ズボン
paper *kami* 紙
Pardon the intrusion. *Ojamashimasu.* お邪魔します。
parents *(go)ryooshin (polite with go)* (ご)両親
park *kooen* 公園
party *paatii* パーティー
passing over a matter *fumon* 不問
patient *kanja* 患者
pay (to) *harau, haraimasu* 払う、払います
payment *(o)shiharai (polite with o)* (お)支払い
pen *pen* ペン

pencil *enpitsu* 鉛筆
pepper *koshoo* 胡椒
perform (to) (music) *ensoosuru, ensooshimasu* 演奏する、演奏します
perhaps *tabun* 多分
perm *paama* パーマ
person *hito* 人
person *mono* (humble), *kata* (polite) 者、方
  a person in charge *tantoo no mono* (humble) 担当の者
  one person *hitori* 一人
  two people *futari, nimeesama* (polite) 二人、二名様
personal computer *pasokon* パソコン
pharmaceutical company *seeyakugaisha* 製薬会社
phonetic-ideographic characters *keesee moji* 形声文字
photograph, photography *shashin* 写真
piano *piano* ピアノ
pictorial characters *shookee moji* 象形文字
pig *buta* 豚
pin *pin* ピン
pink *pinku* (noun) ピンク
pizza *piza* ピザ
place *tokoro* 所
  place of origin *(go)shusshin* (polite with go) (ご)出身
  place of work *kinmuchi* 勤務地
plan *keekaku* 計画
plant (to) *ueru, uemasu* 植える、植えます
plant (to) (seeds) *maku, makimasu* 蒔く、蒔きます
play (to) *asobu, asobimasu* (a game); *fuku, fukimasu* (a wind instruments); *hiku, hikimasu* (piano); *tataku, tatakimasu* (a percussion instrument) 遊ぶ、遊びます;吹く、吹きます;弾く、弾きます; たたく、たたきます
  play sports (to) *suppootsu o suru, supootsu o shimasu* スポーツをする、スポーツをします
Please. *Doozo.* どうぞ。
  Please. (asking for a favor) *Onegaishimasu.* お願いします。
  Please … … *te kudasai.* ～てください。
  Please don't … … *naide kudasai.* ～ないでください。
  Please give me … … *o kudasai.* ～をください。

poison *doku* 毒
police *keesatsu* 警察
police booth *kooban* 交番
police officer *keesatsukan* 警察官
polish (to) *migaku, migakimasu* 磨く、磨きます
pool *puuru* プール
poor at *heta, nigate* 下手、苦手
pop *poppusu* ポップス
popular (to be) *ninki ga aru, ninki ga arimasu* 人気がある、人気があります
popularity *ninki* 人気
pork *butaniku* 豚肉
Portuguese *porutogarugo* (language) ポルトガル語
post office *yuubinkyoku* 郵便局
potato *jagaimo* じゃがいも
practice (to) *renshuusuru, renshuushimasu* 練習する、練習します
prefix meal *teeshoku* 定食
preparation *junbi, yooi* 準備、用意
presentation *happyoo* 発表
  group presentation *gruupu happyoo* グループ発表
president of a company *shachoo* 社長
pretty *kiree* きれい
price *nedan* 値段
  prices (of commodities) *bukka* 物価
  have been priced down (to) *oyasuku natte imasu* (polite) お安くなっています
probably *tabun* 多分
  will probably *daroo, deshoo* だろう、でしょう
problem *mondai* 問題
promotion *kiyoo* 起用
promptly *hayabaya, soosoo* 早々
properly *kichinto, chanto* (infml.) きちんと、ちゃんと
provide (to) *shikyuusuru, shikyuushimasu* 支給する、支給します
psychology *shinrigaku* 心理学
pulse *myaku* 脈
put (to) *oku, okimasu* 置く、置きます
  put into (to) *ireru, iremasu* 入れる、入れます
  put into a salad (to) *sarada ni ireru, sarada ni iremasu* サラダに入れる、サラダに入れます
  put on (to be) *noru, norimasu* 載る、載ります
  have been put on (to) *notte iru, notte imasu* 載っている、載っています
qualification *shikaku* 資格

question *shitsumon* 質問
quickly *hayaku* 早く
quiet *shizuka, jimi (color)* 静か、地味
quite *nakanaka* なかなか
  quite good *nakanaka ii* なかなかいい
radio *rajio* ラジオ
rain *ame* 雨
  It's raining. *Ame desu./Ame ga futte imasu.* 雨
  です。/雨が降っています。
read (to) *yomu, yomimasu* 読む、読みます
  reading books *dokusho* 読書
not readily (in negative) *nakanaka* なかなか
  not come readily *nakanaka konai, nakanaka
  kimasen* なかなか来ない、なかなか来ません
  Are you ready? *Junbi wa ii desu ka.* 準備はい
  いですか。
really *hontoo ni* 本当に
  Really? *Hontoo desu ka./Soo desu ka.* 本当です
  か。/そうですか。
reason *riyuu* 理由
  for that reason *sorede* それで
receive (to) *morau, moraimasu; itadaku,
itadakimasu (humble)* もらう、もらいます；いただ
く、いただきます
  receive a favor of … ing (to) *… te
  morau, … te moraimasu; … te itadaku, … te
  itadakimasu (humble)* 〜てもらう、〜てもらいま
  す；〜ていただく、〜ていただきます
recently *saikin* 最近
reception desk *uketsuke* 受付
receptionist *uketsukegakari* 受付係
red *akai (adjective), aka (noun)* 赤い、赤
red wine *aka wain* 赤ワイン
refrigerator *reezooko* 冷蔵庫
regarding *kansuru* 関する
relatives *(go)shinseki (polite with go)* (ご)親戚
relax (to) *rirakkusususu, rirakkusushimasu* リ
ラックスする、リラックスします
released from hospital (to be) *taiinsuru,
taiinshimasu* 退院する、退院します
replace (a person) (to) *kawaru, kawarimasu* 代
わる、代わります
report *repooto* レポート
reservation *yoyaku* 予約
  make a reservation (to) *yoyakusuru,
  yoyakushimasu* 予約する、予約します
restaurant *resutoran* レストラン
restroom *otearai* お手洗い

resume *rirekisho* 履歴書
return *okaeshi (polite)* お返し
return (to) *kaeru, kaerimasu ; modoru,
modorimasu* 帰る、帰ります；戻る、戻ります
  have returned (to) *kaette iru, kaette imasu;
  modotte iru, modotte imasu* 帰っている、帰って
  います；戻っている、戻っています
reward *shooyo* 賞与
ride (to) *noru, norimasu* 乗る、乗ります
right *migi* 右
  Right? *Soo desu ne. (rising intonation)* そうで
  すね。
  That's right. *Soo desu.; Soo desu ne.; Soo desu
  yo.* そうです。；そうですね。；そうですよ。
right side *migigawa* 右側
rink *rinku* リンク
river *kawa* 川
road *michi* 道
rock *rokku* ロック
Rome *rooma* ローマ
room *heya* 部屋
rudeness *shitsuree* 失礼
rules *kiyaku* 規約
run (to) *hashiru, hashirimasu* 走る、走ります
sake *nihonshu* 日本酒
salad *sarada* サラダ
  chicken salad *chikin sarada* チキンサラダ
  green salad *guriin sarada* グリーンサラダ
  mixed salad *mikkusu sarada* ミックスサラダ
  seafood salad *shiifuudo sarada* シーフードサ
  ラダ
salary *(o)kyuuryoo (polite with o), kyuuyo* (お)
給料、給与
  salary increase *shookyuu* 昇給
salt *shio* 塩
salty *shiokarai* 塩辛い
same *onaji* 同じ
Saturday *doyoobi* 土曜日
say (to) *iu, iimasu; moosu, mooshimasu
(humble); ossharu, osshaimasu (honorific)* 言
う、言います；申す、申します；おっしゃる、おっしゃ
います
scallop *hotate* 帆立
scared (to be) *bikkurisuru, bikkurishimasu* びっ
くりする、びっくりします
scarf *sukaafu* スカーフ
schedule *sukejuuru* スケジュール
school *gakkoo* 学校

seafood salad *shiifuudo sarada* シーフードサラダ

seasoning *choomiryoo* 調味料

second *futatsume* 二つ目

second (day of the month) *futsuka* 二日

section manager *kachoo* 課長

see (to) *goran ni naru, goran ni narimasu (honorific); haikensuru, haikenshimasu (humble); ome ni kakaru, ome ni kakarimasu (humble)* ご覧になる、ご覧になります; 拝見する、拝見します; お目にかかる、お目にかかります

   I see. *Hee.; Soo desu ka.; Soo ka.* へえ。; そうですか。; そうか。

   See you later/then. *Sorede wa mata./Sore ja(a) mata. (infml.)* それではまた。/それじゃ(あ)また。

   seeing movies *eega kanshoo (lit., movie appreciation)* 映画鑑賞

   seen (to be) *mieru, miemasu* 見える、見えます

seed *tane* 種

selfish *katte* 勝手

seminar *seminaa* セミナー

September *kugatsu* 九月

set (counter for written materials) *bu* 部

seven *nana, shichi, nanatsu (native Japanese number)* 七、七、七つ

seven minutes *nanafun* 七分

seven o'clock *shichiji* 七時

seventeen *juunana, juushichi* 十七

seventh (day of the month) *nanoka* 七日

seventy *nanajuu* 七十

several times *nando ka* 何度か

severe *hidoi* ひどい

shade *sheedo* シェード

Shall we ... ? *... mashoo ka.* 〜ましょうか。

she *kanojo* 彼女

shellfish *kai* 貝

Shepherd *shepaado* シェパード

sherbet *shaabetto* シャーベット

shirt *shatsu* シャツ

shoes *kutsu* 靴

shopping *kaimono* 買い物

shopping cart *kaato* カート

short *mijikai* 短い

   short (to be) *tarinai, tarimasen* 足りない、足りません

shortcake *shooto keeki* ショートケーキ

shortly *kondo* 今度

shot *chuusha* 注射

shoulders *kata* 肩

   have stiff shoulders (to) *kata ga kotte iru, kata ga kotte imasu* 肩が凝っている、肩が凝っています

shower *shawaa* シャワー

   take a shower (to) *shawaa o abiru, shawaa o abimasu* シャワーを浴びる、シャワーを浴びます

showy *hade* 派手

shrimp *ebi* えび

shrine *jinja* 神社

siblings *kyoodai (one's own), gokyoodai (someone else's)* 兄弟、ご兄弟

side *hoo* 方

   the side of ... *(... no) yoko* (〜の)横

   this side *temae* 手前

sightseeing *kankoo* 観光

simple *kantan* 簡単

since *node* ので

singer *kashu* 歌手

sit down (to) *suwaru, suwarimasu* 座る、座ります

six *roku, muttsu (native Japanese number)* 六、六つ

six minutes *roppun* 六分

six o'clock *rokuji* 六時

sixteen *juuroku* 十六

sixth (day of the month) *muika* 六日

sixty *rokujuu* 六十

size *saizu* サイズ

ski, skiing *sukii* スキー

skillful *joozu* 上手

skirt *sukaato* スカート

sky *sora* 空

sleep *suimin* 睡眠

   get some sleep (to) *suimin o toru, suimin o torimasu* 睡眠をとる、睡眠をとります

sleep (to) *neru, nemasu* 寝る、寝ます

sliced raw fish *sashimi* 刺身

slowly *yukkuri* ゆっくり

small *chiisai* 小さい

smoke a cigarette (to) *tabako o suu, tabako o suimasu* 煙草を吸う、煙草を吸います

snow *yuki* 雪

   It's snowing. *Yuki desu./Yuki ga futte imasu.* 雪です。/雪が降っています。

so *kara (conjunction), sorede (conjunction), soo (pronoun)* から、それで、そう

   do so (to) *soo suru, soo shimasu* そうする、そうします

Is that so? *Soo desu ka.* そうですか。

so-so *maa maa* まあまあ

sober (color) *jimi* 地味

soccer *sakkaa* サッカー

social insurance *shakaihoken* 社会保険

society *shakai* 社会

sofa *sofaa* ソファー

soft drink *juusu* ジュース

software *sofuto, sofutowea* ソフト、ソフトウェア

soil *tsuchi* 土

solid (color) *muji* 無地

some other day *gojitsu* 後日

someone *dare ka* 誰か

something *nani ka* 何か

sometimes *tokidoki* 時々

somewhere *doko ka* どこか

son *musuko* (one's own), *musukosan* (someone else's) 息子、息子さん

Sorry for the trouble. *Sumimasen.* すみません。

  I'm sorry. *Gomennasai./Sumimasen.* ごめんなさい。/すみません。

  I'm very sorry. *Mooshiwake arimasen.* (polite)/*Mooshiwake gozaimasen.* (polite) 申し訳ありません。/申し訳ございません。

sour *suppai* すっぱい

south side *minamigawa* 南側

soy bean paste *miso* 味噌

soy milk *toonyuu* 豆乳

soy sauce *shooyu* 醤油

spacious *hiroi* 広い

spaghetti *supagetti* スパゲッティ

Spain *supein* スペイン

Spanish *supeingo* (language), *supeinjin* (person) スペイン語、スペイン人

Spanish cuisine *supein ryoori* スペイン料理

speak (to) *hanasu, hanashimasu* 話す、話します

special ability/skill *tokugi* 特技

spicy *karai* 辛い

spoon *supuun* スプーン

sport *supootsu* スポーツ

  play sports (to) *suppootsu o suru, supootsu o shimasu* スポーツをする、スポーツをします

sprain *nenza* 捻挫

  have a sprain (to) *nenzasuru, nenzashimasu* 捻挫する、捻挫します

spring *haru* 春

squid *ika* いか

stairs *kaidan* 階段

stand up (to) *tatsu, tachimasu* 立つ、立ちます

station *eki* 駅

stay home (to) *uchi ni iru, uchi ni imasu* 家にいる、家にいます

staying over night *haku* 泊

stiff (to get) *koru, korimasu* 凝る、凝ります

  have stiff shoulders (to) *kata ga kotte iru, kata ga kotte imasu* 肩が凝っている、肩が凝っています

still *mada* まだ

stomach *i* 胃

stomachache *fukutsuu* 腹痛

  have a stomachache (to) *onaka ga itai, onaka ga itai desu* お腹が痛い、お腹が痛いです

store *mise* 店

store clerk *ten-in* 店員

straight *massugu* まっすぐ

strange *myoo* 妙

stream *ogawa* 小川

street *michi* 道

stress *sutoresu* ストレス

  under a lot of stress (to be) *sutoresu ga tamatte iru, sutoresu ga tamatte imasu* ストレスが溜まっている、ストレスが溜まっています

stripes *shima* 縞

stroke (for writing characters) *kaku* 画

  number of strokes *kakusuu* 画数

  stroke order *kakijun* 書き順

strong *tsuyoi* 強い

student *gakusee* 学生

  college student *daigakusee* 大学生

  graduate school student *daigakuinsee* 大学院生

  high school student *kookoosee* 高校生

  teacher and student *shitee* 師弟

study (to) *benkyoosuru, benkyooshimasu* 勉強する、勉強します

  study abroad (to) *ryuugakusuru, ryuugakushimasu* 留学する、留学します

subject (letter, e-mail) *kenmee* 件名

subway *chikatetsu* 地下鉄

sugar *satoo* 砂糖

suitcase *suutsukeesu* スーツケース

summer *natsu* 夏

  summer vacation *natsu yasumi* 夏休み

sumo wrestling *sumoo* 相撲

Sunday *nichiyoobi* 日曜日

sunny *hare* 晴れ

It's sunny. Hare desu./Harete imasu. 晴れです。/晴れています。

supermarket *suupaa* スーパー

surgery *shujutsu* 手術

surprised (to be) *bikkurisuru, bikkurishimasu* びっくりする、びっくりします

sushi *sushi* 寿司

sweater *seetaa* セーター

sweet *amai* 甘い

swim (to) *oyogu, oyogimasu* 泳ぐ、泳ぎます

swimming *suiee* 水泳

table *teeburu* テーブル

take (to) *ukeru, ukemasu* 受ける、受けます

take (photos) (to) *toru, torimasu* 撮る、撮ります

take (time) (to) *kakaru, kakarimasu* かかる、かかります

take a bath (to) *ofuro ni hairu, ofuro ni hairimasu* お風呂に入る、お風呂に入ります

take a day off (to) *yasumu, yasumimasu* 休む、休みます

take a day off from work (to) *kaisha o yasumu, kaisha o yasumimasu* 会社を休む、会社を休みます

take a medical consultation (to) *shinsatsu o ukeru, shinsatsu o ukemasu* 診察を受ける、診察を受けます

take a shower (to) *shawaa o abiru, shawaa o abimasu* シャワーを浴びる、シャワーを浴びます

take lessons on (to) *narau, naraimasu* 習う、習います

take off (shoes, clothes) (to) *nugu, nugimasu* 脱ぐ、脱ぎます

take some rest (to) *yasumu, yasumimasu* 休む、休みます

take (someone or animal) (to) *tsurete iku, tsurete ikimasu* 連れて行く、連れて行きます

take (something) (to) *motte iku, motte ikimasu* 持って行く、持って行きます

talk show *tookushoo* トークショー

tall *takai* 高い

taxi *takushii* タクシー

tea (Japanese kind) *ocha* お茶

teach (to) *oshieru, oshiemasu* 教える、教えます

teacher *kyooshi, sensee* 教師、先生

Prof./Dr. Tanaka *Tanaka sensee* 田中先生

teacher and student *shitee* 師弟

telephone *(o)denwa (polite with o)* (お)電話

telephone number *(o)denwabangoo (polite with o)* (お)電話番号

television *terebi* テレビ

tell (to) *oshieru, oshiemasu* 教える、教えます

tell a lie (to) *uso o tsuku, uso o tsukimasu* 嘘をつく、嘘をつきます

(check one's) temperature *netsu o hakaru, netsu o hakarimasu* 熱を測る、熱を測ります

temple *(o)tera (polie with o)* (お)寺

tempura *tenpura* 天ぷら

ten *juu, too (native Japanese number)* 十、十

ten thousand *ichiman* 一万

ten thousand yen *ichiman en* 一万円

ten minutes *juppun* 十分

ten o'clock *juuji* 十時

tennis *tenisu* テニス

tennis court *tenisu kooto* テニスコート

tenth (day of the month) *tooka* 十日

terrible *hidoi* ひどい

textbook *kyookasho* 教科書

the … th … me ～目

Thank you. *Arigatoo gozaimasu./Arigatoo gozaimashita.* ありがとうございます。/ありがとうございました。

Thank you very much. *Doomo arigatoo gozaimasu./Doomo arigatoo gozaimashita.* どうもありがとうございます。/どうもありがとうございました。

No, thank you. *Kekkoo desu.* 結構です。

that (conjunction) *to* と

that (demonstrative) *sono (far from the speaker but close to the listener) ; sore (far from the speaker but close to the listener); ano (far from both the speaker and the listener); are (far from both the speaker and the listener)* その;それ;あの;あれ

that pen *sono pen (far from the speaker but close to the listener); ano pen (far from both the speaker and the listener)* そのペン; あのペン

that way *sochira (far from the speaker but close to the listener) (polite); achira (far from both the speaker and the listener) (polite)* そちら; あちら

then *dewa, ja(a) (infml.), sorede wa, sore ja(a) (infml.)* では、じゃ(あ) 、それでは、それじゃ(あ)

and then *sorekara, soshite* それから、そして

See you then. *Sorede wa mata./Sore ja(a) mata. (infml.)* それではまた。/それじゃ(あ)また。

there *asoko (far from both the speaker and the listener) ; soko (far from the speaker but close to the listener)* あそこ;そこ

There is ... *aru, arimasu (inanimate); iru, imasu (animate); gozaimasu (polite); irassharu, irasshaimasu (honorific); oru, orimasu (humble)* ある、あります; いる、います; ございます; いらっしゃる、いらっしゃいます; おる、おります

they *karera (people) ; kanojora (people, feminine) ; kanojotachi (people, feminine) ; sorera (inanimate)* 彼ら; 彼女ら; 彼女達; それら

thing *koto* こと

think (to) *omou, omoimasu* 思う、思います

third *mittsume* 三つ目

third (day of the month) *mikka* 三日

thirteen *juusan* 十三

thirty *sanjuu* 三十

five thirty *goji sanjuppun* 五時三十分

thirty minutes *sanjuppun* 三十分

this *kore, kono, kochira (polite)* これ、この、こちら

this morning *kesa* 今朝

this pen *kono pen* このペン

this time *kondo* 今度

this way *kochira (polite)* こちら

this week *konshuu* 今週

this weekend *konshuumatsu* 今週末

this year *kotoshi* 今年

thousand *sen* 千

ten thousand *ichiman* 一万

ten thousand yen *ichiman en* 一万円

thousand yen *sen en* 千円

three *san, mittsu (native Japanese number)* 三、三つ

three minutes *sanpun* 三分

three o'clock *sanji* 三時

throat *nodo* 喉

have a sore throat (to) *nodo ga itai, nodo ga itai desu* 喉が痛い、喉が痛いです

Thursday *mokuyoobi* 木曜日

time *jikan* 時間

this time *kondo* 今度

Times Square *taimuzu sukuea* タイムズスクエア

(sent) to *atesaki* 宛先

from ... to ... *... kara ... made* 〜から〜まで

tobacco *tabako* 煙草

today *kyoo* 今日

together *issho ni* 一緒に

all together *zenbu de* 全部で

toilet *toire* トイレ

Tokyo *Tookyoo* 東京

tomato *tomato* トマト

tomorrow *ashita, asu* 明日

the day after tomorrow *asatte* あさって

tonight *konban* 今晩

too (also) *mo* も

too, too much *sugiru, sugimasu* すぎる、すぎます

tooth *ha* 歯

tour guide *tenjooin, tsuaagaido* 添乗員、ツアーガイド

town *machi* 町

trade *booeki* 貿易

trading company *booekigaisha* 貿易会社

traffic light *shingoo* 信号

before the traffic light *shingoo no temae* 信号の手前

train *densha* 電車

transfer (a phone line) (to) *kawaru, kawarimasu* 代わる、代わります

transportation *kootsuu* 交通

transportation costs *kootsuuhi* 交通費

travel *ryokoo* 旅行

travel company *ryokoosha* 旅行社

treatment *taiguu* 待遇

tree *ki* 木

big tree *taiboku* 大木

tree shadow *kokage* 木陰

true *hontoo* 本当

Is that true? *Hontoo desu ka.* 本当ですか。

try ... ing (to) *... te miru, ... te mimasu* 〜てみる、〜てみます

T-shirt *tiishatsu* ティーシャツ（Tシャツ）

Tuesday *kayoobi* 火曜日

tunnel *tonneru* トンネル

turn (to) *magaru, magarimasu* 曲がる、曲がります

twelve *juuni* 十二

twelve o'clock *juuniji* 十二時

twentieth (day of the month) *hatsuka* 二十日

twenty *nijuu* 二十

two *ni, futatsu (native Japanese number)* 二、二つ

two minutes *nifun* 二分

two o'clock *niji* 二時

two people *futari, nimeesama (polite)* 二人、二名様

typhoon *taifuu* 台風

under … *(… no) shita* (〜の)下

under a lot of stress (to be) *sutoresu ga tamatte iru, sutoresu ga tamatte imasu* ストレスが溜まっている、ストレスが溜まっています

understand (to) *wakaru, wakarimasu* 分かる、分かります

United States (the) *amerika* アメリカ

university *daigaku* 大学

unskillful *heta* 下手

until *made* まで

up to now *ima made ni, kore made ni* 今までに、これまでに

urine *nyoo* 尿

use (to) *tsukau, tsukaimasu* 使う、使います

vacation *yasumi* 休み

summer vacation *natsu yasumi* 夏休み

van *ban* バン

various *kakushu* 各種

vegetable *yasai* 野菜

very *totemo, taihen* とても、大変

very much *totemo* とても

vest *besuto* ベスト

vigorous *genki* 元気

violin *baiorin* バイオリン

visible (to be) *mieru, miemasu* 見える、見えます

visit (to) *tazuneru, tazunemasu* 訪ねる、訪ねます

vitamin supplement *bitaminzai* ビタミン剤

volleyball *bareebooru* バレーボール

voucher *ken* 券

waist *koshi* 腰

wait (to) *matsu, machimasu* 待つ、待ちます

I/We will be waiting for you. *Omachishite orimasu. (polite)* お待ちしております。

Please wait. *Omachi kudasai. (polite)* お待ちください。

waiting room *machiaishitsu* 待合室

waitress *weitoresu* ウェイトレス

wake-to-sleep transition *netsuki* 寝つき

Wales *weeruzu* ウェールズ

walk (to) *aruku, arukimasu* 歩く、歩きます

five minute walk *aruite gofun* 歩いて五分

want (to) *hoshii, hoshii desu* 欲しい、欲しいです

(Someone) wants *hoshigatte iru, hoshigatte imasu* 欲しがっている、欲しがっています

want to (to) *tai, tai desu* たい、たいです

warm *atatakai* 暖かい

wash (to) *arau, araimasu* 洗う、洗います

washing machine *sentakuki* 洗濯機

watch *tokee* 時計

watch (to) *miru, mimasu; goran ni naru, goran ni narimasu (honorific); haikensuru, haikenshimasu (humble)* 見る、見ます; ご覧になる、ご覧になります; 拝見する、拝見します

water *(o) mizu (polite with o)* (お)水

we *watashitachi* 私達

web designer *webudezainaa* ウェブデザイナー

Wednesday *suiyoobi* 水曜日

week *shuu* 週

a week *isshuukan* 一週間

last week *senshuu* 先週

next week *raishuu* 来週

this week *konshuu* 今週

weekday *heejitsu* 平日

weekend *shuumatsu* 週末

this weekend *konshuumatsu* 今週末

Welcome. *Yookoso.* ようこそ。

Welcome (to our store). *Irasshaimase.* いらっしゃいませ。

well *yoku* よく

well … *anoo, etto, hee, uun* あのう、えっと、へえ、ううん

Well done. *Yoku dekimashita.* よくできました。

west side *nishigawa* 西側

Western style *yoofuu* 洋風

what *nan(i)* 何

What about … ? *Doo desu ka.* どうですか。

what kind of *donna* どんな

what time *nanji* 何時

What's the matter? *Doo shimashita ka./Doo nasaimashita ka. (polite)* どうしましたか。/どうなさいましたか。

wheat *komugi* 小麦

when *itsu (question); tara, to, toki (conjunction)* いつ; たら、と、時

where *doko, dochira (polite)* どこ、どちら

which (one) *dono* どの

which one *dore, dochira, dochira no hoo* どれ、どちら、どちらの方

which pen *dono pen* どのペン

which way *dochira (polite)* どちら

white *shiroi* 白い
white night *byakuya* 白夜
white wine *shiro wain* 白ワイン
who *dare, donate (polite)* 誰、どなた
why *dooshite, naze, nande (infml.)* どうして、な
ぜ、なんで
　Why don't we ... ? *... masen ka.* 〜ませんか。
wife *kanai (one's own), tsuma (one's own),
okusan (someone else's)* 家内、妻、奥さん
wind *kaze* 風
window *mado* 窓
window shopping *windooshoppingu* ウィンドー
ショッピング
wine *wain* ワイン
　red wine *aka wain* 赤ワイン
　white wine *shiro wain* 白ワイン
winter *fuyu* 冬
with *to* と
woman *onna no hito* 女の人
(I) wonder ... *... kana(a)./ ... kashira.* 〜かな
(あ)。/〜かしら。
woods *hayashi* 林
wool *uuru* ウール
　100% wool *uuru hyakupaasento* ウール100パ
ーセント
word *kotoba* 言葉
word processor *waapuro* ワープロ
work *o(shigoto) (polite with o), kinmu (fml.)* (お)
仕事、勤務
　place of work *kinmuchi* 勤務地
　take a day off from work (to) *kaisha o
yasumu, kaisha o yasumimasu* 会社を休む、
会社を休みます
work (to) *hataraku, hatarakimasu* 働く、働きます
　work overtime (to) *zangyoosuru,
zangyooshimasu* 残業する、残業します
Wow. *Hee.* へえ。
write (to) *kaku, kakimasu* 書く、書きます
yard *niwa* 庭
year *nen* 年
　for a year *ichinenkan* 一年間
　next year *rainen* 来年
　this year *kotoshi* 今年
yellow *kiiroi (adjective), kiiro (noun)* 黄色い、黄色
yen *en* 円
　ten thousand yen *ichiman en* 一万円
　thousand yen *sen en* 千円
yes *hai, ee (infml.), un (infml.)* はい、ええ、うん

　Yes, it is. *Soo desu ne.* そうですね。
yesterday *kinoo* 昨日
　the day before yesterday *ototoi* おととい
yet *mada (+negative)* まだ
you (subject pronoun) *anata (sg.), anatagata
(pl.), anatatachi (pl.)* あなた、あなた方、あなた達
young *wakai* 若い
younger brother *otooto (one's own), otootosan
(someone else's)* 弟、弟さん
younger sister *imooto (one's own), imootosan
(someone else's)* 妹、妹さん
your (sg.) *anata no* あなたの
zen *zen* 禅
zero *ree, zero* 零、ゼロ